FONTAINEBLEAU FUN BLOC

INTRO

J'ai conçu ce livre afin qu'il soit un guide très pratique pouvant être utilisé quelque soit la langue parlée et ainsi il plaira aux grimpeurs de toute nationalité et du monde entier qui viennent en visite à Fontainebleau. J'ai présumé que le lecteur ne connait pas du tout la forêt et j'ai donc fourni des cartes détaillées permettant de localiser les parkings et les différents sites d'escalade. Je vous conseille de visiter www.jingowobbly.com afin de trouver toutes les informations nécessaires pour votre voyage, votre hébergement, les périodes où venir, les choses à faire, la géologie, etc. Cette information est d'ordre général et peut être mise à jour régulièrement mais il n'est pas nécessaire de l'avoir sur vous lors de vos visites quotidiennes dans la forêt.

CARTES: la carte de navigation sur la couverture intérieure est le point de départ qui vous permet d'identifier les 4 sites qui sont dans ce guide. Il y a des informations de base comme le nombre de passages dans chaque niveau, l'ombrage, la distance à pieds et si le site est adapté pour les enfants. Cela devrait vous permettre d'avoir suffisamment d'information afin de choisir le site qui vous convient pour y passer la journée. Deuxièmement vous trouverez les cartes des parkings qui sont essentielles afin de vous diriger de ces derniers vers les rochers (et de revenir!) dans ce qui peut être une forêt très compliquée. Troisièmement chaque site a une carte aérienne qui illustre chaque bloc avec des points de couleur qui montrent précisément chaque passage connu à ce jour. Il faut noter que les cartes aériennes sont élargies à une taille maximum afin que les blocs soient bien définies et qu'elles sont orientées pour qu'elles soient pratiques à utiliser (donc pas toujours orientées nord). Les coins pique-nique sont illustrés ainsi que la facilité d'accès sur les différents sentiers avec une poussette (voir le volet pour le détail des symboles utilisés).

CIRCUITS: Tous les sites d'escalade ont des circuits avec des numéros de couleur peints sur les rochers qui sont parfaits pour localiser votre position exacte dans le labyrinthe de blocs. Les numéros durent entre 5 et 10 ans avant que dame nature les fasse disparaître. De nombreux numéros peuvent donc manquer et quelques fois des circuits entiers peuvent être re-numérotés, alors attention! Suivre un circuit enfants ou un jaune facile à travers la forêt est très amusant mais lorsque la difficulté augmente ils deviennent insignifiants – surtout puisque les circuits rouge varient de 3a à 7a.

BLOCS ET VOIES: Dans ce livre j'ai donné un nom à chaque bloc et à chaque voie surtout afin qu'ils soient trouvés facilement dans n'importe quelle base de données sur internet. J'ai fait de nombreuses recherches pendant des années afin de trouver les noms historiquement les plus appropriés à chaque passage mais dans les cas où aucun nom n'est connu, j'ai suggéré un nom temporaire en italique pour identification. Toutes les informations données dans ce guide sont l'arrête centrale à partir de laquelle les sites internet vous donneront plus d'information détaillée, des videos, etc. Certains blocs sont très hauts donc l'utilisation d'une corde en moulinette est hautement recommandée.

TOPOS PHOTOS: Si vous venez sur un site d'escalade pour la première fois, ils seront indispensables. J'ai apporté beaucoup d'attention aux images et j'ai utilisé le flash pour illuminer les blocs les plus difficiles (plus de 20,000 images ont été prises pour ce livre). Toutes les lignes de traverse représentent les prises des mains avec la position de chaque prise marquée précisément. L'édition finale des TOPOS PHOTOS a été vérifiée par de nombreux grimpeurs qui vivent et grimpent à Fontainebleau et qui sont à l'origine de nombreuses premières ascensions. Pour les

COTATIONS: Page 6 pour V Grades.

GUIDES D'ESCALADE: Il y a environ 300 circuits et plus de 35,000 passages dans les forêts autour de Fontainebleau, assez pour remplir 5 à 10 guides d'escalade de styles différents. Cependant 82% (820 km2) de cet endroit n'a aucun bloc d'escalade et vous pourriez littéralement errer pendant des années avant de trouver les blocs. Vous pouvez visiter Jingowobbly et les autres sites d'escalade pour voir quels sont les guides disponibles.

LA FORET: C'est un environnement fragile, s'il vous plait ramenez vos déchèts avec vous et ne laissez aucune trace de votre passage. Le GPS ne fonctionne pas très bien sous les arbres mais il y a en général un bon signal pour les téléphones portables. Là où les voies ont de très petites prises s'il vous plait ne les taillez pas car elles sont une cour de récréation parfaite pour les grimpeurs très légers. Si vous marquez une prise avec de la magnésie, merci de le faire de façon très minimaliste (c'est facile) et nettoyez cette marque avec une brosse à dents à poils doux avant de partir. Il n'y a pas de toilettes dans la forêt donc planifier votre journée en fonction de cela. Si vous avez besoin d'utiliser la forêt pour aller aux toilettes, merci de le faire à une bonne distance et à au moins 50 mètres des blocs d'escalade.

P	🚶		Sectors	Circuits - grade	Hors / Off circuit problems
p206	8 min	🌳🧗	91.1 (Sud) - p. 235	3b	4 / 2 / 0 / 0
	10 min		91.1 (Centre) - p. 236-8	2c 3c 5b	2 / 15 / 15 / 5
	15 min	🧗	91.1 (Nord) - p. 239	2c 3c 5b	1 / 2 / 5 / 0
p206	7 min		95.2 (Ouest-centre) - p. 210	3c	2 / 15 / 12 / 19
	9 min	🧗🧗	95.2 (Nord) - p. 214	3a 5b	8 / 6 / 10 / 7
	14 min	🧗	95.2 (Sud) - p. 218	4a 4c 6a	8 / 13 / 4 / 21
p98	5 min	🧗☺	Apremont Bizons (Enfants) - p. 99	1b	1 / 3 / 5 / 0
	6 min	🌳🌳	Apremont Bizons (Bois) - p. 100	3a 4a 5c	8 / 4 / 28 / 13
	7 min	🌳☺	Apremont (Centre) - p. 106	1c 4b 5a 5c	14 / 12 / 12 / 35
	11 min		Apremont (Chaos) - p. 112	3a 3c 4a 5b 5c 6a 6c	3 / 6 / 17 / 26
p8	1 min	🌳☺	Beauvais, Noires - p. 8	4a 5a 5c	3 / 0 / 0 / 0
	1 min	🌳☺	Beauvais, Loutte-Télégraph - p. 10	2a 2c 4a 1a 1b 1c 2b 4a	5 / 9 / 2 / 5
	1 min	🌳🌳☺	Beauvais, Nainville (Bois) - p. 14	1b 2b 3b 5c	2 / 2 / 6 / 10
	1 min	🌳☺	Beauvais, Nainville (Crête) - p. 20	1b 1c 4c 5c 6c	0 / 1 / 3 / 5
	6 min		Beauvais, Nainville (Côte) - p. 22	3b 4c 5c 6c	4 / 7 / 8 / 11
p182	4 min	🌳	Bois Rond, Le - p. 186	3b 3c 5a 6a	2 / 16 / 42 / 32
p312	1 min	🌳☺	Buthiers (Piscine) - p. 308	1a 2a 3b 5a 5c 6b	9 / 5 / 34 / 54
p207	2 min	🌳☺	Cailleau (Rocher) - p. 286	1c 3c 4a 4c 6a	4 / 4 / 10 / 17
p182	4 min	🌳☺	Canche aux Merciers - p. 166	1a 1b 2b 3a 3c 4c 6a	5 / 5 / 56 / 50
p62	1 min	🌳🧗☺	Canon, Rocher - p. 40	1b 3a 2c 3c 4c 5a 6b	7 / 8 / 57 / 71
p198	2-5 min	🧗	Chats, Gorge aux - p. 198	3b 5a 6b	6 / 10 / 26 / 32
p120	18 min	🧗	Cuisinière (Franchard) - p. 142	3b 4b 5c 6a	12 / 24 / 90 / 102
p206	16 min		Cul de Chien (Toit) - p. 246	3a 4b 5c	18 / 11 / 13 / 15
	16 min	🌳	Cul de Chien (Nord) - p. 251	4b 5c	6 / 0 / 4 / 0
p92	1 min	🌳	Cuvier (Bas) - p. 64	3b 5b 5b 6a 6b	21 / 33 / 112 / 103
	6 min	🌳	Cuvier Est (Bellevue) - p. 92	6b	14 / 35 / 32 / 28
p207	12 min		Diplodocus - p. 274	3a 3c 5a	4 / 5 / 16 / 7
p307	2 min	☺	Eléphant (Est) - p. 294	1b 3b 5a 6a	11 / 16 / 12 / 28
	7 min	🧗	Eléphant (Haute) - p. 306	2c	5 / 2 / 3 / 0
cover	3 min	🌳☺	Ermitage (Enf), Franchard - p. 118	1b	0 / 0 / 0 / 0
p182	5 min	🌳🌳☺	Feuillardière - p.182-183	1a 1b 1c 3b	0 / 0 / 0 / 0
p206	17 min		Fin, Rocher (Côte) - p. 278	2c 4a 5a 6a	4 / 7 / 24 / 27
	21 min	🌳🌳	Fin, Rocher (Bois) - p. 285	5a	5 / 6 / 3 / 5
p207	1 min	🌳	Guichot, Rocher - p. 256	3b 5a 6b	3 / 6 / 22 / 15
p120	1 min	🌳	Isatis, Franchard (Croc) - p. 121	3a 4a 5a 5b 6b	4 / 3 / 39 / 49
	4-8 min	🧗	Isatis, (Angle Ben & Memel) - p. 122	4a 5a 5b 6b	12 / 14 / 21 / 39
	11 min	🧗	Isatis, Franchard (Ice) - p. 140	5b	4 / 1 / 20 / 25
p207	7 min	🧗	Potala - p. 262	3a 4a 4c 6a	5 / 20 / 60 / 28
p206	11 min	🧗☺	Potets, Rocher des - p. 208	1a 1c 3a 3c	12 / 4 / 2 / 6
p207	4 min	🌳☺	Sabots, Rocher - p. 224 (☺ p.234)	1b 3a 3b 5a 6b	3 / 13 / 24 / 52
p39	1 min	🧗☺	Saint Germain (Côte) - p.38	1c	0 / 0 / 0 / 0
	5 min	🧗🧗☺	Saint Germain (Bois) - p.30	3a 4a 5a 6b	2 / 2 / 6 / 13
p182	10 min	🌳	Télégraphe-Noisy - p.180	5b	0 / 4 / 3 / 1

Page 4-5 Introduction
Page 6, Fun bloc - 127 Circuits in ascending order of difficulty
Page 7, Circuits - Histoire / history & concept
Page 55, Cotations / Fontainebleau grading
Page 143, Fontainebleau technique, tips & Conservation
Page 318-320, Index

Fontainebleau Rock is fragile - please read page 143 - and preserve the forest.

Fontainebleau Fun Bloc
Escalade-Bouldering
by David Atchison-Jones (Author, Illustrator, Photographer & Graphic Design)

Jingo Wobbly – FONT BLOC volume 1
First Published in April 2012 (reprinted 2025) This title is updated for each reprint,
by Jingo Wobbly Publishing (www.jingowobbly.com)
(An imprint of Vision PC).
Holmwood House, 52 Roxborough Park, Harrow-on-the-Hill, London. HA1 3AY   Great Britain

Copyright © David Atchison-Jones 2012, 2014, 2016, 2018, 2019, 2021, 2022, 2023, 2025

All rights reserved. No part of this publication may be reproduced, stored in a retrieval system, or transmitted in any form or by any means, electronic, mechanical, photocopying, recording or otherwise, without prior written permission of the copyright owner, and especially not to be copied or published online.

A CIP catalogue record is available from the British Library - Made & printed in EU

ISBN   978-1-873 665 15-2

This book by definition is a climbing guidebook, and not a climbing safety book, and has no instructions or directions with regard to any safety aspect of climbing or general safety in climbing areas. Please seek professional safety advice before ever entering any climbing environment.

A climbing guidebook, is a collection of past climbing knowledge from a variety of sources. It cannot be regarded as either fact or fiction, since the information has been generally handed down across the generations, and is always open to the interpretation of the reader. We do of course however, make every effort to ensure that the information included in the guidebook is as up to date, and as accurate as possible at the time of going to press, but we unfortunately cannot guarantee any complete accuracy. Any information included within the sponsor advertisements are the sole responsibility of the advertiser. The publisher and editor cannot accept responsibility for any consequences arising from the use of this book, and do not accept any liability whatsoever for injury or damage caused by anyone arising from the use of this book.

The inclusion of any boulder or cliff in this guide, does not mean that anybody has any right of access whatsoever. All climbers and visitors should be aware that there may be strict access and conservation issues at any of the areas included in this guide, and should read and understand all notices, before climbing.

If there is any information that you feel is improper, or that you feel could be updated, please write to us or email us (info@jingowobbly.com) at our publishing address, where we will gladly collect the information for future editions. Latest information can be found at **www.jingowobbly.com**

Editorial acknowledgements: A giant thank you to everyone who has contributed to the making of this book over several years, especially those who have checked and climbed routes personally, and to all the spotters involved with the climbing. I would like to thank specially a few individuals whose knowledge of the forest is exceptional and have shared their immense knowledge first hand without hesitation; **Philippe Le Denmat, Eric Letot, Neil Hart, Loic Le Denmat, Dominique Yvorel, Jean-Yves Derouck, Jo Montchaussé, Jacky Godoffe, Jean Pierre Bouvier, Victor Pinto, Florian Bourdon.** A huge thanks everyone who has assisted with the gigantic photographic endeavour for this volume, both in climbing for the camera, and apologetically those who didn't make it through the final edit. Mega thanks also to other open information sources and contributors to websites (**Jean-Pierre Roudneff & Bernard Théret**, in particular), forums etc. Thanks to all previous guidebook writers (**Jo, Jacky, Jean-Jacques Naels & Bart Van Raiij**, in particular), collators, contributors, photographers, etc. Thanks to all of the folk who help behind the scene with climbing access work, crag maintenance, circuit painting and future welfare of the climbing environment. Thanks to Virginie and Eric for the translations. Many thanks to Paula and Gilbert for the musical, gastronomic and tranquil delights of Maison Mathieu. Big hugs to Sally, whose wicked sense of humour and musical shenanigans kept me going through endless hours of photoshop and graphic design. Thanks to Carsten and Choupie in scouting the forest for changes. Final thanks to Carrie, who wins best wife, climbing partner, everything partner for the umpteenth year running.

This book is dedicated to
Sally Rose - Pianist (1962-2012)
'a girl with inspirational jolity, and whose fun giggling will be remembered forever.'

Cover photo: **6b DIRECT DU CULOT**, *James Doherty ; Buthiers Piscine*
Title Page: **6a LE JETÉ D'OR**, *Linus Mühlpointer; Rocher 91.1* ▷
Back cover photo: **5b RAGE DE DENT**, *Sarah Fee; Cul de Chien*

INTRODUCTION | 5

I have designed this book to be a highly effective practical guide that can be used essentially without the use of language, and therefore usefully appeal to a wide cross section of nationalities from all over the world that visit Fontainebleau. I assume that the reader does not know the area at all, and have provided complete maps to locate all of the parking and climbing locations. Visit **www.jingowobbly.com** where you will find plenty of basic information about general climbing, crash pad hire, geology of the area, forests, travel, accomodation etc. This web information can obviously be updated, but once you are climbing - surely you only want to carry the climbing pages.

MAPS: The *Navigation map* on the inside cover is designed as your main start point, and should be used to identify the 45 areas covered. There is basic information shown such the number of problems in each grade, type of shade cover, walk in times, and kids suitablilty. This layout should provide enough information for you to choose a venue for the day that is ideally suited. Secondly, you will find the *Parking maps* essential to find your way from the car park to the boulders (and back!), in what can be – a very complicated forest. Thirdly, each area has an incredibly accurate *Aerial plan* that illustrates every boulder in perfect outline, and has coloured dots that exactly pinpoint every single problem known to date. Note – Aerial plans are enlarged to maximum size for boulder definition, then orientated for practical use (not always north). Nice picnic spots are illustrated, along with level of difficulty for a buggy on the different footpaths. (See back flap for all symbols used.)
CIRCUITS: Page 7 (Circuits are often updated each year with minor changes - sometimes major).
BOULDERS and PROBLEMS: I have named every boulder and problem in this book, principally so they can be searched easily in the future on any web database. I have done many years of research to find the historically most appropriate name for each problem, but in cases where no name seems to be commonly known, I have suggested a temporary name in italics for basic identification. By setting all this down in this book, it should provide a backbone-skeleton, from which websites can provide a huge amount of more detailed info, videos etc. which can be easily searched and accessed. Some blocs are very high, so using a top rope on occoasions is highly advisable.
PHOTOTOPOS: If you are new to an area, these prove invaluable. I have taken very special care with the images, and used flash to light the more difficult boulders. (Over 20,000 images were shot for this book.) All traverse lines represent handholds, with any hold markers being very precisely positioned. The final edit to all of the photo-topos, have been checked by many climbers who live and climb in the Fontainebleau area, and have been responsible for many of the first ascents.
GRADES: Font grades are notoriously tough, but they are very fair and have stood the test of time: Grade 2; easy enough in tennis shoes, but is certainly proper vertical climbing - not so easy. Grade 3; technical so you will need proper rock shoes and be able to use very precise footholds. Grade 4; you either need very strong fingertips - or arms. Grade 5; you need both strong fingers and arms. Grade 6; you need additional core strength, and the abitliy to use a micro grain of sand as a foothold. Grade 7; you need even more core strength and compression on sloping holds.
GUIDEBOOKS: There are around 300 circuits and over 35,000 problems scattered in the forests around Fontainebleau, plenty to fill 5-10 different guidebooks with different styles. However, 82% (820 sq km) of the forest area has no bouldering remotely, so you could wander around literally for years before ever finding the boulders. Our Volume 2 book called "Top Secret" covers 9000 problems in the quieter areas. There are also many other guidebooks available by other authors.
THE FOREST: This is a fragile environment, please take all of your litter home, and leave no traces. GPS does not work very well under trees, but there is generally a good phone signal in most parts. Where problems have incredibly small holds, please do not chip or improve them, they are the ideal playground for very lightweight climbers. If you mark a hold with chalk, please do in a minimalistic way (its easy), then remove with a soft toothbrush before leaving. There are no toilets in the forest, so plan your day sensibly. If you do need to use the forest as a loo, please travel a good distance from the outcrop and always 50 metres from any possible climbing boulder.
Camping: Do not wild camp anywhere in the forest, please use campsites to support the local economy.

FUN BLOC - 127 CIRCUITS (Volume 1 - 2025 edition)

- ☐ ⚪ **1a ENF-** Franchard Ermitage (~)
- ☐ 🌸 **1a ENF-** Feuillardière (~)
- ☐ ⚪ **1a ENF-** Canche-Merciers Est (~)
- ☐ ⚪ **1b ENF** Beauvais Télé-Lout (~)
- ☐ ⚪ **1b ENF** Beauvais Nainville (~)
- ☐ 🌸 **1b ENF** Beauvais Télé-Lout (~)
- ☐ ⚪ **1b ENF-** Feuillardière (~)
- ☐ ⚪ **1b ENF** Rocher Canon (~)
- ☐ ⚪ **1b ENF** Apremont Bizons (~)
- ☐ ⚪ **1b ENF** Canche aux Merciers (~)
- ☐ 🟢 **1b ENF** Roche aux Sabots (~)
- ☐ ⚪ **1b ENF** Éléphant (~)
- ☐ ⚪ **1b ENF** Buthiers Piscine (~)
- ☐ ⚪ **1c ENF+** Feuillardière (~)
- ☐ ⚪ **1c ENF+** Beauvais Télégraphe (~)
- ☐ ⚪ **1c ENF+** Beauvais Nainville-C (~)
- ☐ ⚪ **1c ENF+** Saint Germain (~)
- ☐ ⚪ **1c ENF+** Rocher Cailleau (~)
- ☐ ⚪ **1c+ F** Beauvais Nainville-Côte (~)
- ☐ 🟡 **2a F** Beauvais Télé-Lout (~)
- ☐ 🟡 **2a F** Buthiers Piscine (1)
- ☐ 🟣 **2a+ F** Canche aux Merciers (1)
- ☐ 🟡 **2b PD** Beauvais Lout-Télé (1)
- ☐ 🟡 **2b PD** Beauvais Nainville (1)
- ☐ 🟡 **2b+ PD-** Canche-Merciers (1+)
- ☐ 🟡 **2c PD+** Beauvais Loutteville (1)
- ☐ 🟡 **2c PD+** Rocher Canon (1)
- ☐ 🟡 **2c PD** Rocher Fin (1)
- ☐ 🟡 **2c PD-** Éléphant (1+)
- ☐ 🟡 **2c+ PD+** 91.1 (1)
- ☐ 🟡 **2c+ PD+** Diplodocus (1)
- ☐ 🟣 **3a AD-** Rocher Canon (1)
- ☐ 🟠 **3a PD+** 95.2-Nord (~)
- ☐ 🟠 **3a AD-** Saint Germain (1)
- ☐ 🟠 **3a AD-** Apremont Bizons (1)
- ☐ 🟡 **3a PD** Isatis (1)
- ☐ 🟡 **3a PD** Potets (1)
- ☐ 🟠 **3a AD-** Cul de Chien (1)
- ☐ 🟠 **3a PD+** Gorge aux Chats (1)
- ☐ 🟠 **3a PD+** Potala (1)
- ☐ 🟠 **3a+ PD** Rocher Cailleau (1+)
- ☐ 🟠 **3a+ PD+** Apremont Gorges (1+)
- ☐ 🟠 **3a+ AD** Cuisinière (1)
- ☐ 🟠 **3b AD** Bois Rond (1)
- ☐ 🟠 **3b AD+** Cuvier (1)
- ☐ 🟠 **3b AD+** Sabots (1)
- ☐ 🟠 **3b AD** 91.1 Sud (1)
- ☐ 🟠 **3b AD** Guichot (1)
- ☐ 🟠 **3b AD** Buthiers Piscine (1)
- ☐ 🟠 **3b AD** Beauvais Hameau (1)
- ☐ 🟠 **3b AD+** Éléphant (2++)
- ☐ 🟠 **3b+ AD+** Beauvais Nainville (1)
- ☐ 🟠 **3b+ AD+** Bois Rond (1)
- ☐ 🟠 **3b+ AD** Rocher Canon (1+)
- ☐ 🟠 **3b AD** Canche aux Merciers (1+)
- ☐ 🟢 **3b+ AD+** Apremont Gorges (2+)
- ☐ 🟠 **3c AD+** Diplodocus (1)
- ☐ 🟠 **3c+ AD+** 95.2-Ouest (1)
- ☐ 🟠 **3c+ AD+** 91.1 (1)
- ☐ 🟠 **4a AD+** Rocher Fin (1)
- ☐ 🔵 **4a D-** Saint German (1)
- ☐ 🟠 **4a AD** Isatis (1+)
- ☐ 🟠 **4a AD+** Beauvais R-Noires (1+)
- ☐ 🟠 **4a AD+** 95.2-Sud (1+)
- ☐ 🟠 **4a AD+** Apremont Bizons (1)
- ☐ 🔵 **4a D-** Beauvais Téléegraphe (1+)
- ☐ 🔵 **4a AD+** Rocher Cailleau (2+)
- ☐ 🔵 **4a+ AD+** Potala (1)
- ☐ 🔵 **4b D** Cul de Chien (1)
- ☐ 🔵 **4b D** Cuisinière (1+)
- ☐ 🔵 **4b D** Apremont Outremer (1+)
- ☐ 🔵 **4b+ D** Canon No.5 (1+)
- ☐ 🔵 **4b+ D+** Canche aux Merciers (1+)
- ☐ 🔵 **4c D** Beauvais Nainville (1)
- ☐ 🔵 **4c D+** Potala (1)
- ☐ 🔵 **4c D+** 95.2 (2+)
- ☐ 🔵 **4c D** Rocher Cailleau (2+)
- ☐ 🔵 **4c+ D++** Diplodocus (2+)
- ☐ 🔴 **5a D+** Rocher Fin (1)
- ☐ 🔴 **5a D+** Gorge aux Chats (1+)
- ☐ 🔴 **5a TD-** Saint Germain (1)
- ☐ 🔴 **5a D+** Roche aux Sabots (1)
- ☐ 🔵 **5a D+** Isatis (1)
- ☐ 🔵 **5a D+** Guichot (1)
- ☐ 🔴 **5a TD-** 91.1 (2+)
- ☐ 🔴 **5a D++** Canon No.4 (1+)
- ☐ 🔴 **5a TD-** Bois Rond (1+)
- ☐ 🔴 **5a D+** Beauvais R-Noires (2+)
- ☐ 🔴 **5a D+** Buthiers Piscine (2+)
- ☐ 🔴 **5a TD-** Éléphant (4+X☠)
- ☐ 🔵 **5a+ D++** Télégraphe Noisy (2+)
- ☐ 🔵 **5a D+** Beauvais Loutteville (2+)
- ☐ 🔴 **5b TD** Isatis-Franchard (1+)
- ☐ 🔵 **5b TD-** Bas Cuvier (2)
- ☐ 🔴 **5b TD-** 91.1 (2)
- ☐ ⚪ **5b TD-** Apremont Gorges (2+)
- ☐ 🔴 **5b TD-** 95.2 (2+)
- ☐ 🔵 **5c TD** Beauvais Nainville (1)
- ☐ 🔴 **5c TD+** Cul de Chien (1+)
- ☐ 🔴 **5c TD-** Beauvais R-Noires (1)
- ☐ 🔴 **5c TD** Apremont Bizons (2+)
- ☐ 🔴 **5c TD** Buthiers Piscine (2+)
- ☐ 🔴 **5c ED-** Apremont Gorges (5++)
- ☐ 🔴 **5c+ TD+** Cuisinière-Franchard (2+)
- ☐ 🔴 **5c+ TD+** Bas Cuvier (2+)
- ☐ 🔴 **6a TD+** Potala (1+)
- ☐ ⚪ **6a ED-** Cuisinière-Franchard (3+)
- ☐ 🔴 **6a TD+** Canche aux Merciers (1+)
- ☐ ⚪ **6a ED-** 95.2 (1+)
- ☐ ⚪ **6a ED-** Rocher Fin (1+)
- ☐ 🔴 **6a ED-** Apremont Gorges (2+)
- ☐ 🔴 **6a ED-** Rocher Cailleau (2+)
- ☐ ⚫ **6a ED-** Éléphant (4+X☠)
- ☐ 🔴 **6a+ ED-** Saint Germain (1+)
- ☐ 🔴 **6a+ ED-** Rocher Canon (1+)
- ☐ 🔴 **6a+ ED-** Gorge aux Chats (2+)
- ☐ 🔴 **6a+ ED-** Bois Rond (1+)
- ☐ 🔴 **6a+ ED-** Roche aux Sabots (1+)
- ☐ 🔴 **6a+ ED-** Guichot (1+)
- ☐ ⚪ **6a+ ED** Isatis-Franchard (2+)
- ☐ ⚫ **6b ED-** Beauvais Nainv-Bois (1)
- ☐ ⚫ **6b ED-** Bas Cuvier (2+)
- ☐ ⚫ **6b ED** Buthiers Piscine (3+p☠)
- ☐ ⚪ **6c ED+** Beauvais Nainv-Côte (2+)
- ☐ ⚪ **6c ED+** Apremont Gorges (2+)
- ☐ ⚪ **7a ED+** Bas Cuvier (2+)
- ☐ ⚪ **7a+ ED+** Rocher Canon (2+)

Historic Niveau/Circuit grades:
- ⚪ **1a ENF-** Enfants - Blocs 1 metre
- 🌸 **1b ENF** Enfants - Blocs 2 metre
- 🟢 **1c ENF+** Enfants - Blocs 3 metre
- 🟡 **2a PD-** Peu Difficile
- 🟡 **2b PD** Peu Difficile (little difficult)
- 🟡 **2c PD+** Peu Difficile plus
- 🟠 **3a AD-** Assez Difficile
- 🟠 **3b AD** Assez Difficile (quite difficult)
- 🟠 **3c AD+** Assez Difficile plus
- 🔵 **4a D-** Difficile
- 🔵 **4b D** Difficile (difficult)
- 🔵 **4c D+** Difficile plus
- 🔴 **5a TD-** Trés difficile
- 🔴 **5b TD** Trés difficile (very difficult)
- 🔴 **5c TD+** Trés difficile plus
- ⚫⚪ **6a ED-** Extreme difficile
- ⚫⚪ **6b/c ED** Extreme difficile
- ⚫⚪ **7a/7b ED+** Extreme difficile plus

Circuit numbers: 3cm in size
About 1.5m up from ground.
Start with hand either side of arrow.
A coloured dot may show the start foothold under an overhang.
Dot to the right of number - next problem is somewhere to the right.

Fonatinebleau Grades / V Grade comparison

2a-c	3a-b	3c	4a-c	5a-b	5c-6a	6b-c	7a	7b	7c
🟡	🟠	🟠	🔵	🔴	🔴	⚫	🟣	🟣	🟣
V0	V1	V2	V3	V4	V5	V6	V7	V8	V9

If your spotter doesn't catch you... its your fault... "you" chose the wrong spotter, make sure to choose wisely.

FONTAINEBLEAU CIRCUITS - Fun Bloc (127) & Top Secret (150)

Fontainebleau est un site d'escalade unique en son genre, car chaque "bloc" offre généralement un grand nombre de problèmes différents dans la plupart des niveaux. Des circuits d'escalade colorés ont été créés, en peignant des numéros séquentiels avec des flèches qui vont d'un bloc à l'autre, et en regroupant les problèmes d'une difficulté similaire avec une couleur. À l'origine, l'idée était de suivre un itinéraire à travers la forêt, qui était facile à suivre puisqu'une fois la mousse et le lichen nettoyés, le sentier était évident. L'escalade de bloc est devenue plus populaire, et avec de nombreux circuits de différents niveaux, des flèches ont été peintes sur le dessus de chaque bloc, pour vous indiquer la direction du problème suivant. Cependant, si vous ne parveniez pas à franchir un problème, trouver le suivant était un véritable cauchemar. Aujourd'hui, la plupart des grimpeurs utilisent un crash pad - les flèches au sommet ont donc disparu, et un point situé de part et d'autre du numéro indique où se trouve le problème suivant. Chaque circuit se voit attribuer une note globale de type voie de montagne historique, illustrée à gauche. Comme en montagne, certains itinéraires plus faciles peuvent avoir une section très difficile pour le niveau, ce qui vous oblige à tirer sur un boulon. Fontainebleau est similaire, parfois il y a des problèmes inclus dans un circuit en dehors de la gamme normale de grades (pourquoi - je ne sais pas ?), il est préférable de simplement l'éviter et de passer à côté. Je trouve que faire 80% des problèmes d'un circuit est très satisfaisant, certains peuvent ne pas convenir à votre style d'escalade, d'autres n'ont pas vraiment leur place sur le circuit. Certains problèmes peuvent tout simplement être trop dangereux pour vous ; ils peuvent certainement l'être, alors ne soyez pas stupide - "revenez peut-être" - avec plus de tampons, de spotters ou même une corde. J'ai toujours aimé traiter les circuits comme un défi à vue, en les faisant entièrement en une journée - avec un maximum de 10 chutes. J'ai réussi presque tous les circuits de cette manière (sauf le ED), mais pour faire cela en TD+, vous devez être à l'aise en 7b, ce qui veut tout dire, c'est un défi complet. Pour la plupart des visiteurs, faire la moitié d'un circuit est raisonnable en une journée, et vous êtes encore fort et frais pour le jour suivant. La note globale que j'attribue à chaque circuit illustre la note requise pour surmonter environ 80 % des problèmes et passer une bonne journée. Je donne une évaluation globale du crash pad. (~) bloc à bloc, (1) pad ok, (2+) pads et parreurs (p) panique, (X☠) sérieux risques pour la santé.

Fontainebleau is a unique climbing area, because each actual "boulder," usually offers so many different problems across most of the grades. Coloured climbing circuits have been created, by painting sequential numbers with arrows that go from boulder to boulder, and group problems of a similar difficulty with a colour. Originally, the idea was to follow a route through the forest, which was easy to follow since once the moss and lichen had been cleaned off - the trail was obvious. Bouldering became more popular, and with many circuits of different levels, arrows were then painted on top of each boulder, to point you in the direction of the next problem. However, if you didn't get up a problem - finding the next one was a nightmare. Today, most climbers use a crash pad - so the arrows at the top have disappeared, and a dot to either side of the number illustrates where the next problem is. Each **"Circuit"** is given an overall historic mountain route style grade, illustrated on the left page. Just like in the mountains, some easier routes might have a super hard section for the grade - so you pull on a bolt. Fontainebleau is similar, sometimes there are problems included on a circuit outside the normal grade range (why - I do not know?), it is best to simply avoid and pass by. I find that doing 80% of the problems on a circuit very satisfying, some might not suit your style of climbing, some don't really belong on the circuit. Some problems may simply be too dangerous for you; they certainly can be, so don't be stupid - "return maybe" - with more pads, spotters or even a rope. I've always enjoyed treating circuits as an onsight challenge, doing them complete in one day - with a maximum of 10 falls. I've managed nearly all of the circuits like this (except the ED), but to do this in TD+, you have to be comfortable in 7b, which says it all: it's a full on challenge. For most visitors, doing half a circuit is sensible in a day, and then you are still strong and fresh for the next day (local climbers usually take 2 rest days after a full day). The overall grade I give for each circuit, illustrates the grade required for getting up around 80% of the problems and having a good day out. I give an overall crash pad assessment. (~) bloc to bloc, (1) 1 pad ok-ish, (2+) 2 pads and (+) spotter, (p) Scary, (X☠) Serious health hazard.

Cotation/Grades: Page 55   Fontainebleau Technique & Tips: Page 143

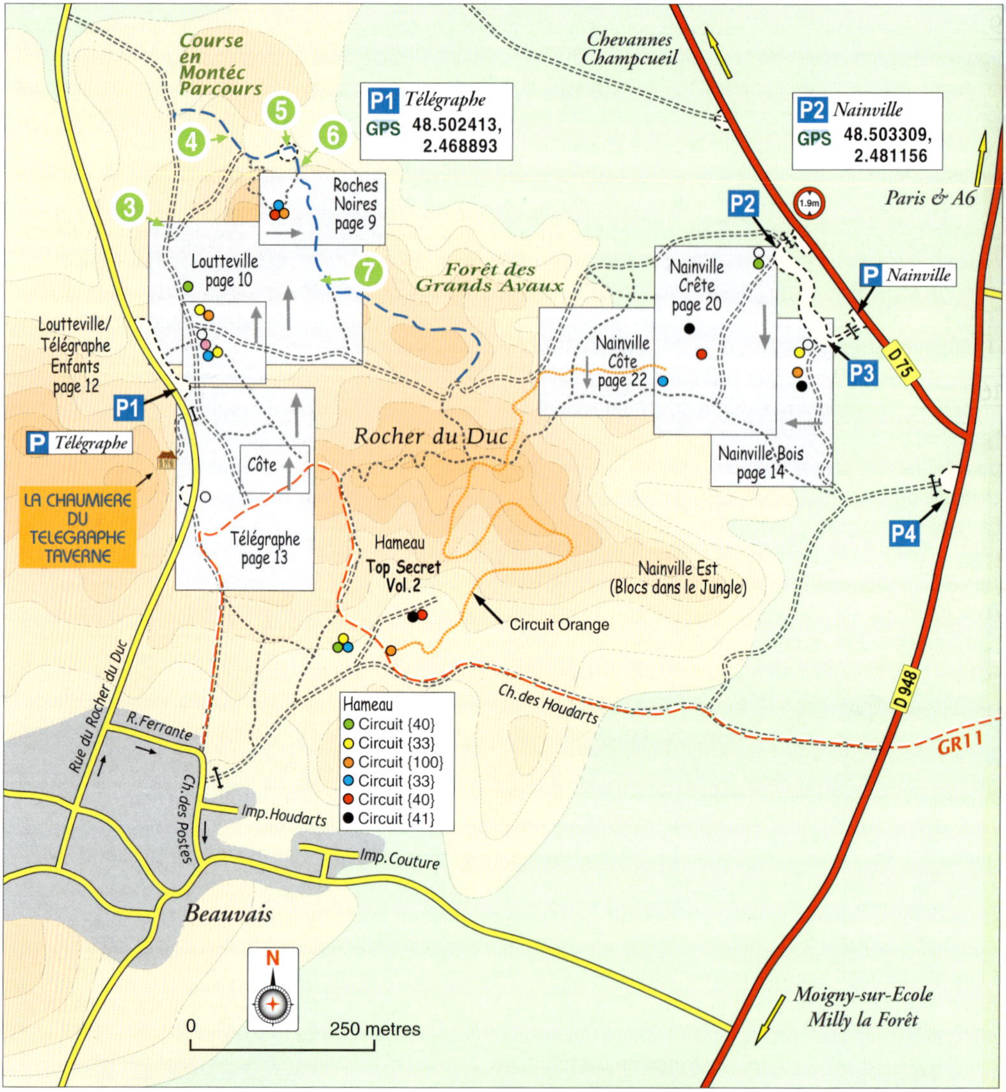

BEAUVAIS

Map of Beauvais climbing area showing parking locations (P1 Télégraphe GPS 48.502413, 2.468893; P2 Nainville GPS 48.503309, 2.481156; P3; P4), sectors (Roches Noires page 9, Loutteville page 10, Loutteville/Télégraphe Enfants page 12, Côte, Télégraphe page 13, Hameau Top Secret Vol.2, Nainville Crête page 20, Nainville Côte page 22, Nainville Bois page 14, Nainville Est (Blocs dans le Jungle)), and the Course en Montéc Parcours with numbered stops 3–7. Notable features: Forêt des Grands Avaux, Rocher du Duc, Circuit Orange, Ch. des Houdarts, GR11, La Chaumière du Télégraphe Taverne. Roads: D75, D948. Directions to Chevannes Champcueil, Paris & A6, Moigny-sur-Ecole, Milly la Forêt. Village of Beauvais with Rue du Rocher du Duc, R. Ferrante, Ch. des Postes, Imp. Houdarts, Imp. Couture.

Hameau
- 🟢 Circuit {40}
- 🟡 Circuit {33}
- 🟠 Circuit {100}
- 🔵 Circuit {33}
- 🔴 Circuit {40}
- ⚫ Circuit {41}

Scale: 0 – 250 metres. North arrow.

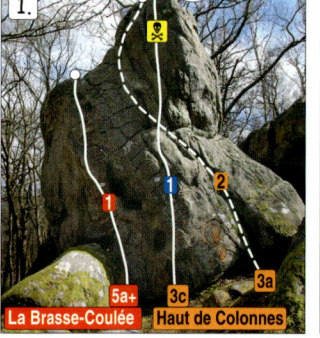

1. (6m) — **La Brasse-Coulée** 5a+ (1), **Haut de Colonnes** 3c (1) / 3a (2)

2. (3m) — **Le Trou** 5b- (2), **Le Ventre** 5c (2), **Les Oreilles** 4c (3)

5. (6m) — **L'Octrol** 5b- (5) / 2c, **Les Draperies** 3c (5) / 7 / 6 / 2b

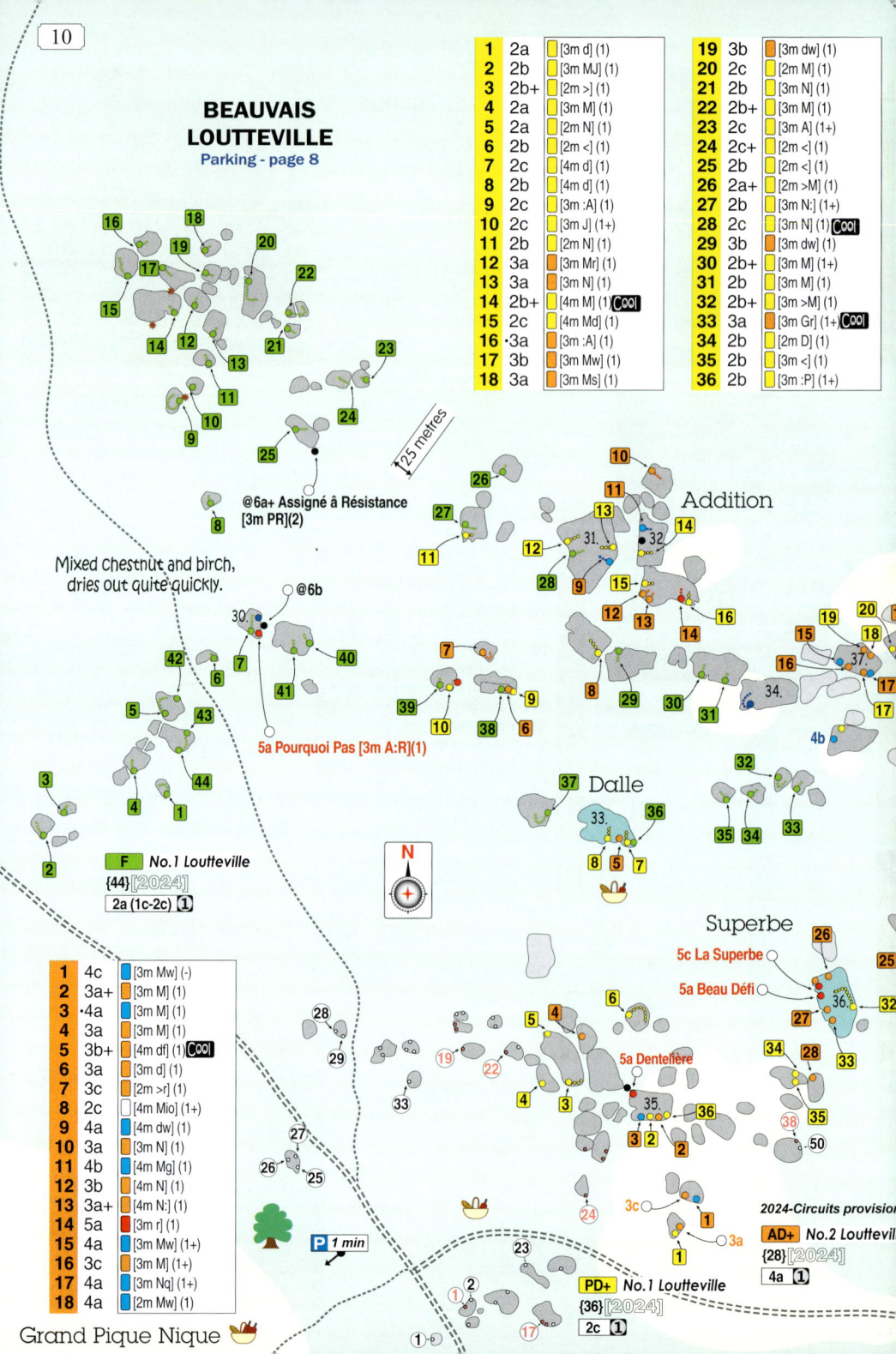

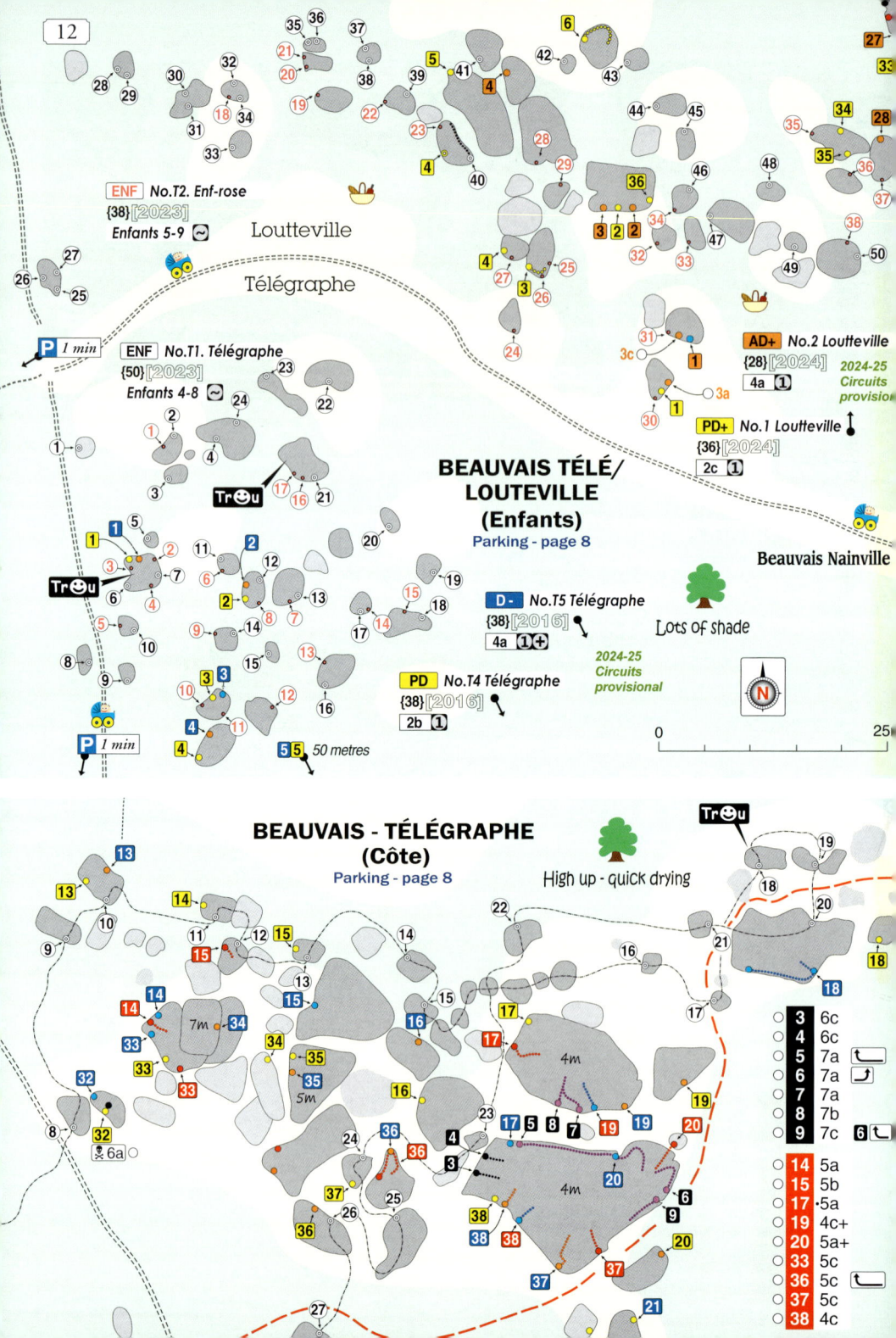

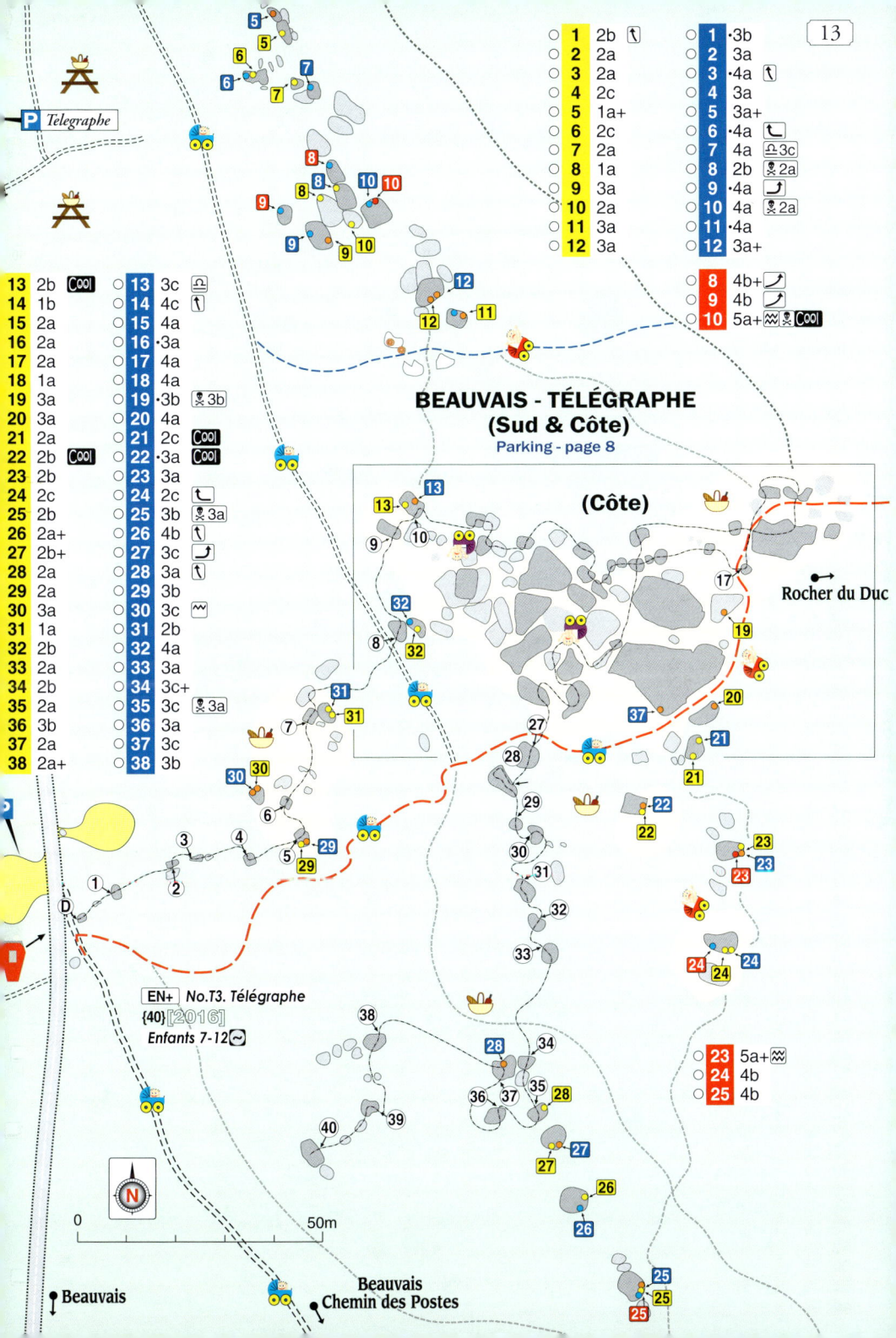

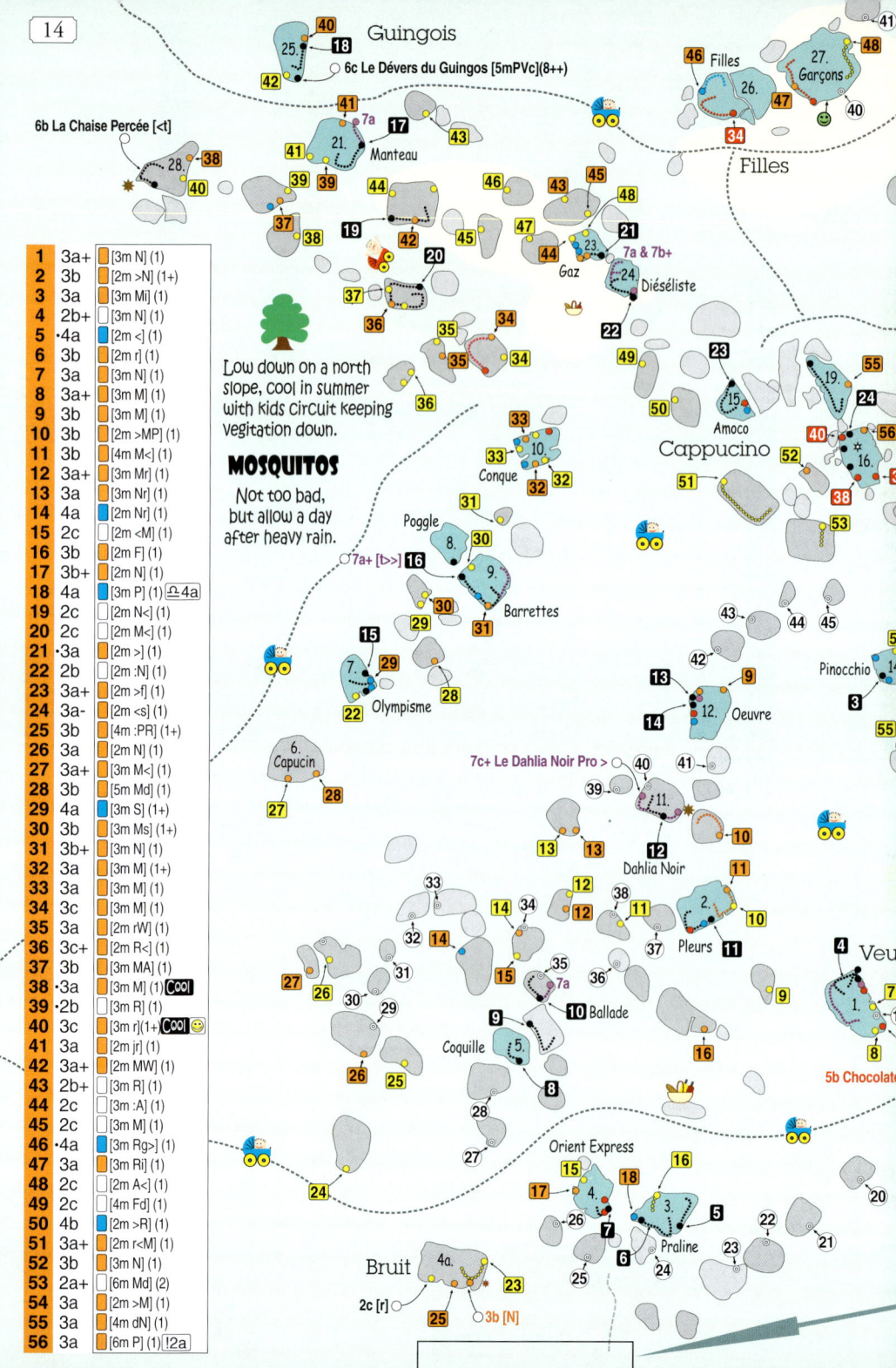

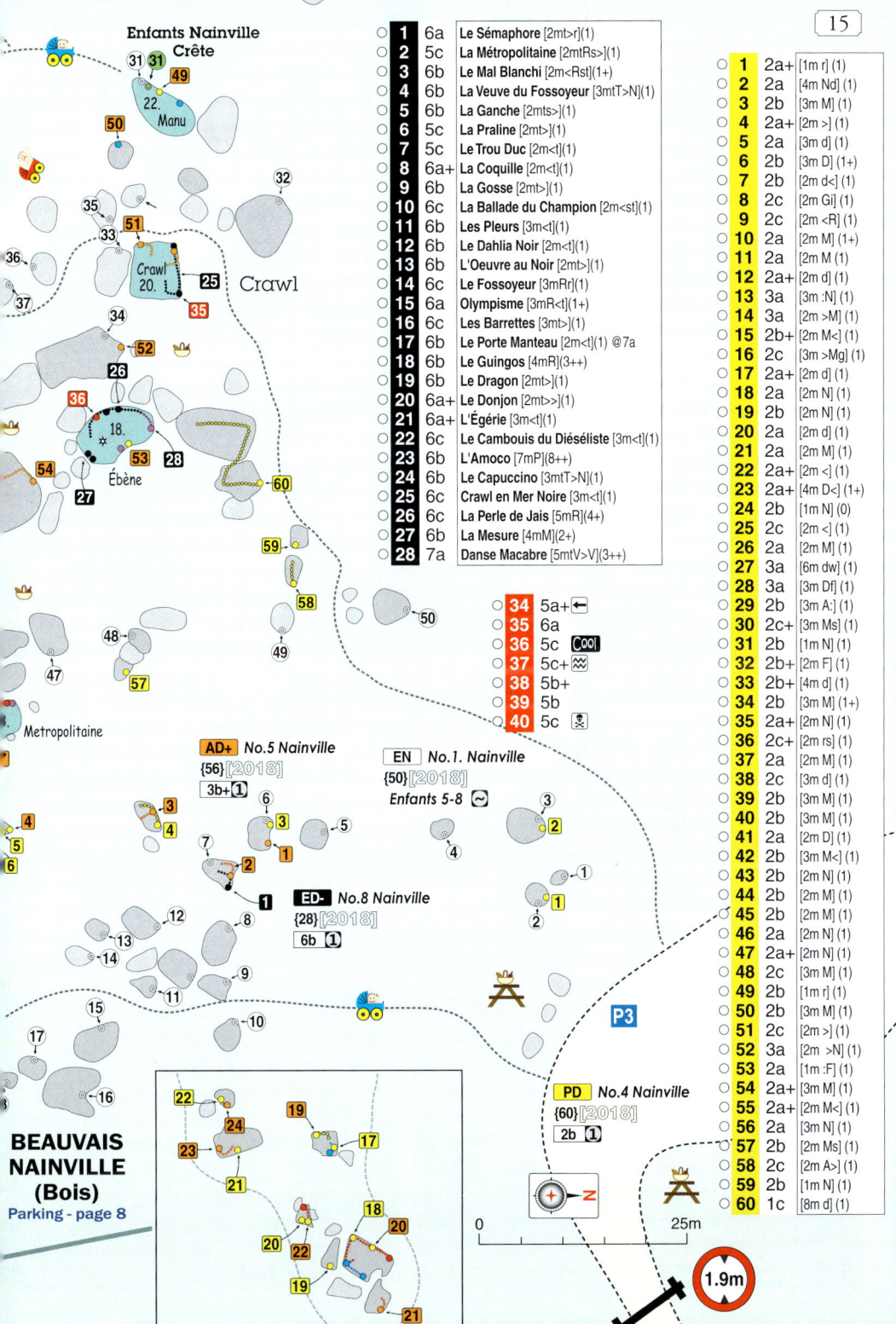

BEAUVAIS - NAINVILLE (Bois)

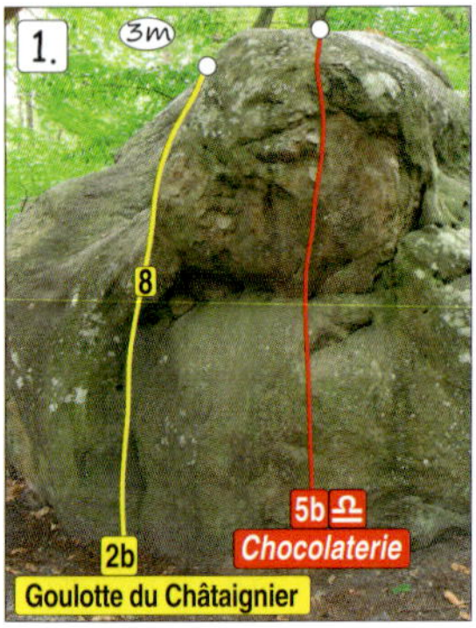

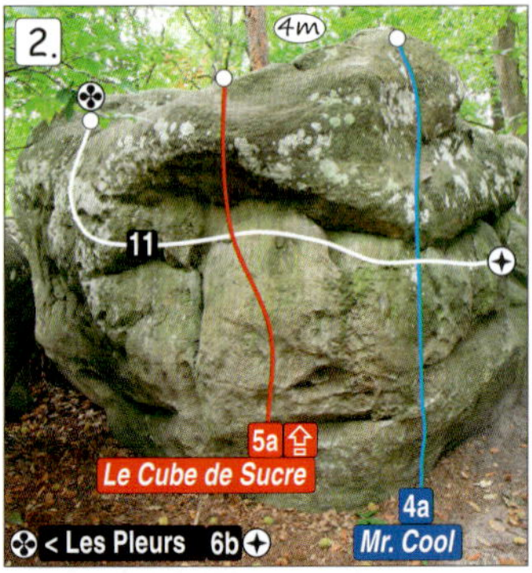

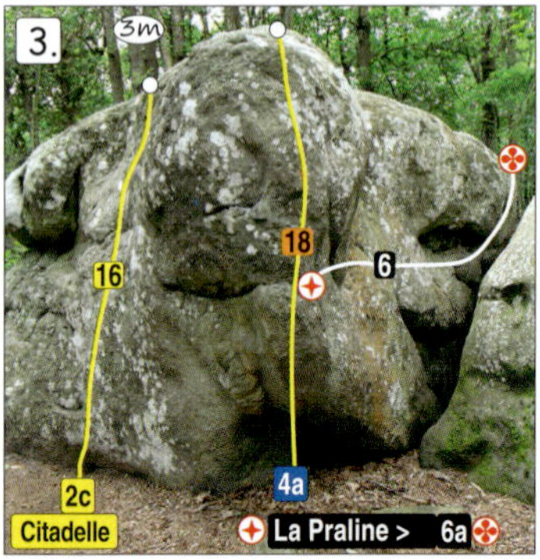

BEAUVAIS - NAINVILLE (Bois)

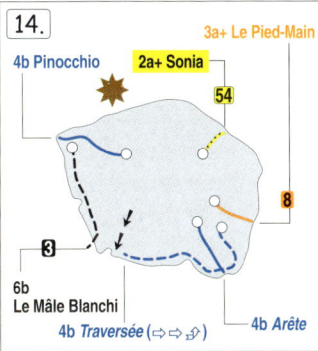

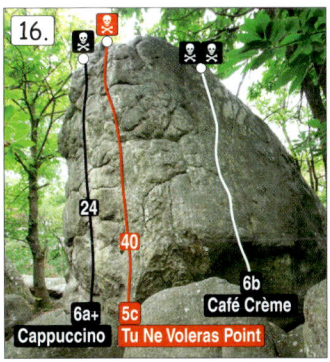

Beauvais Parking - page 8

BEAUVAIS - NAINVILLE (Bois)

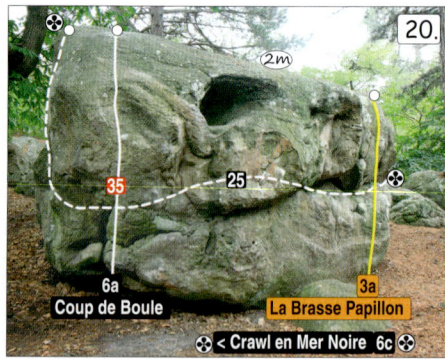

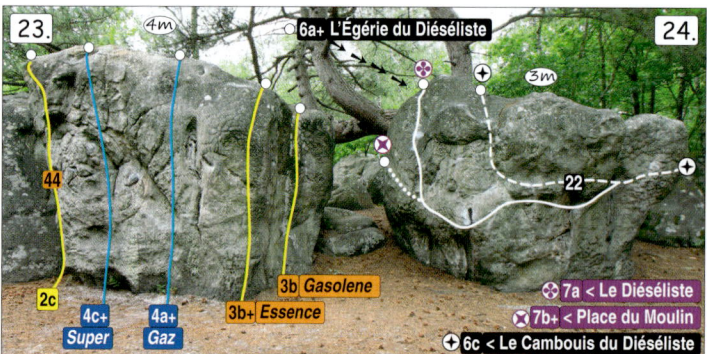
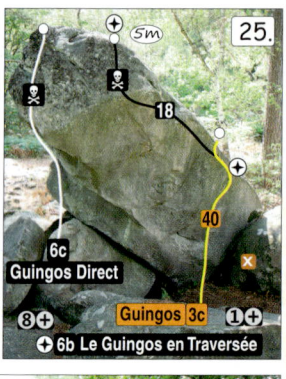

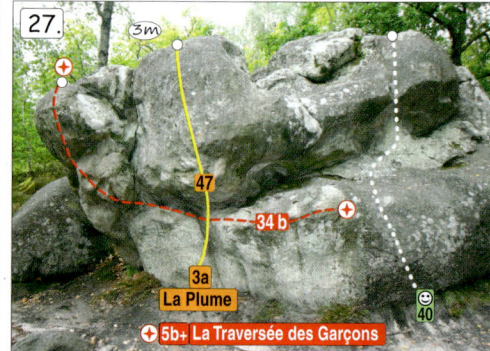

3b+ Circuit Orange, *Mathilde & Didier* [Beauvais Bois] ▷

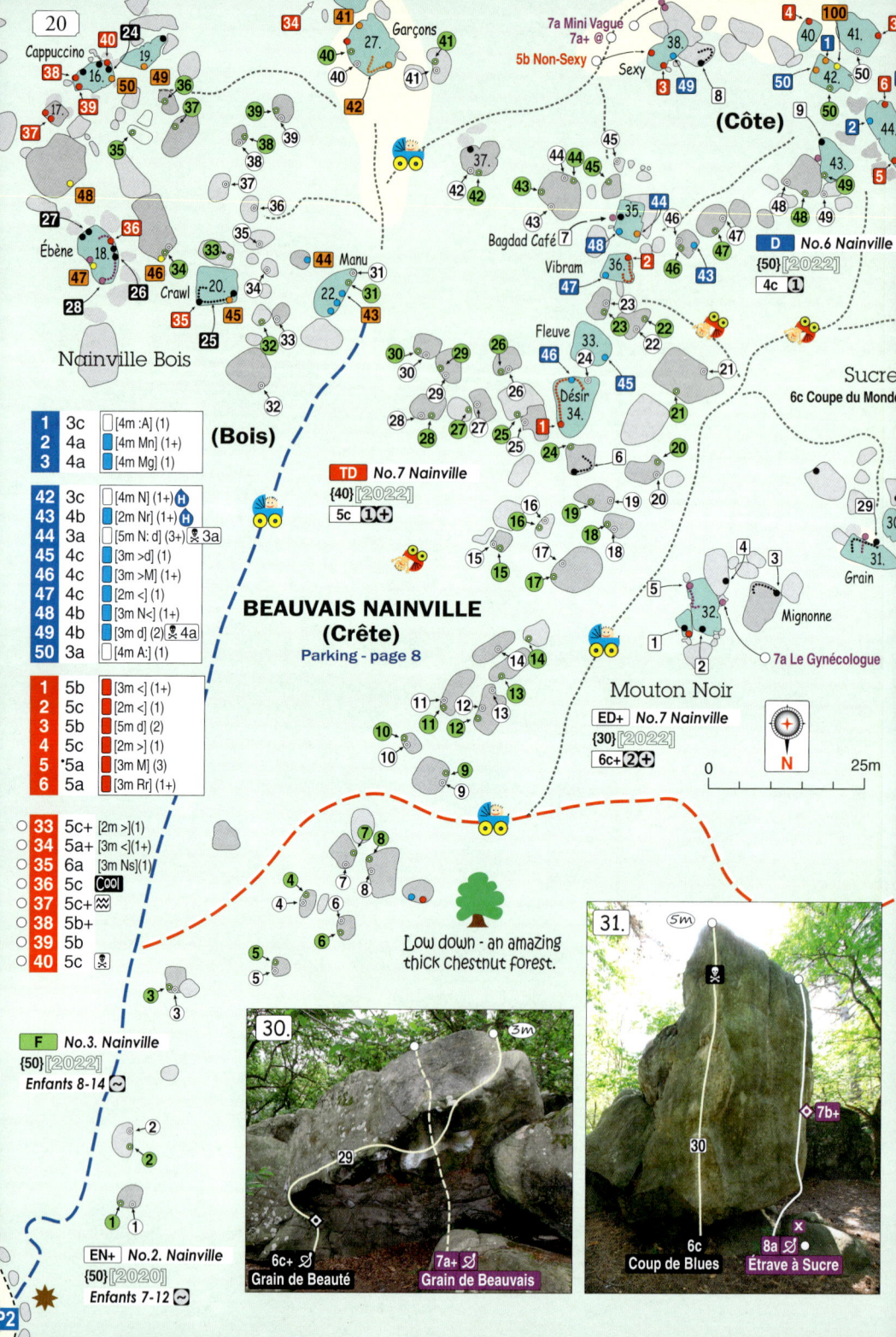

BEAUVAIS - NAINVILLE (Crête)

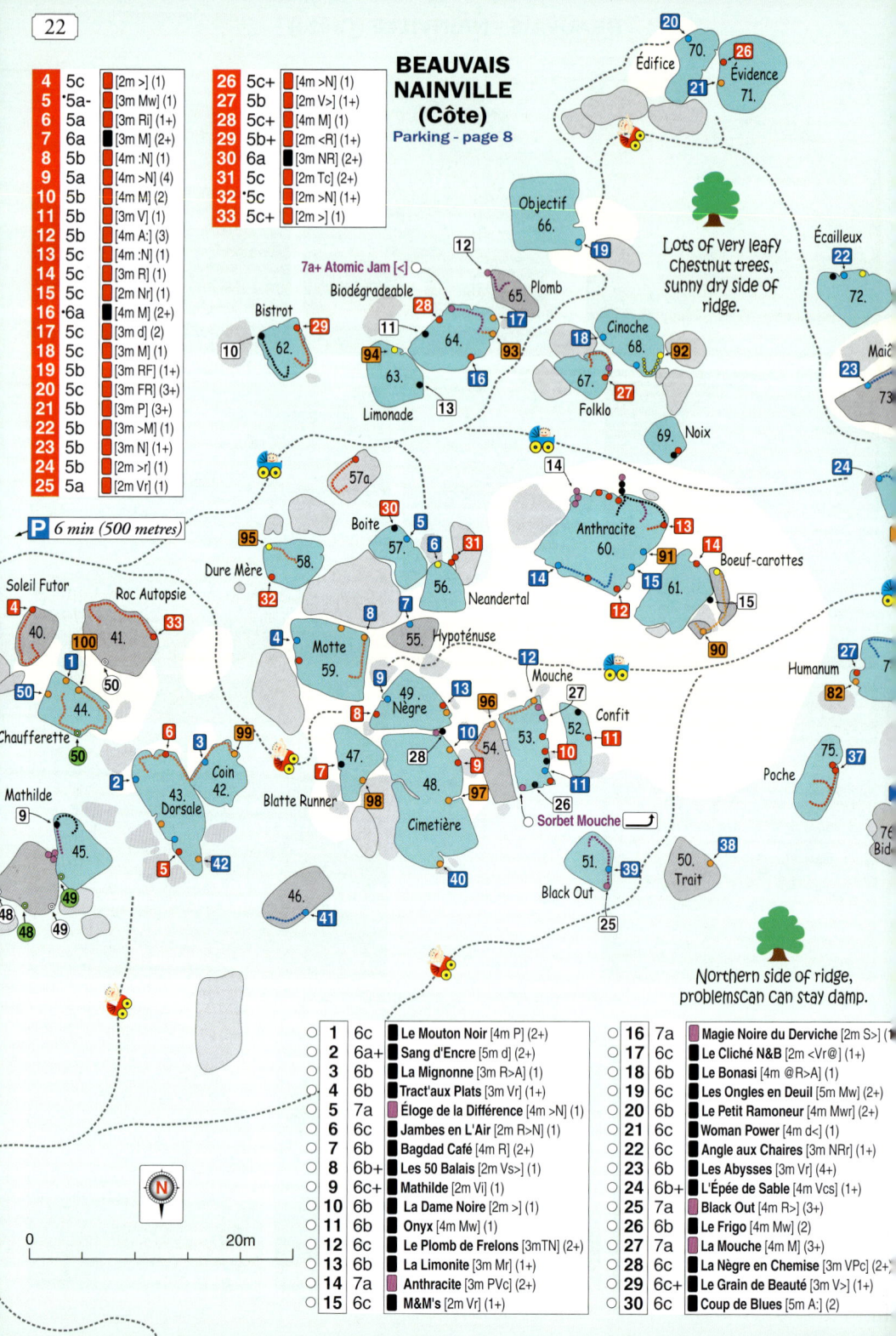

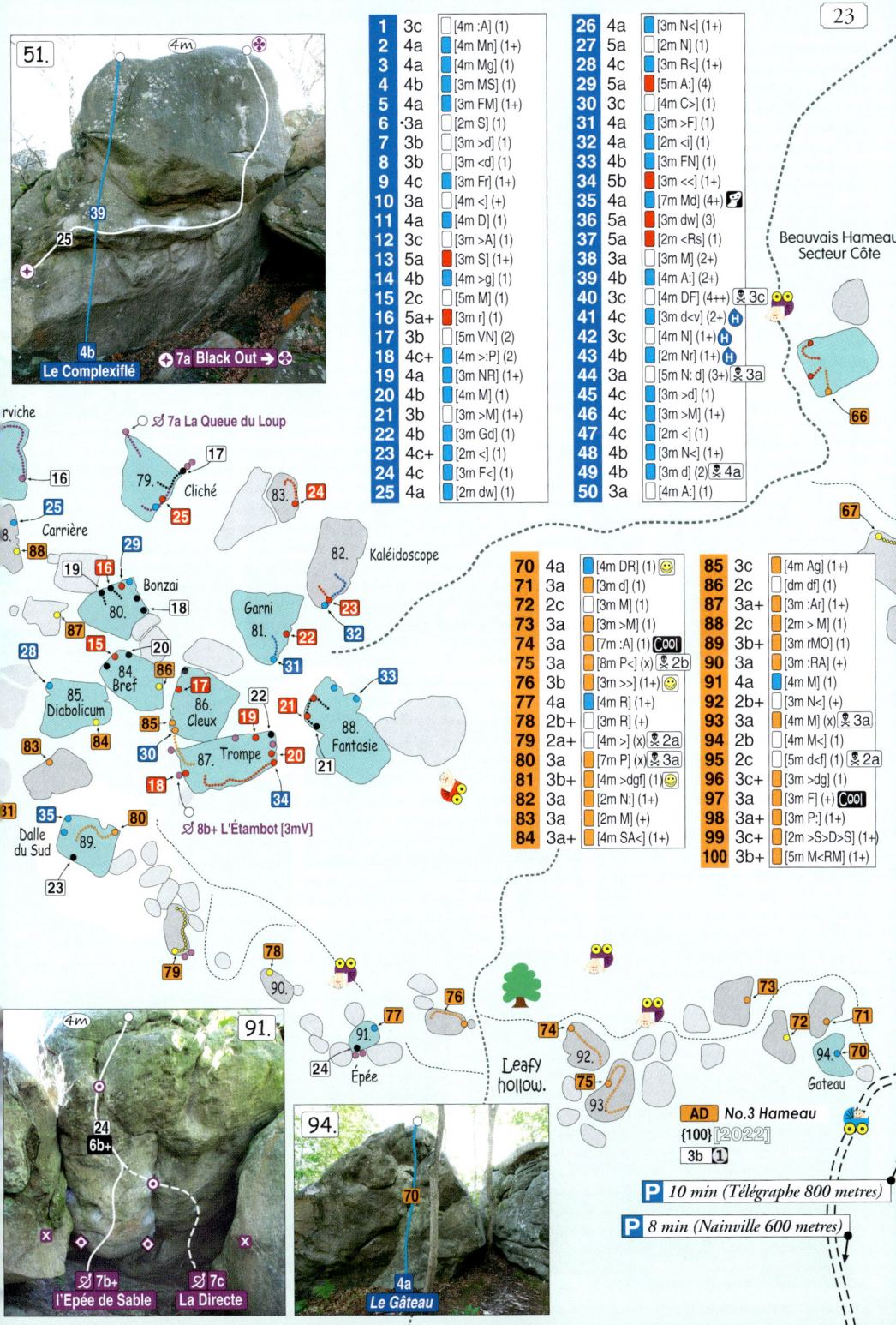

BEAUVAIS - NAINVILLE (Côte)

BEAUVAIS - NAINVILLE (Côte)

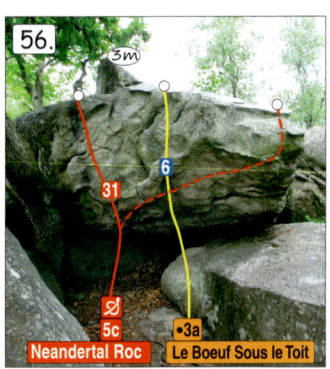

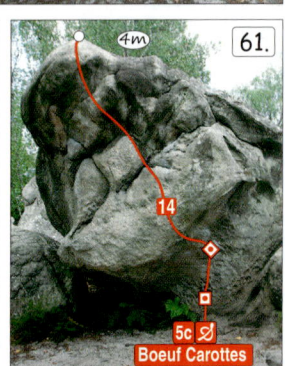
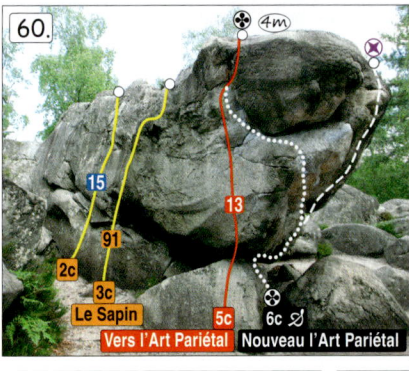
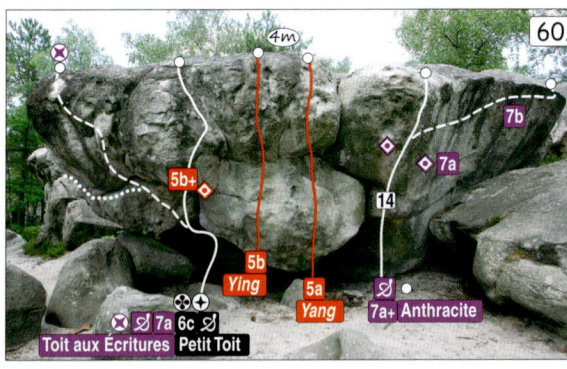

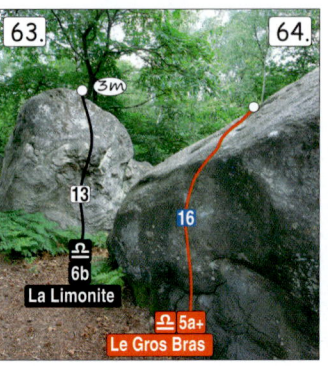

BEAUVAIS - NAINVILLE (Côte)

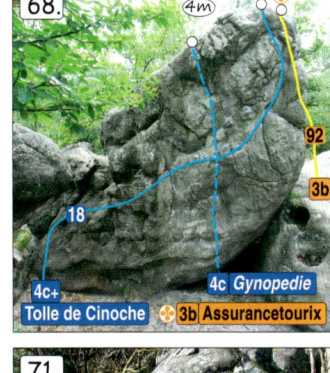
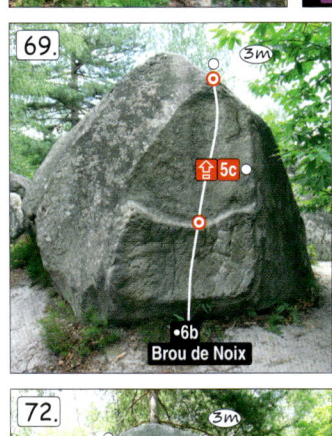

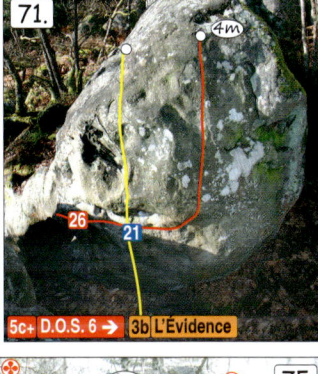

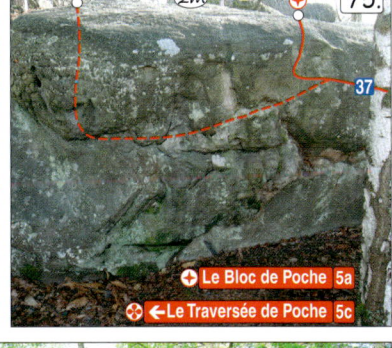

BEAUVAIS - NAINVILLE (Côte)

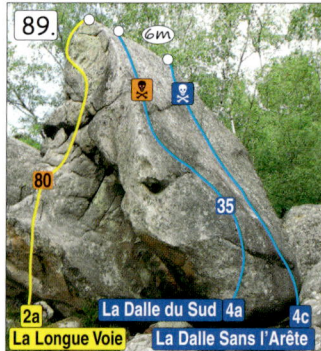

Beauvais Parking - page 8   7a LE CLICHÉ PROLONGÉ, *Laurie Barascud* [Beauvais Nainville Côte-bloc 79] ≫

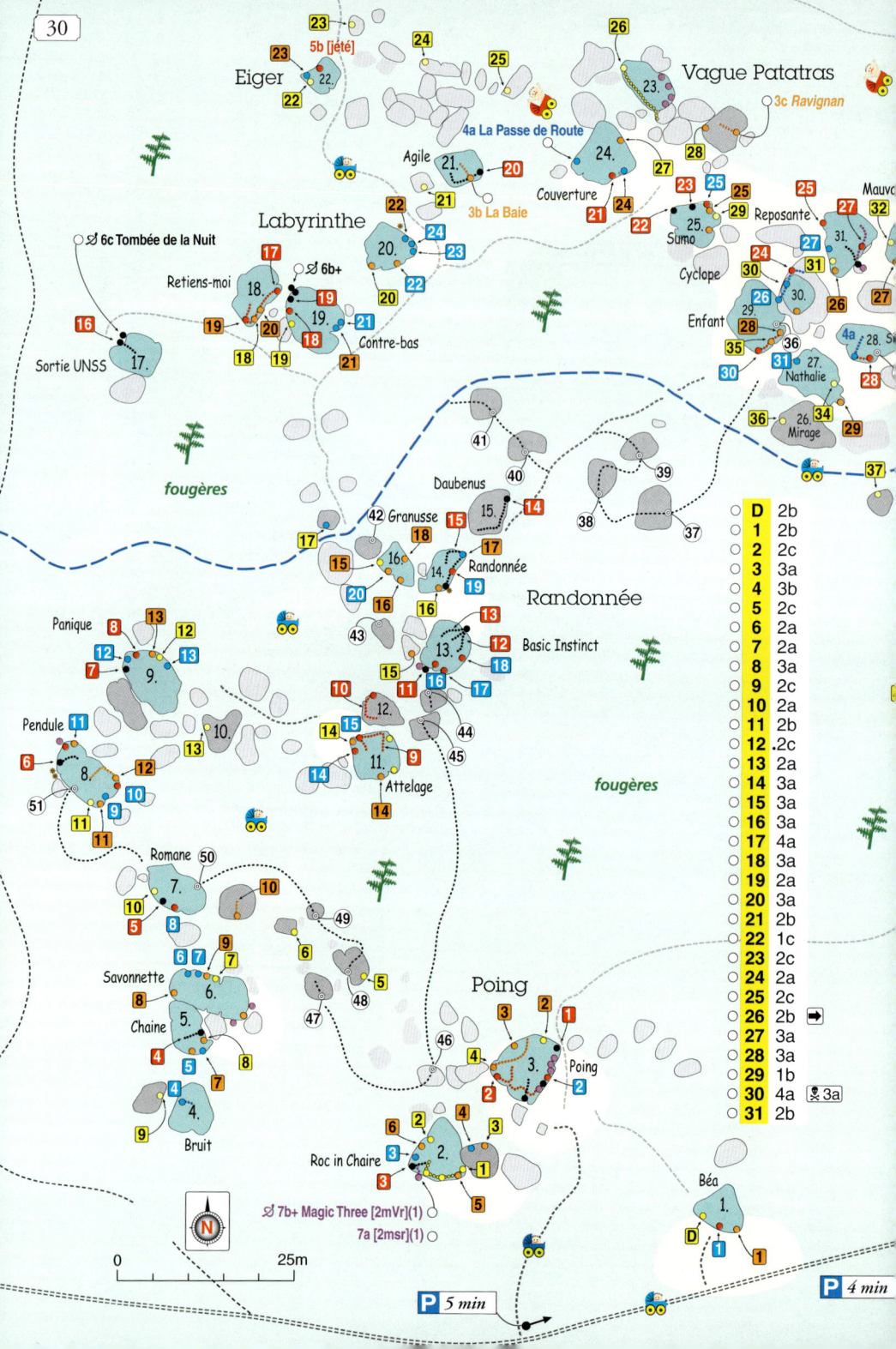

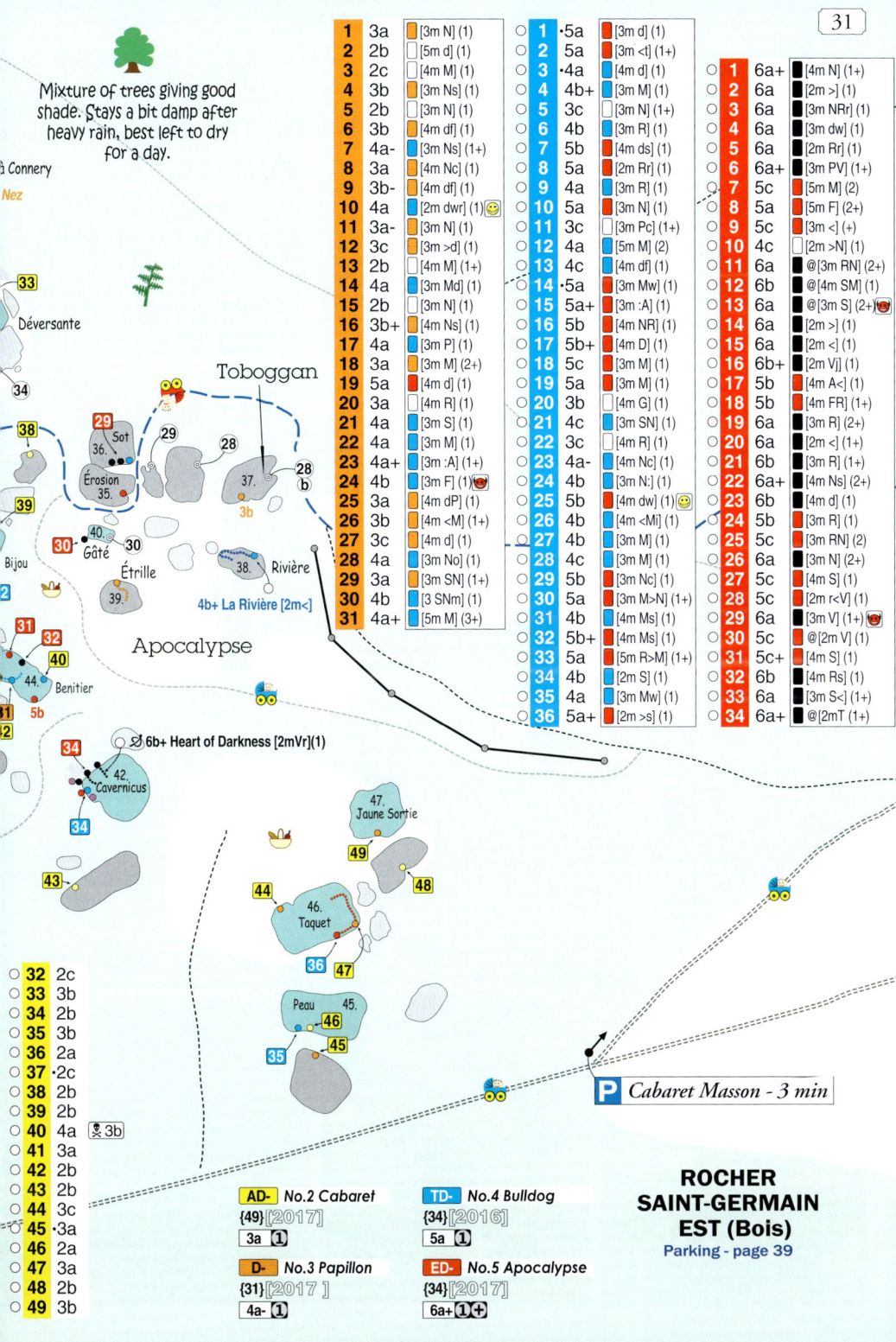

ROCHER SAINT-GERMAIN EST

ROCHER SAINT-GERMAIN EST

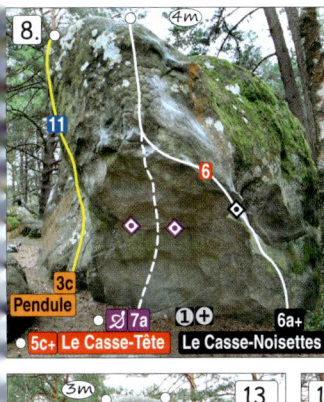

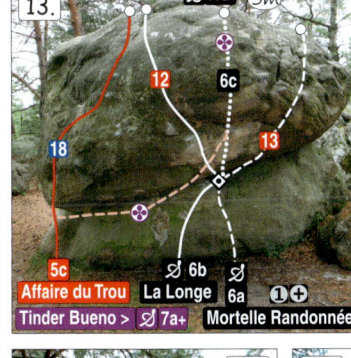
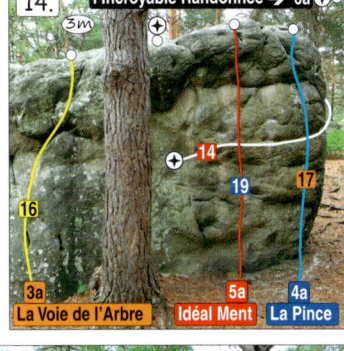

Rocher Saint-Germain Parking - page 39

ROCHER SAINT-GERMAIN

ROCHER SAINT-GERMAIN

Aerial plan - 30

Rocher Saint-Germain Parking - page 39

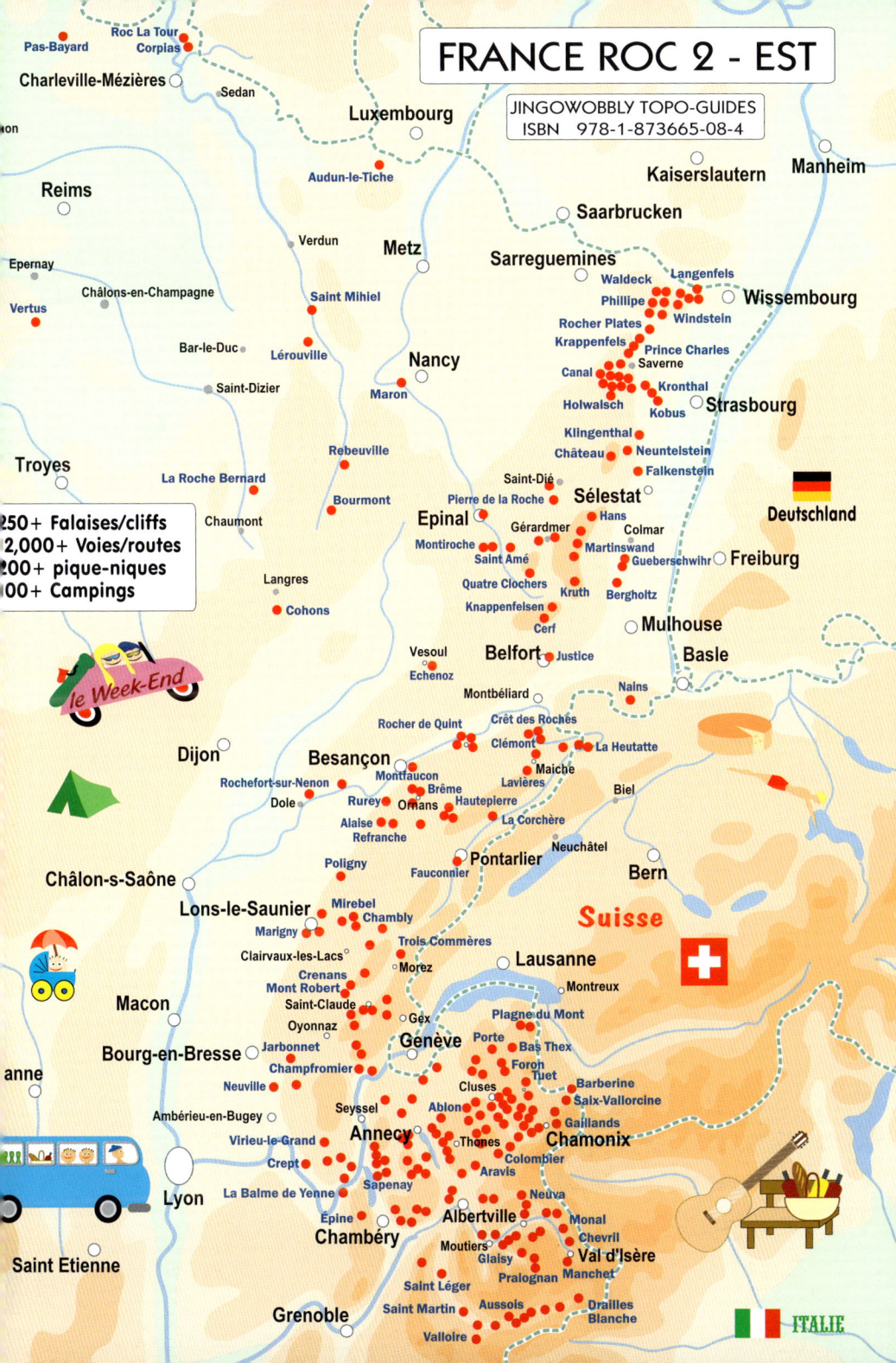

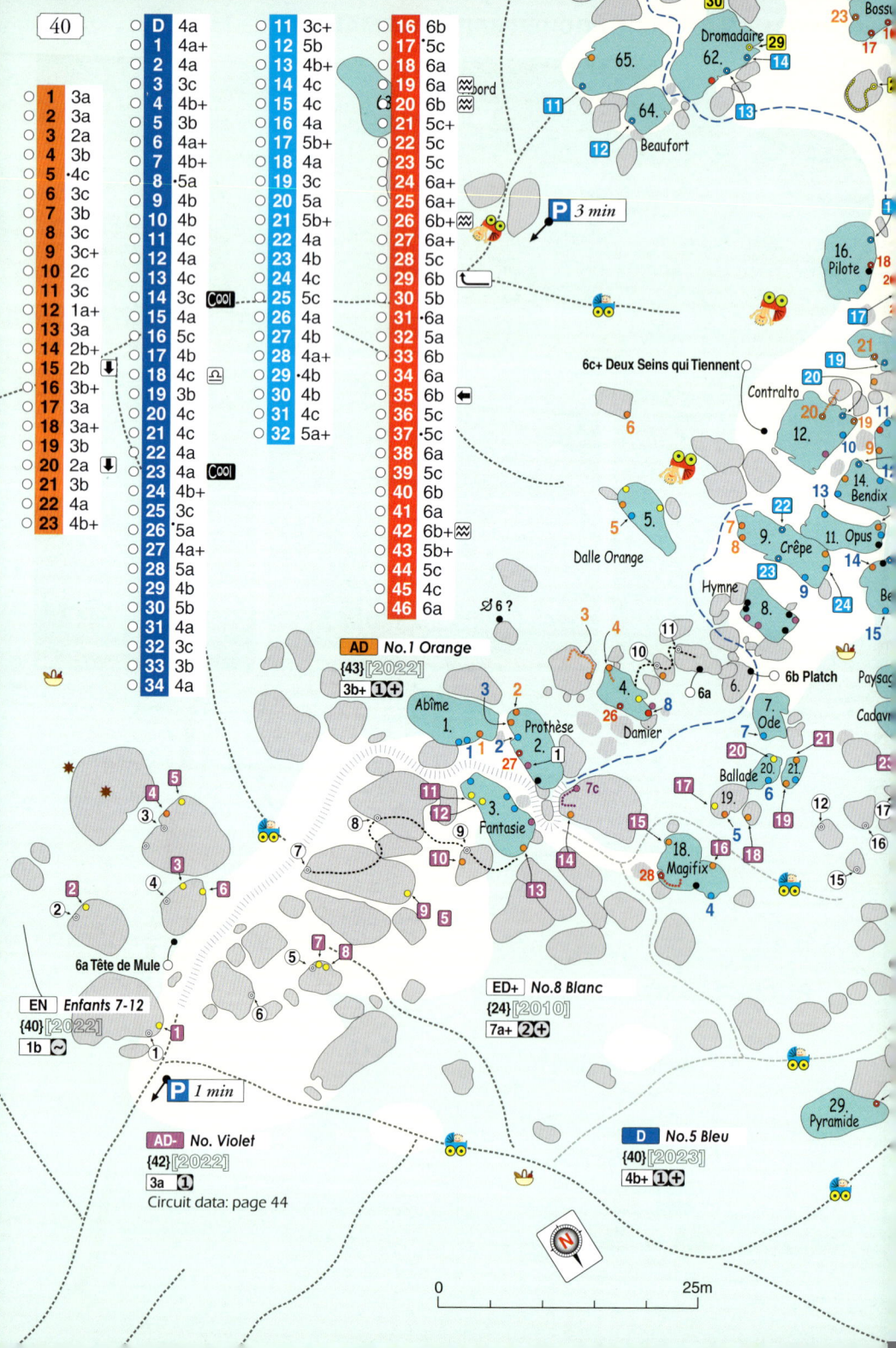

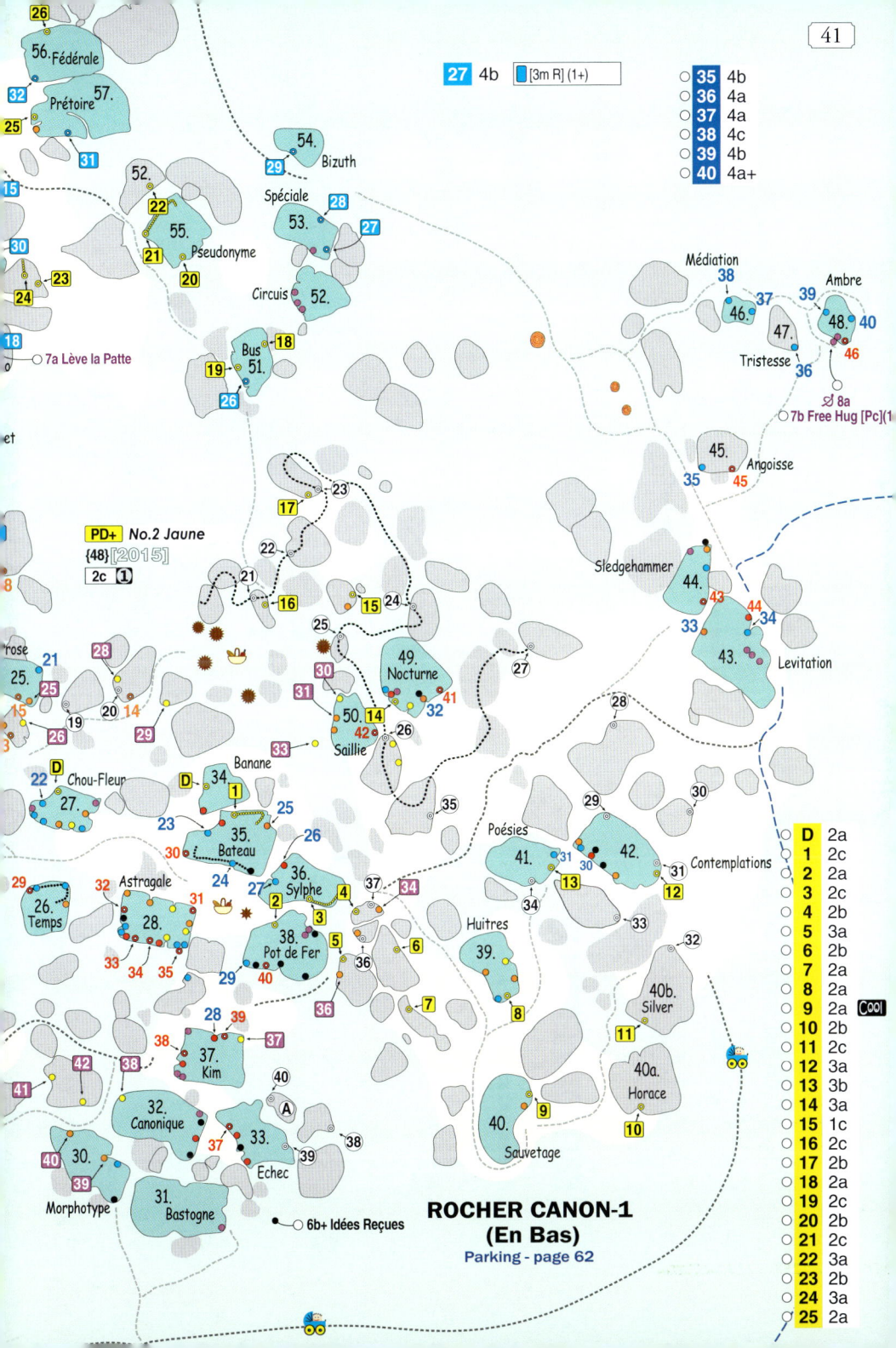

ROCHER CANON-2 (Côte)
Parking - page 62

6b La Spontex
6a Noir Zazate
7a L'Artif du Ciel
8c La Valse aux Adieux [>]
7a+ Le Mur de la Honte

ED- No.6 Roug
{46} [2011]
6a+ 1+

D++ No.4 Bleu
{40} [2014]
5a 1+

Named features: Theorie 88, Canon 89, Compressman 83, 84, Metal 85, Cachent, Maschine 86, Chasseur 87, Raie, Clarion, Voltaire 42, Gap 82, Bombé 80, Chaînon Mar 81, Appuyette 79, Bloc 77, Talon 78, Honte 76, Mouche 75, 73, Carrie 67, 66, Intermédiaire, Copains d'Abord 63, 65, 64, Bea

#	Grade	Info
1	5a	[3m dw] (1)
2	4a	[6m M] (3)
3	5a	[6m S] (1) Cool
4	5b	[4m dw] (1) ☺
5	•5b	[3m M] (1)
6	5a+	[4m Mw] (1)
7	4b	[3m R] (1)
8	5c+	[3m Nc] (1)
9	5b+	[3m M] (1)
10	4a	[3m M] (2)
11	4a	[4m N] (2+)
12	5b	[3m S] (1+)
13	4b+	[3m Ri] (1+)
14	4c	[3m :A] (2+)
15	4b	[4m :A] (1)
16	4a	[3m M] (1)
17	5b+	[5m A] (3+)
18	4a	[6m SM] (7+)
19	3c	[3m FD] (1)
20	5a	[5m MD] (3+)
21	5b+	[4m NR] (1)
22	4a	[4m Fg] (1)
23	4b	[3m R] (2+)
24	4c	[5m NS] (2)
25	5c	[4m VA] (2+)
26	4a	[4m R :A] (1)
27	4b	[3m R] (1+)
28	4a+	[3m Ri] (1)
29	•4b	[3m Ms] (1+)
30	4b	[3m R] (1+)
31	4c	[3m Rs] (1)
32	5a+	[2m Rw] (1)
33	3b	[3m N:] (1)
34	5a+	[3m R] (1)
35	4c	[3m M] (1+)
36	4c	[3m N:] (1)
37	4c	[3m >M] (1+)
38	5a+	[2m Rr] (1)
39	5a+	[4m As] (1+)
40	4b	[5m :A] (1) Cool

P 5 min
P 3 min

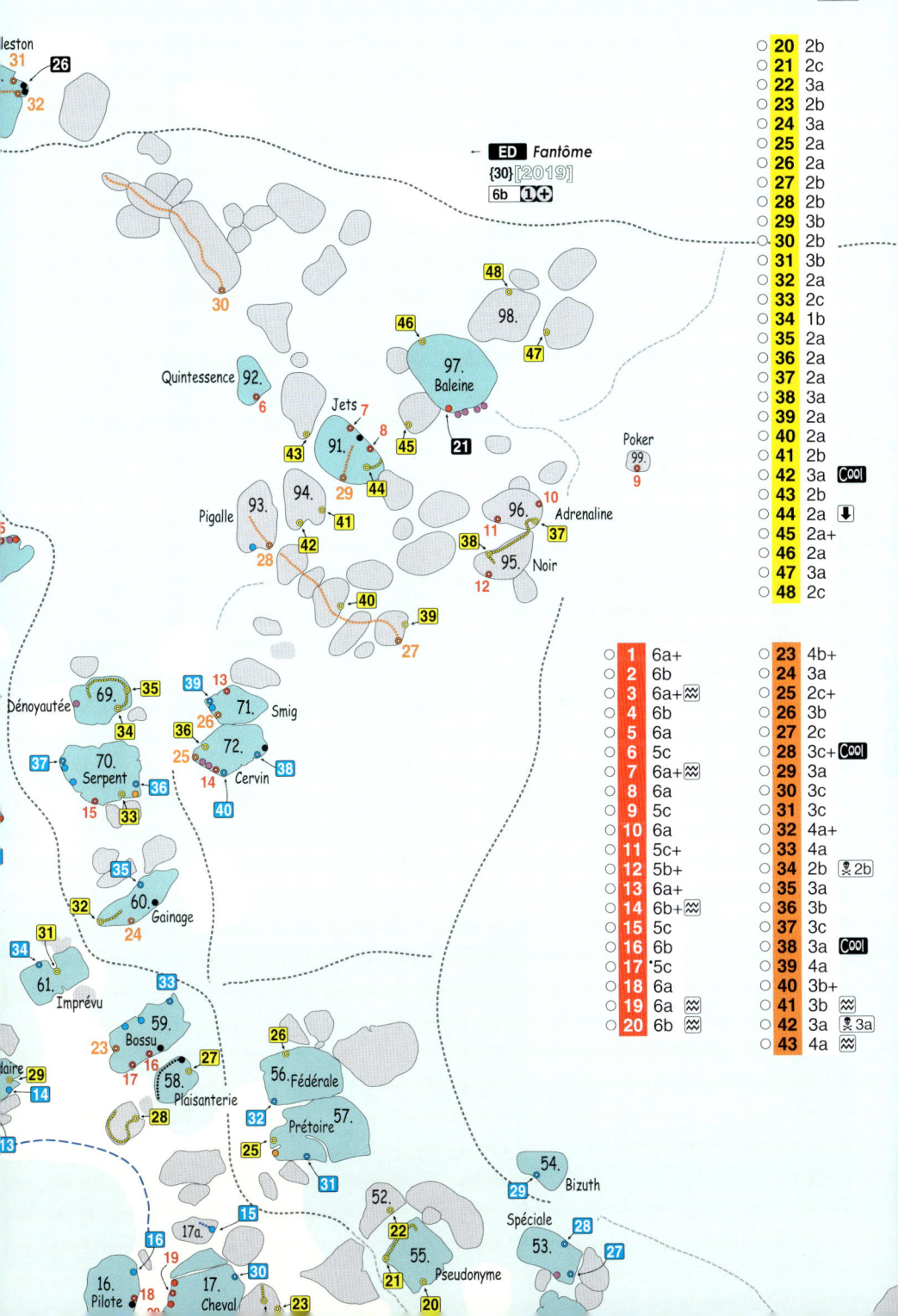

Circuits: Rocher Canon (PD-AD) - 2024

#			#			#			#		
1	2c		1	2b	[2m N] (1)	1	3a	[4m D] (2+)	1	4a+	[4m R] (2+)
2	2a		2	2c	[3m N] (1)	2	3a	[3m N<] (2+)	2	4a	[4m D] (1+)
3	2c		3	2c	[2m M] (1)	3	3a	[2m >] (1)	3	3c	[4m N] (2)
4	2b		4	3a	[3m N] (1)	4	3b	[4m dgf] (1)	4	4b+	[4m PVc] (1)
5	3a		5	2c	[3m df] (1)	5	4c	[3m N] (1)	5	3b	[5m N:] (1) Cool
6	2b		6	2a+	[2m N] (1)	6	3c	[3m M] (1+)	6	4a+	[4m Mi] (2+)
7	2a		7	2a+	[3m d] (1)	7	3b	[3m M] (1)	7	4b+	[4m R] (3+)
8	2a		8	2a+	[3m dN] (1)	8	3c		8	·5a	[4m NR] (2+)
9	2a	Cool	9	2b+	[2m N] (1)	9	3c+	[6m dw] (1)	9	4b	[4m RM] (3+)
10	2b		10	3a	[3m df] (1)	10	2c	[3m R] (2)	10	4b	[5m d] (1+)
11	2c		11	2c	[5m rd] (1) !2a	11	3c		11	4c	[4m M] (1+)
12	3a		12	2c	[4m M] (1) Cool	12	1a+		12	4a	[4m RM] (2)
13	3b		13	2c+	[3m M] (1)	13	3a		13	4c	[2m Vr] (1+)
14	3a		14	3a+	[4m df] (1) Cool	14	2b+		14	3c	[3m Rr] (1)
15	1c		15	3c	[3m Nf] (1)	15	2b		15	4a	[4m df] (1)
16	2c		16	3a	[2m N] (1)	16	3b+	[3m] (1+)	16	5c	[4m N] (1+)
17	2b		17	2a+	[5m N] (1+) Cool	17	3a		17	4b	[4m N] (3+)
18	2a		18	3a	[4m :A] (1)	18	3a+		18	4c	[3m Rr] (2+)
19	2c		19	3c	[5m Ndf] (1) Cool	19	3b	[5m Nd] (2) Cool	19	5a	[4m M] (1)
20	2b		20	2b+	[3m Fr] (1)	20	2c		20	4c	[3m N] (2)
21	2c		21	3b	[3m :Ag] (1)	21	3b		21	4c	[3m AR] (2+)
22	3a		22	2a+	[3m D] (1)	22	4a		22	4a	[3m Ri] (1)
23	2b		23	4a	[3m dw] (1)	23	4b+		23	4a	[4m R] (1) Cool
24	3a		24	3a-	[3m A>] (1+)	24	3a		24	4b+	[5m Ms] (2)
25	2a		25	3a-	[4m M] (1)	25	2c+		25	4c	[3m dgg] (1)
26	2a		26	2b	[3m d] (1)	26	3b		26	·5a	[4m Mw] (1)
27	2b		27	2b	[3m M] (1)	27	2c		27	4a+	[4m F] (1)
28	2b		28	2b+	[4m F:] (1)	28	3c+	Cool	28	5a	[4m M] (2)
29	3b		29	2c	[4m N] (1) Cool	29	3a		29	4b	[3m PR] (2++)
30	2b		30	·2c	[3m N] (1)	30	3c		30	5b	[4m Mw] (1)
31	3b		31	3a+	[3m Ms] (1)	31	3c		31	4a	[3m :N] (1)
32	2a		32	3b	[2m Gg] (1)	32	4a+		32	3c	[4m M] (1)
33	2c		33	2b	[3m Mr] (1)	33	4a		33	3b	[4m M] (1)
34	1b		34	3a	[3m A:] (1)	34	2b	☠ 2b	34	4a	[3m DR] (1+)
35	2a		35	3a	[3m F:] (1)	35	3a		35	4b	[3m VN] (1)
36	2a		36	3a	[2m r] (1)	36	3b		36	4a	[3m NR] (1)
37	2a		37	2b+	[4m N] (1)	37	3c		37	4a	[3m >R] (2+)
38	3a		38	2a+	[2m N] (1)	38	3a	Cool	38	4c	[3m Ro] (1)
39	2a		39	3b	[3m D] (1)	39	4a		39	4b	[4m df] (1)
40	2a		40	3a	[3m M] (1)	40	3b+		40	4a+	[4m ds] (1)
41	2b		41	2c	[3m d] (1)	41	3b				
42	3a	Cool	42	2b	[3m M] (1)	42	3a	☠ 3a			
43	2b					43	4a	[6m dw] (2)			
44	2a										
45	2a+										
46	2a										
47	3a										
48	2c										

Crash Pads: do not drag from problem to problem - fold up and carry to prevent erosion as much as possible.

Use a 30cm square of floor mat to start the problem, the sand falls into the bristles leaving your shoes clean. Also the start point is often not the same as the fall zone.

PINE DECORATION - Les Enfants

Aerial plan - page 40 — **ROCHER CANON-1 (En Bas)** — 45

Rocher Canon Parking - page 62

ROCHER CANON-1 (En Bas)

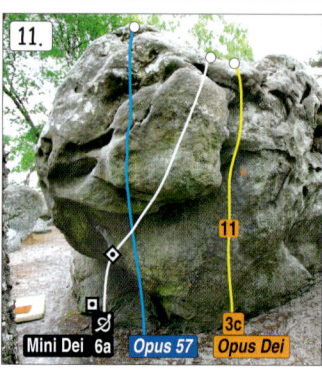

ROCHER CANON-1 (En Bas)

ROCHER CANON-1 (En Bas)

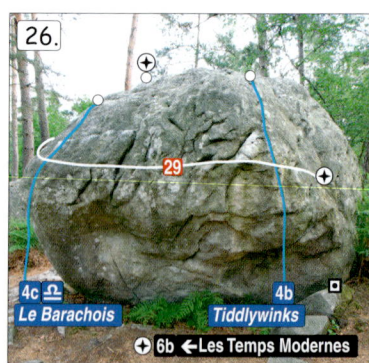

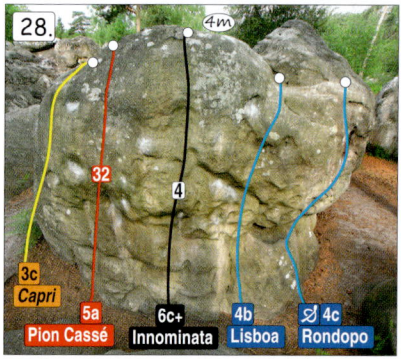

Aerial plan - page 40 — **ROCHER CANON-1 (En Bas)** — 51

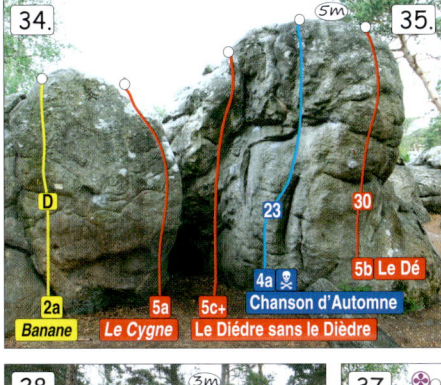

Rocher Canon Parking - page 62

ROCHER CANON-1 (En Bas)

5a+ IMPOSSIBLE 38, Benjamin Von Polheim [Bloc 72 - Cervin] ▷

ROCHER CANON-1 (En Bas)

Aerial plan - page 40

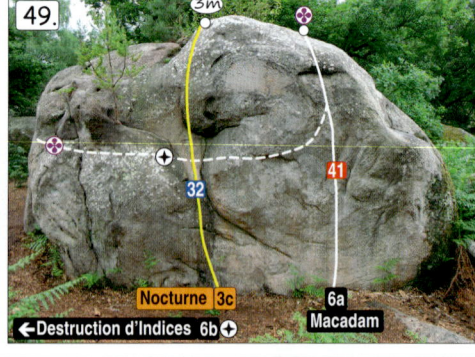

Rocher Canon Parking - page 62

Fontainebleau - Niveau/Grades

J'utilise 5 critères –par ordre d'importance, pour définir les cotations des voies dans ce livre.
1. J'observe dans toute la forêt des grimpeurs différents, et en particulier les méthodes utilisées et quels passages leur posent problème 2. Je grimpe avec un groupe assez large d'amis qui grimpent du 1a au 8c et je rassemble leur opinion sur les cotations moyennes. 3. Je cherche dans les topos et sur les sites Internet les cotations historiques.4. J'ai grimpé moi-même jusqu'au 7c ces 40 dernières années. 5. Je grimpe toujours environ 2000 voies par an à Bleau. La variété de grès et d'escalade à Fontainebleau est unique. De la fine arrête aux murs déversant, dalles, surplombs. Etc. C'est ainsi qu'une échelle de 24 cotations du 1a au 8c a été définie. Les différents auteurs de topos sur Bleau ont tous leur propre personnalité et donc les topos sont différents mais restent uniformes. L'échelle des cotations commence ici doucement avec le 1a (au contraire des ouvrages d'escalade sportive qui commencent au 4) J'ai aussi utilisé des couleurs différentes pour chaque niveau : 1-Jaune pour les voies sans les mains ; 2-Jaune pour les passages raides avec de bonnes prises (sport 4) ; 3-Orange, pour les voies plus techniques où l'utilisation de chaussons d'escalade est nécessaire (sport5) ; 4-Bleu, escalade plus soutenue demandant de la force dans les bras et les doigts (sport6a) ; 5-Rouge, pour les voies vraiment difficiles (sport 6b-7a). 6-Noir, Pour l'escalade spécifique de bloc (sport 7b). 7&8- Mauve, Pour les voies de haut niveau (sport 7c-8c). J'ai trouvé utile de définir 9 caractéristiques corporelles: petit, moyen, grand-maigre, normal, enveloppé-épaules carrées (hommes), taille large, taille fine (femmes), ce qui donne 27 combinaisons par niveau! Si les prises clés sont accessibles seulement pour des grimpeurs d'une certaine taille, je prends leur avis et je le mentionne via un point devant la cotation. Il est évident qu'au dessus du niveau 4, plus ils grimpent à haut niveau plus les grimpeurs ont en général un indice de masse corporelle décroissant. Je pars du principe pour chaque cotation que le grimpeur à l'indice adéquat-voir le tableau ci-contre. J'ai personnellement noté que les blessures aux doigts et aux bras sont plus fréquentes quand on dépasse le niveau adéquat. Ce système n'est pas juste à 100% pour les grimpeurs de niveau 5, en général moins légers. Il devient plus précis pour le haut niveau (Niveau 8) qui requiert d'être léger. La cotation sous entend aussi que les semelles des chaussons sont parfaitement propres. (C'est le sable fin qui polit les prises, pas la magnésie). Partez donc toujours d'un tapis et les pieds propres. Protégez toujours la zone de chute par un crash-pad. Toutes les cotations sont données pour un départ sur une seule épaisseur de crash.

Fontainebleau uses 24 grades to indicate climbs of different difficulty, 1a, 1b, 1c, 2a, etc up to 8c (hardest). Unlike temperature or distance, there are no fixed parameters – so please don't expect any blinding science or rationality! Each guidebook writer generally has their own reasons for giving grades to climbs, and slight variations are possible. It seems fair to explain my methodology. There is a natural split of (1-4) general climbing, and (5-8) specific bouldering. Grade 1: Climbing without your hands touching the rock. Grade 2: Vertical with good holds and where you don't need special climbing shoes. Grade 3: Technical climbing where you do need special shoes, but generally no great strength is required (Sport grade 5). Grade 4: Difficult climbing where you definitely need good strength in either fingers or arms and sometimes both - (Sport 6a). Grades 5-8: These are given for the easiest way possible (which may not be obvious), and do presume that the problem is well practised. Anyone new to Fontainebleau will find them very harsh, but they do however accurately reflect the minimum strength to weight required for a problem. Plus (+) grades usually indicate a slightly more difficult top out, and help to reduce grade inflation. I have chosen the problem MARIE ROSE at Bas Cuvier, for mid level 6a. From here, I then rate climbs easier or harder, with 5a and 7a being only 3 grades apart from a 'common fixed point.' I grade personally about 5000 of the 7000 problems in the book, having done them several times. I also use a BMI (body mass index) system, where I link each grade to a particular BMI. This ensures you genuinely only have grade 5 & 6 climbers commenting on grade 5 & 6 climbs. I have also noticed that over the years, those climbers who exceed this BMI-linking, generally suffer from nasty finger and arm injuries. Climbing the high grades does require great skill, but is certainly not magic! If you are too heavy, don't over train – try to loose weight sensibly. If you are not climbing up to your BMI, then yes – you do need to be a bit more assertive and "crank like a demon." For the 2000 hardest problems, I carefully watch and listen to a selection of different climbers that know the forest intimately, and operate at a very high level. In the past, approximate grades were often given if a problem was different grades for different heights of climber. I prefer to simply give an exact grade for a particular height of climber, which is denoted by the dot in front of a grade.

Camping - 2025

CAMPING LES PRES Pad rental
Chemin des Prés, 77880 Grez sur Loing
Open: Mar-Nov (Aquadis). A large open sunny and shady site with good grass. The Bivouac field for those wanting plenty of space, with in-situ BBQ's. Shop & Boulangerie in the local village a few mins walk. River nearby - popular for swimming in summer. Mosquito repellant essential.
Fast road to Fontainebleau to access all areas.

ILE DE BOULANCOURT Pad rental
77760 Boulancourt, Malesherbes
Open: All year (Some English).
A large site with a mixture of sun and shade, soft grass, trees and a small river (Mosquito repellant useful), and is incredibly tranquil. Nice facilities. Good value for money.
Climbing: Good for Buthiers & Trois Pignons.

HOSTEL Pad rental
Fontainebleau Hostel Camping,
La Chapelle-la-Reine. Open: All year
English spoken, a small site (2.8m height - stone barrier). Simple (no elec), sunny & use of hostel facilities. Climbing: Ideal for Dame Jouanne and Eléphant (by walking trails).

LA MUSARDIERE   Pad rental
La Musardière. 91490 Milly la Forêt.
Open: Feb-Nov
(Some English). A large and spread out site in the woods, highly popular in peak holidays. It's mostly under the trees (not much grass), which can often be very chilly. No shop, but bread van in summer holidays. Star attraction is the 4 swimming pools and lovely shade during a hot summer. Snack bar with frites by the pool.
Climbing: Ideal for walking or cycling direct into the Trois Pignons, very central and popular.

LA BELLE ETOILE    Pad rental
La Belle Etoile Camping, Quai Joffre,
La Rochette, 77000 Melun.
Open: Mar-Oct
English & Dutch spoken, nice open site with lush grass and trees. It has a new big covered pool that stays lovely and warm. Ping pong, volleyball court, swings. Situated by the river Seine & on the edge of Melun (Urban), easy to walk to station and get the train into Paris.
Climbing: Ideal for Canon-Cuvier-Saint Germain.

This 2025 - 4th edition of FUN BLOC, contains the same boulders as the original version in 2012, hence we have kept the same title. However, each year there are many changes in the forest that affect climbers and visitors. It is only sensible to update the book with each printing, and consequently - is why we do not print very many copies of each edition. I also like to take a lot of new photos in the forest, and by producing new editions, it allows me to share my photography with both the climbers who use the forest regularly, and those who have never visited, and therefore might be enticed to do so.

PAINTED CIRCUITS: These last for many years on the rock, but sometimes a whole circuit is changed, with a different start, problems, and tough grade variations. This process often takes around 3 years, and many editions are temporarily painted on the rock. I tend to wait until the circuit is finalised before updating in the book, and there has been a general consensus of grades given to the problems. Historically, harder problems were included on a circuit as variations (so a grade 3 climber could do a whole orange circuit), but today they get their own numbers, so the coloured dots and boxes by the grades will give the visitor a quick warning to the difficulty range.

Climb Fontainebleau
Arbonne-la-Fôret (rondpoint)
Topos for Sale, Crash pads & rock shoes for hire, T shirts, chalk and resin supplies, energy bars and drinks, general climbing boutique.

Karma Climbing Gym
Fontainebleau
A very large indoor climbing wall, both with 15m sport climbing and bouldering (part sometimes closed for national climbing team and events).
Topos for Sale.

S'cape
Fontainebleau
An outdoor shop for trail running, bouldering, skiing and walking . Big shoe range, large selection of crash pads - also for hire.
(no parking on site).

ROCHER CANON-2 (Côte)

ROCHER CANON-2 (Côte)

Aerial plan - page 42

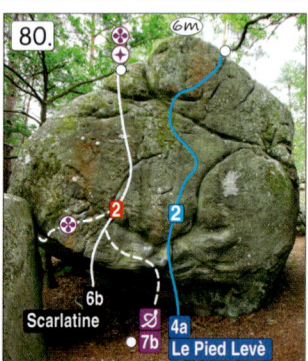

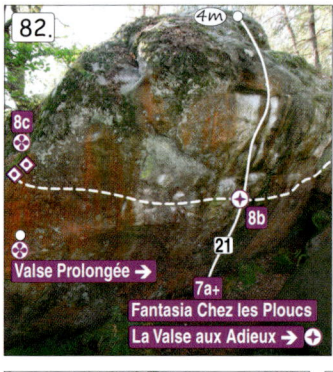

Rocher Canon Parking - page 62

5a ATTRAPE-MOUCHE, Ewa Kotanska [Bloc 75 - Mouche]

ROCHER CANON

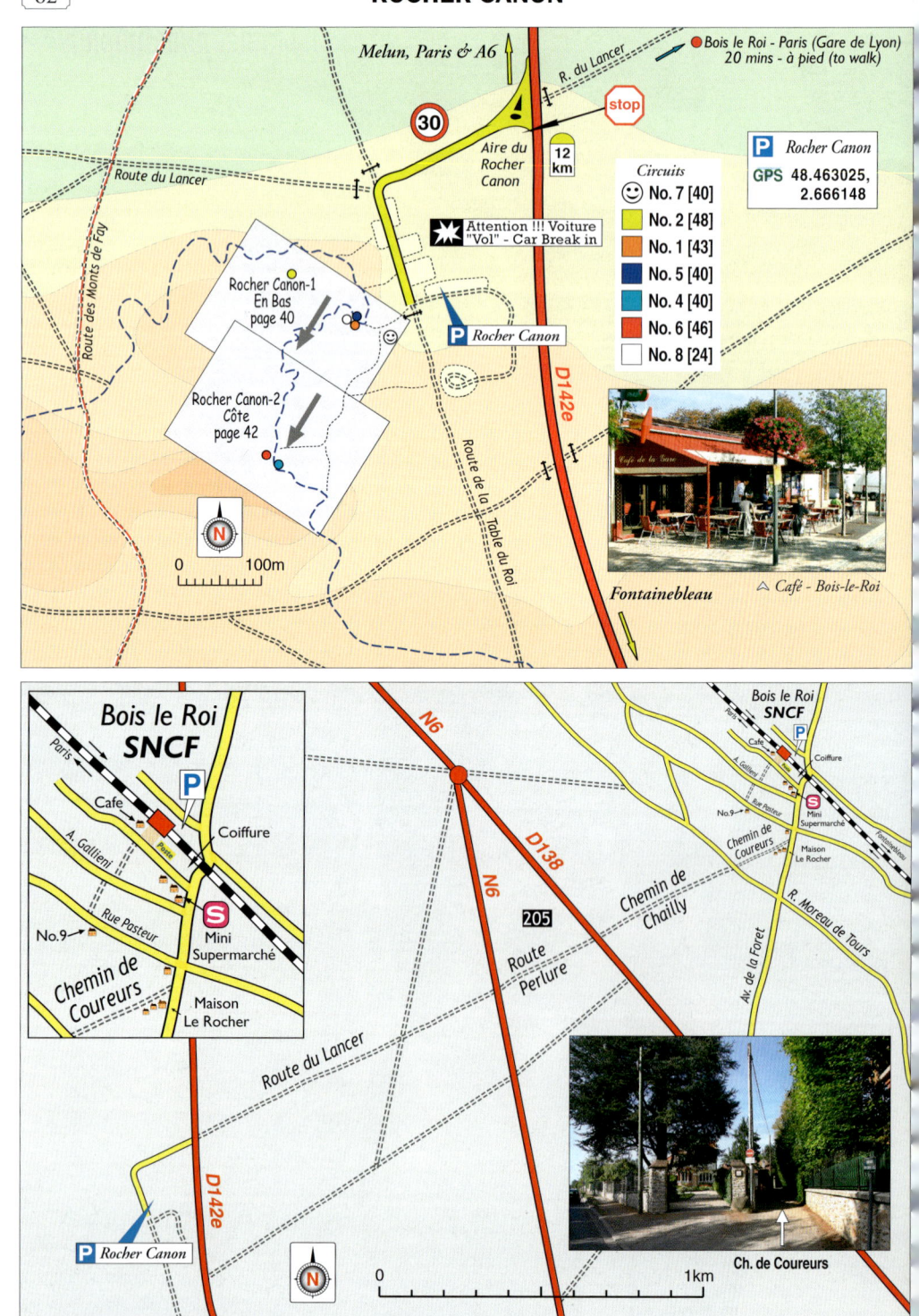

ROCHER CANON-2 (Côte)

Rocher Canon Parking - page 62

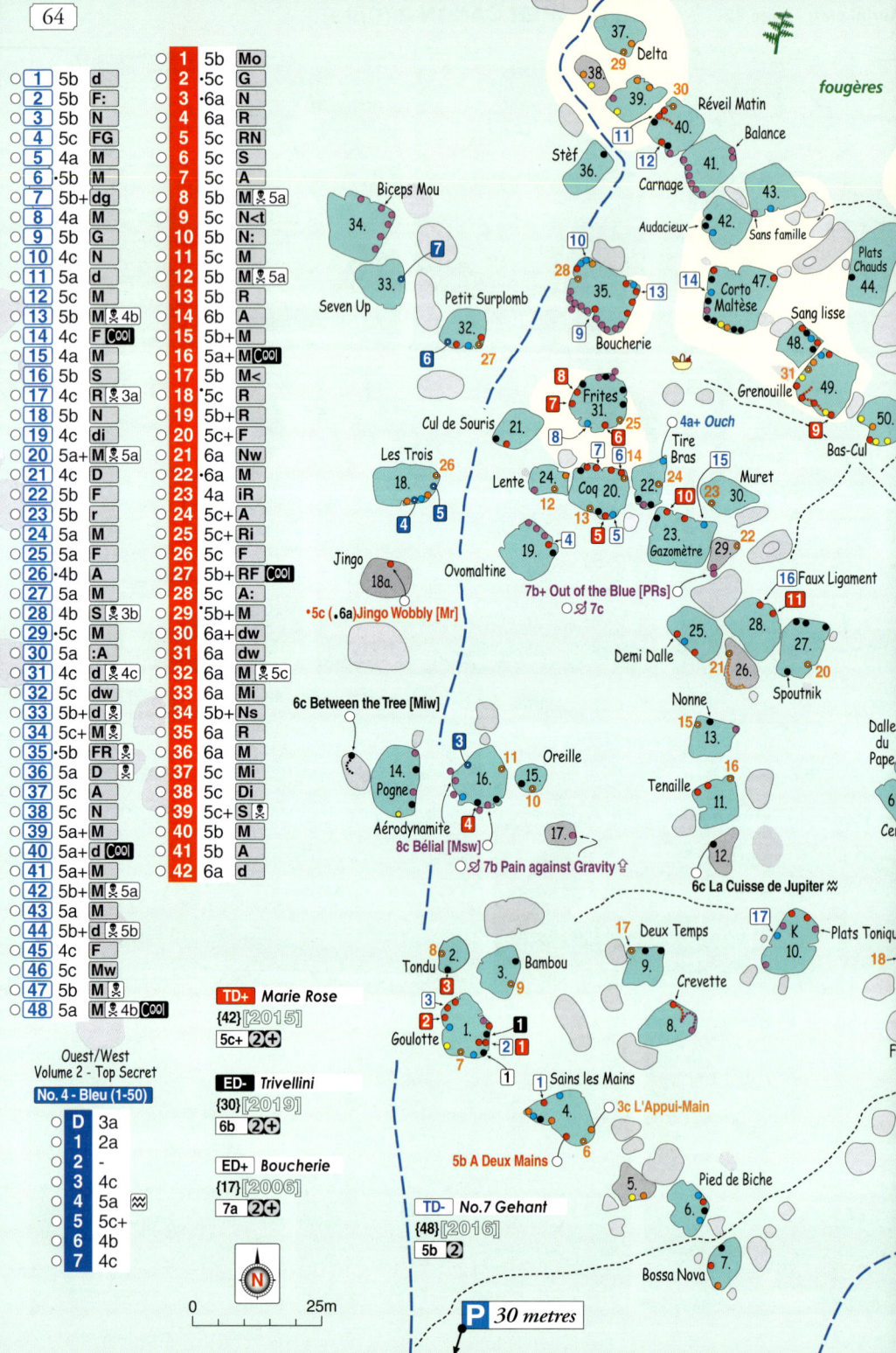

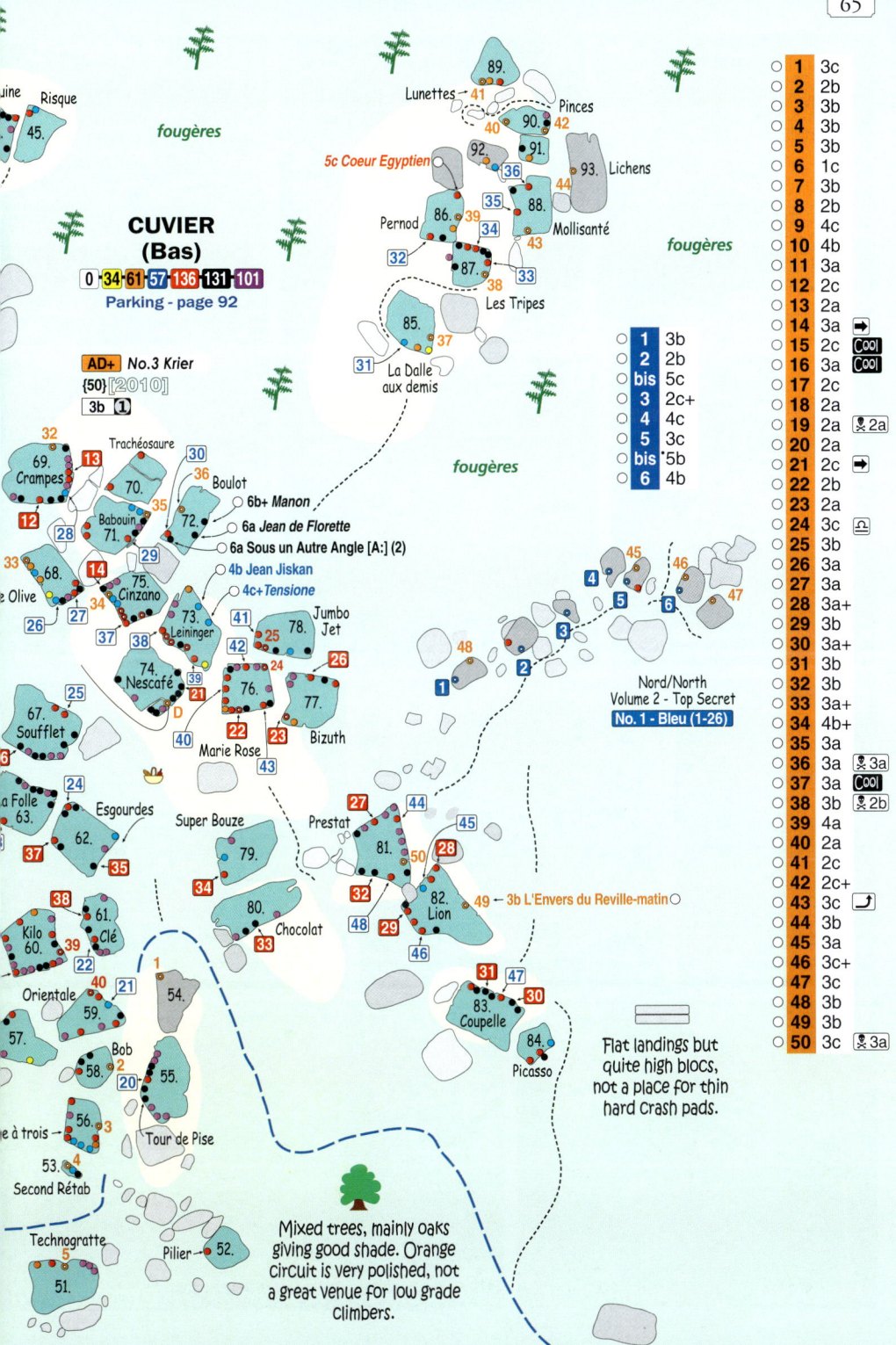

CUVIER (Bas)

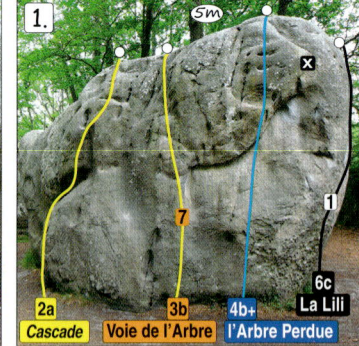

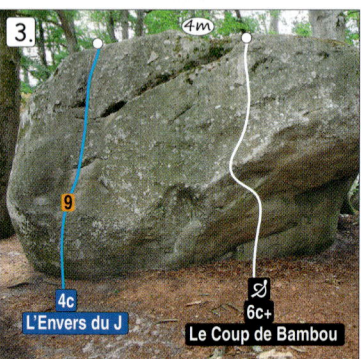
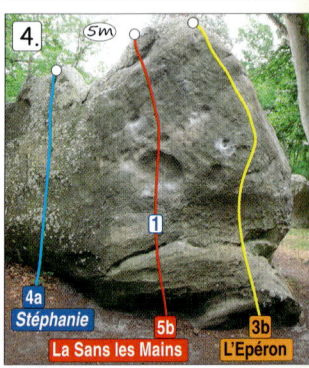

YOU FEEL, YOU CHOOSE.*

Chaque surface a ses secrets: jetés ou prises parfaites. Nous créons à la main les outils pour chaque **discipline verticale**. Depuis 1928, nous chaussons les meilleurs athlètes lors de leurs ascensions, car telle est notre inspiration.

*****VOS RESSENTIS, VOS CHOIX.**

CUVIER (Bas)

Aerial plan - page 64

6a LE TROU SIMON [4], *Lena Decker; (Bloc 16)*

Cuvier Parking - page 92

CUVIER (Bas)

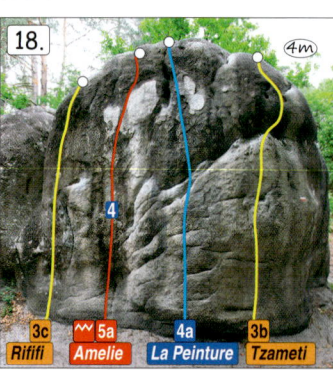

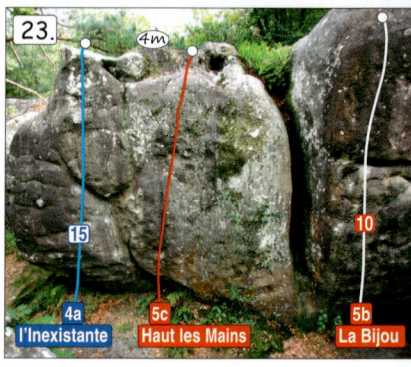

CUVIER (Bas)

Cuvier Parking - page 92

CUVIER (Bas)

Aerial plan - page 6

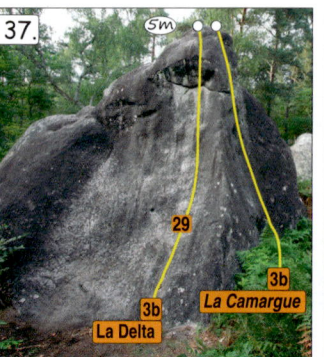

5b LES GRATTONS MORIN [13], Helen Moore [Bloc 35 - Boucherie]

CUVIER (Bas)

Aerial plan - page 6

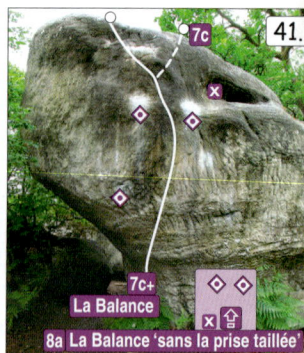

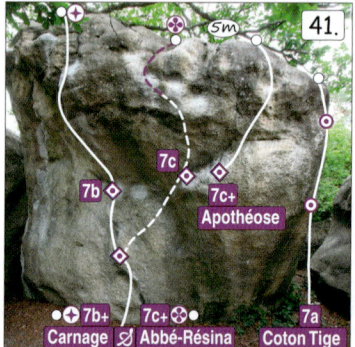
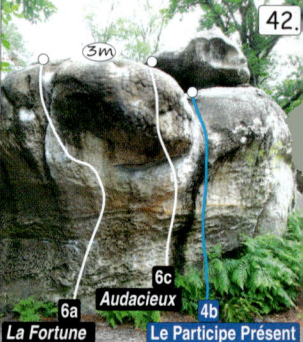

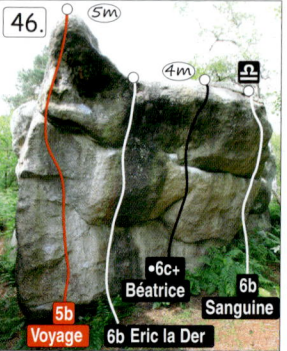

Cuvier Parking - page 92

7c ABBE-RESINA, Léon Bonnevay [Bloc 41 - Carnage]

CUVIER (Bas)

Aerial plan - page 6

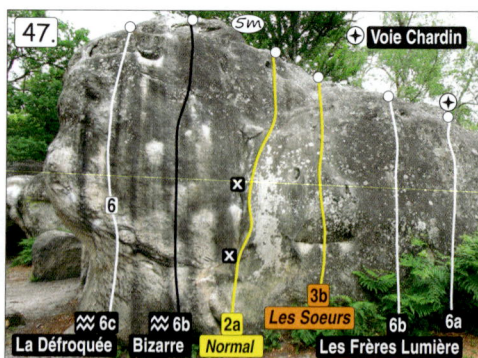

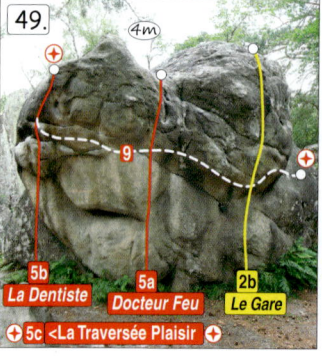

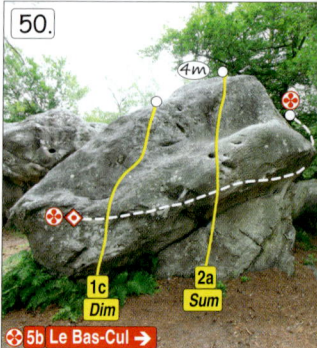

Cuvier Parking - page 92

5c+ LES FRITES 7, Elin Lois Owens [Bloc 31 - Frites] ▶

CUVIER (Bas)

Aerial plan - page 64

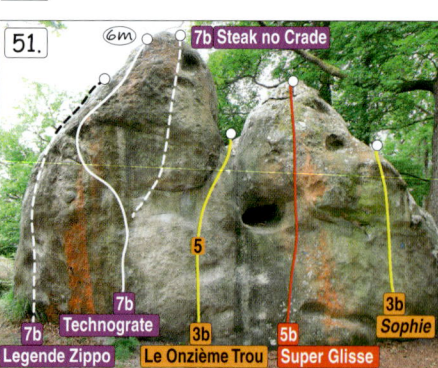

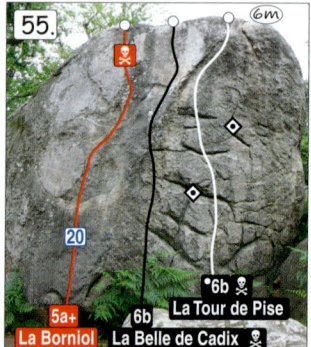

Cuvier Parking - page 92

7a **LA CHICORÉE**, *Selina Greff [Bloc 74 - Nescafe]* ≫

CUVIER (Bas)

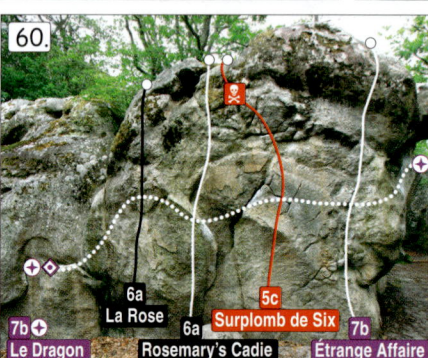

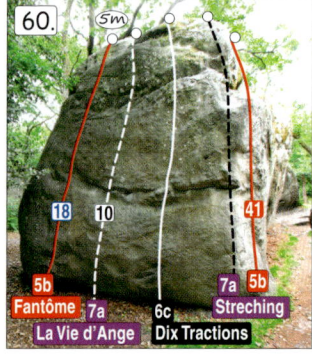

5c LA BICOLORE 38, *Judith & Rem* [Bloc 61 - Clé]

CUVIER (Bas)

5b LE COUP [23], Lauren Hoffman [Bloc 63 - La Folle]

CUVIER (Bas)

Aerial plan - page 64

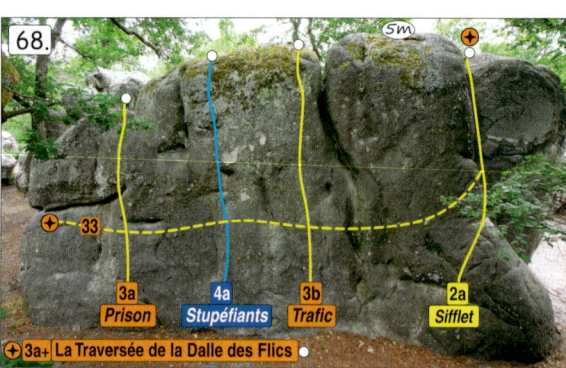

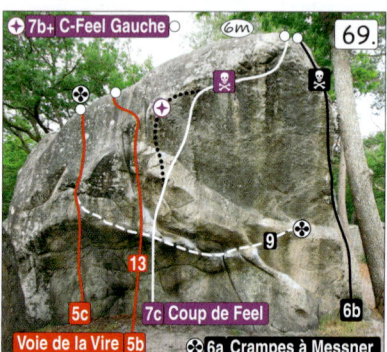

Cuvier Parking - page 92

CUVIER (Bas)

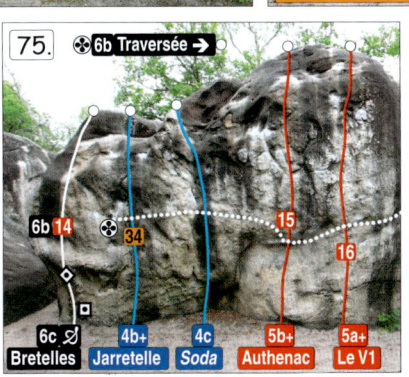

CUVIER (Bas)

Aerial plan - page 64

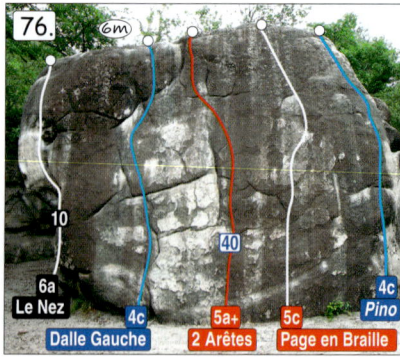

6a MARIE ROSE 22, Alberto Marañon [Bloc 76 - Marie Rose]

CUVIER (Bas)

Aerial plan - page 64

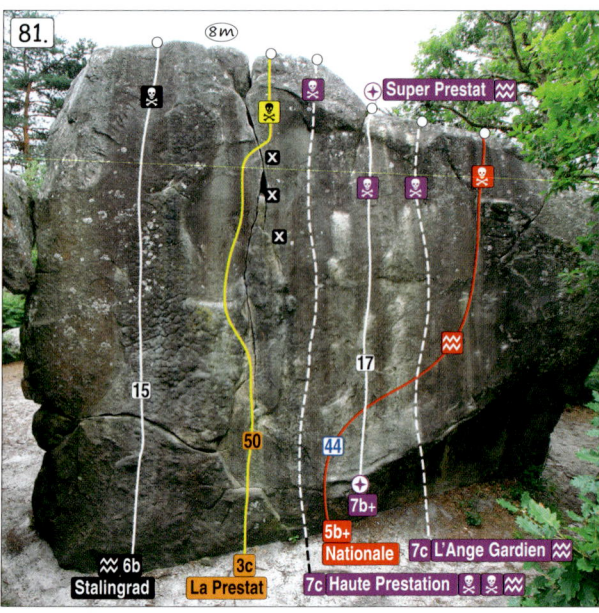
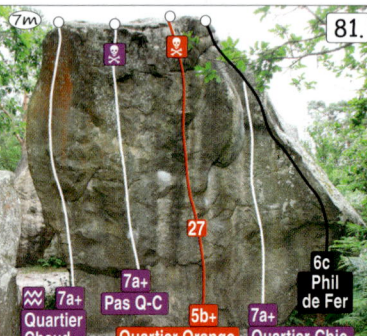

Cuvier Parking - page 92 5b+ LA NATIONALE 44, Julien Rousset [Bloc 81 - Prestat]

CUVIER (Bas)

Aerial plan - page 64

Cuvier Parking - page 92

5b LA PICASSO, *Merlijn van Hamel & Joep Meij, [Bloc 84 - Picasso]* ▷

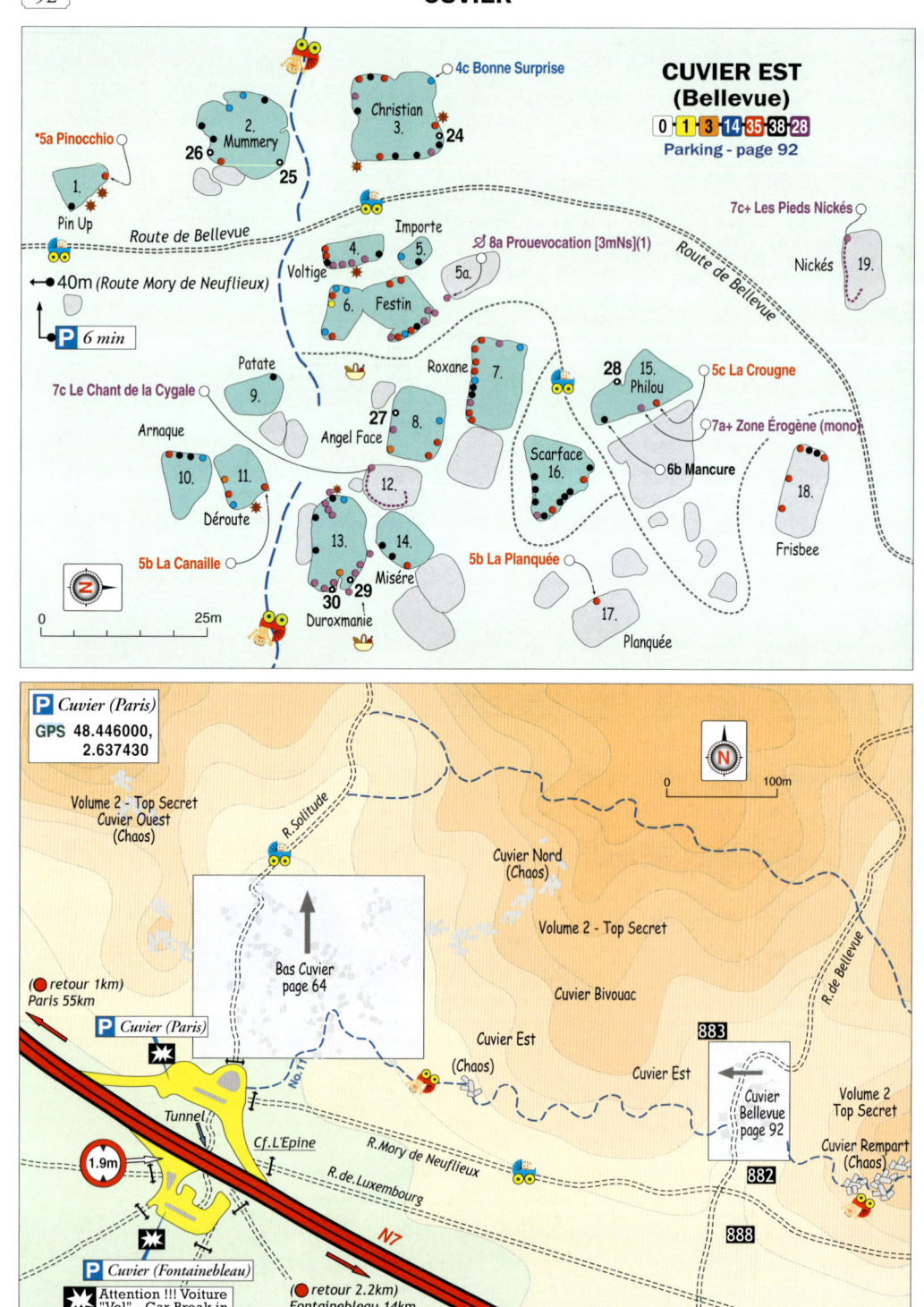

CUVIER EST (Bellevue)

Aerial plan - page 92 | 93

1. 4m — Angle Pin Up 6c / Pinocchio 5a

2. La Psyssure 6b (25)

2. La A 6b / A Mineur 4a

2. La Rampe 4a / Ticketyboo 6a+ / Balibalo 6c / Mummery 6b (26)

2. La Grosse Bête 5c

3. 6a Fissure Droit / La Fissure de Gauche 5a / Drôle la Grimpe 6c+ / Sisyphe 7c / 7b

3. La Loulou 5a / Les 3 Compères 6a

3. Les 3 Compères 6a / L'Amaury 5b

3. Les Cupules 7a / La Butor 6c

3. Pierre qui Roule 6c / 5b / La Branche 5b / La Christian (24)

4. Le Vieux Bleu 5c / Triviale Oblique 5a

4. Lune de Miel Gauche 6c+ / Lune de Miel 7b

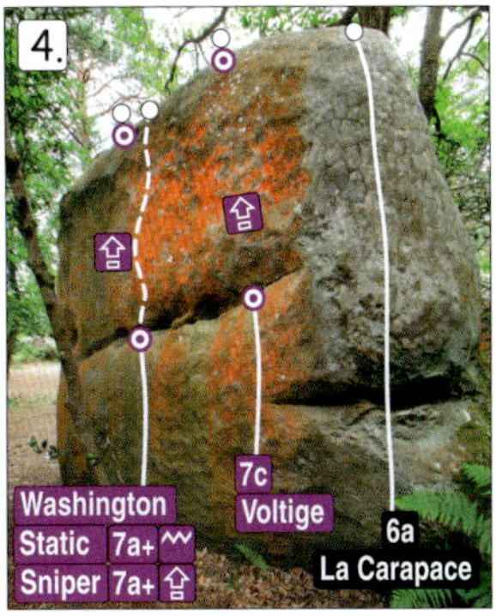

4. Washington Static 7a+ / Sniper 7a+ / Voltige 7c / La Carapace 6a

Cuvier Parking - page 92

BEAUVAIS | SAINT GERMAIN | CANON | CUVIER | AP - BIZONS | APREMONT | ERMITAGE | ISATIS | CUISINIÈRE | CANCHE - A-M | TELEGRAPHE | BOIS ROND | G - CHATS

CUVIER EST (Bellevue)

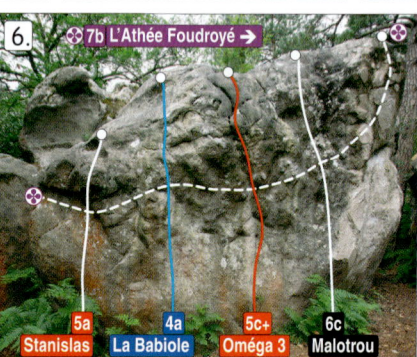

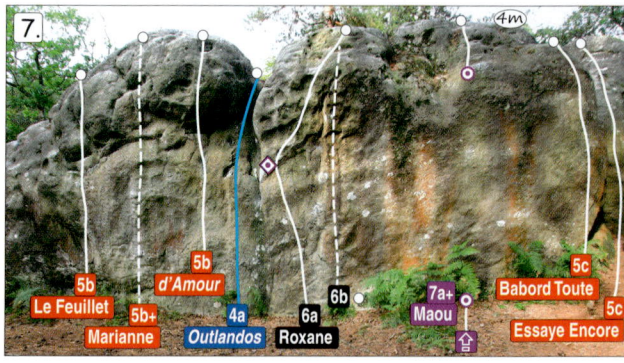
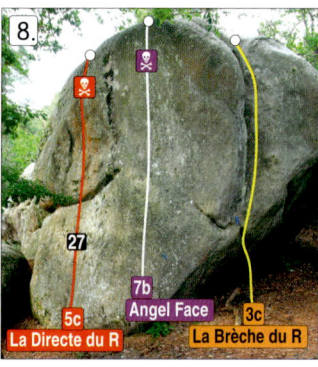

6c BALIBALO, *Philippe le Denmat [Bloc 2 - Mummery]* ▷

CUVIER EST (Bellevue)

Aerial plan - page 92

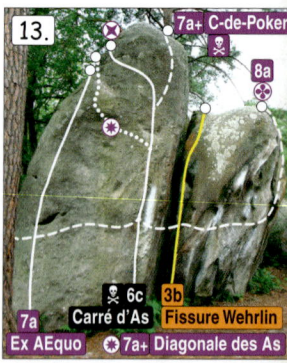

Cuvier Parking - page 92   6a LES TROIS COMPERES, Alexandre Dejean, [Bloc 3 - Chrisitan]

APREMONT

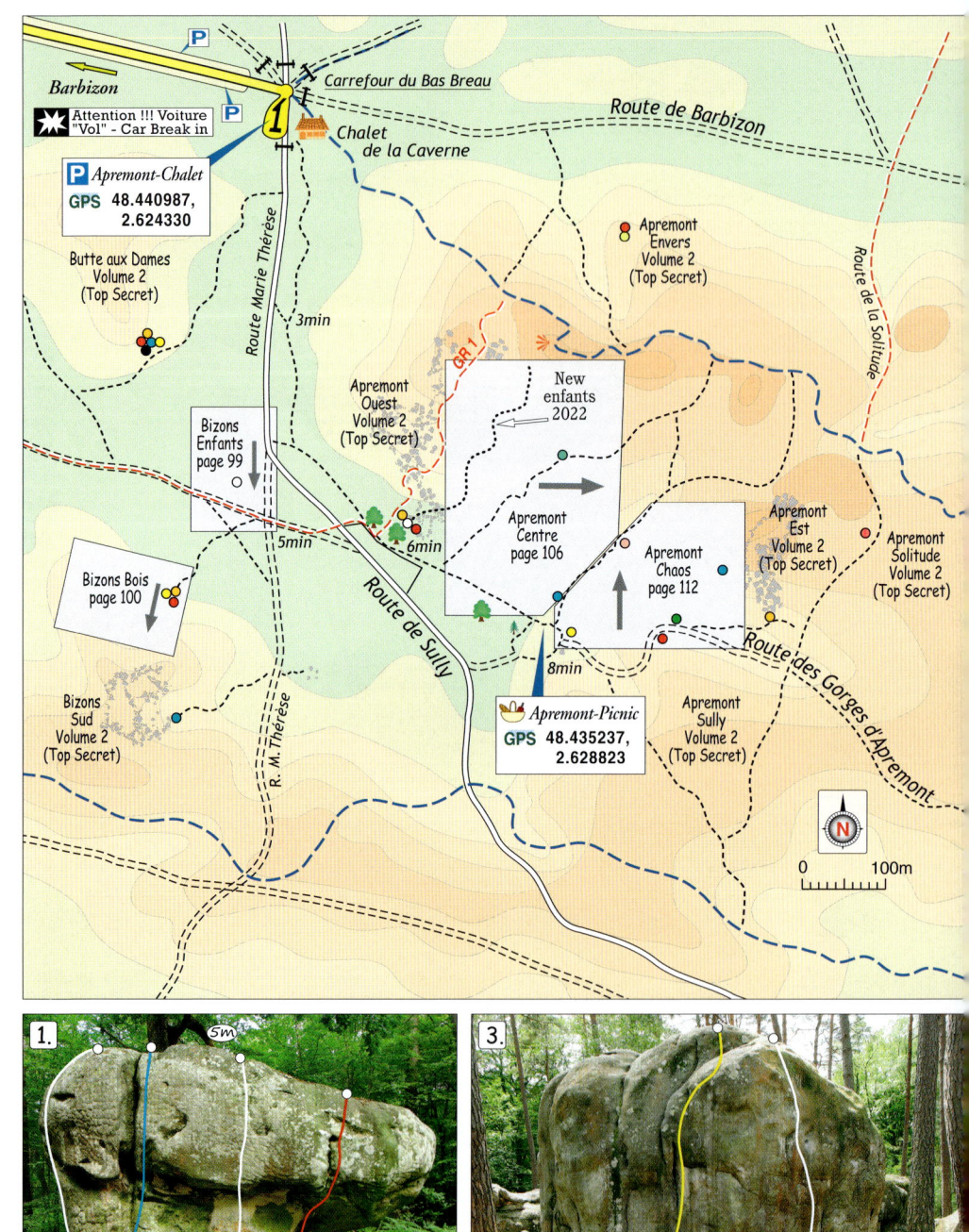

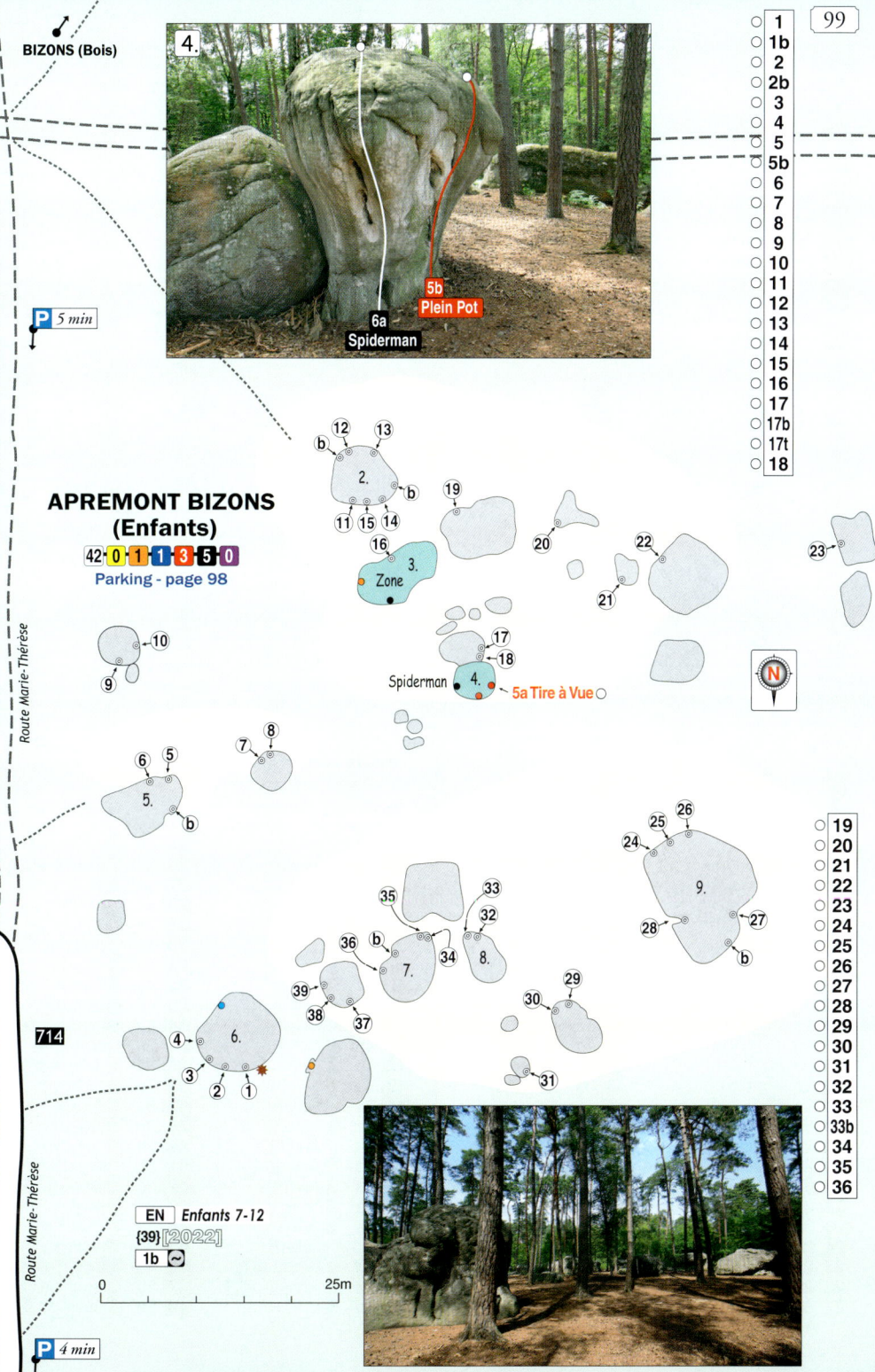

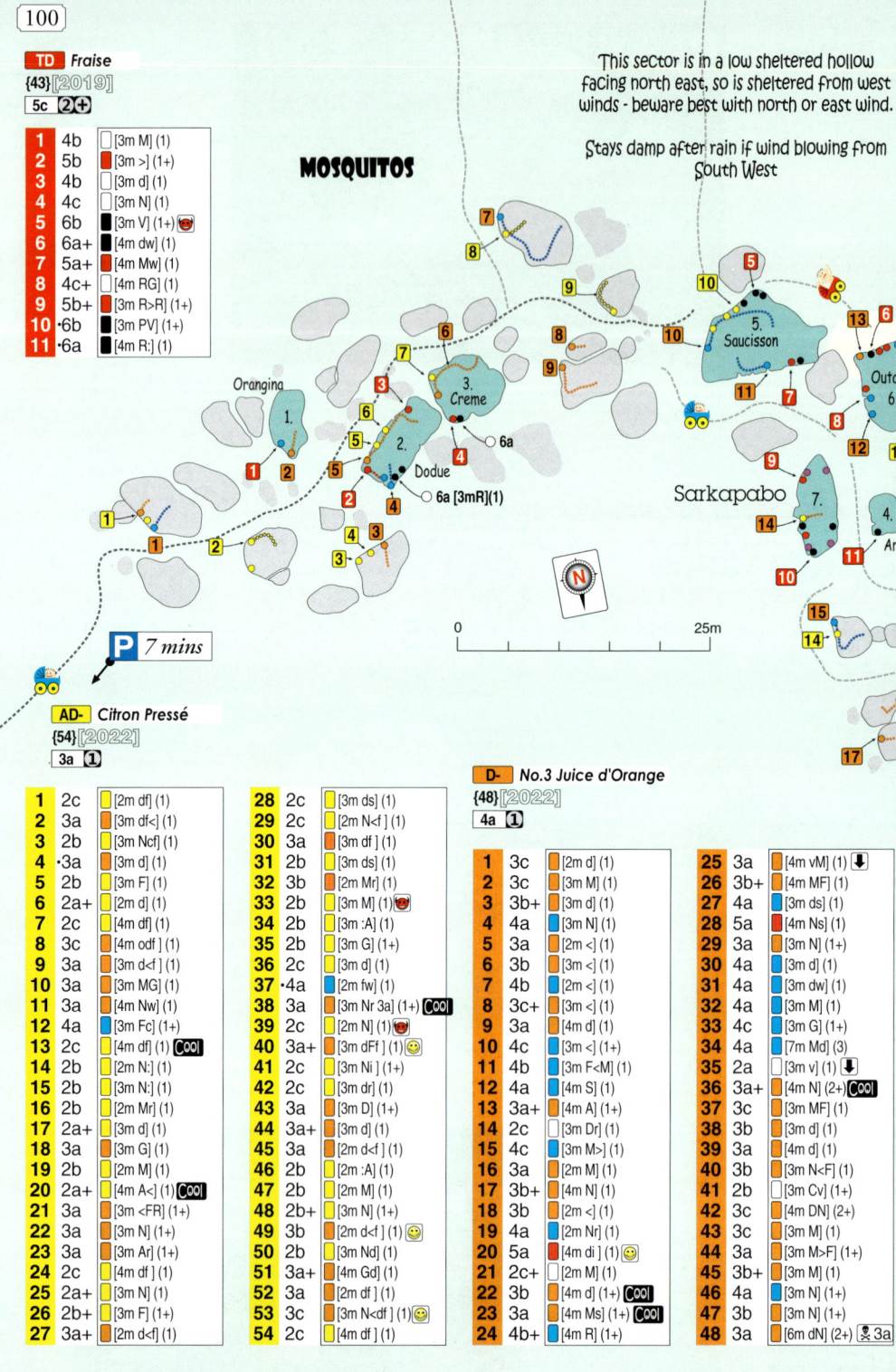

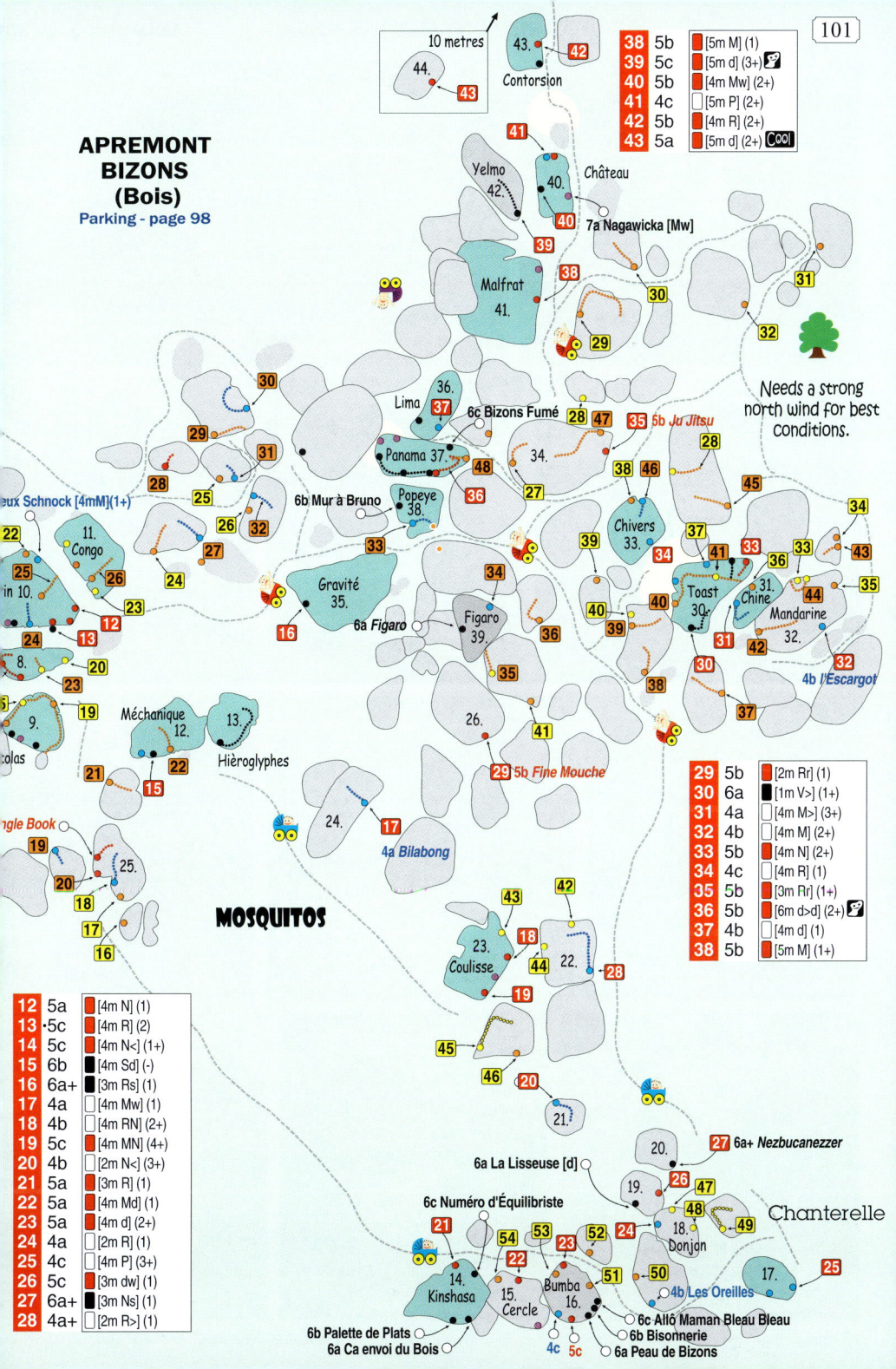

APREMONT BIZONS (Bois)

Aerial plan - page 10

Apremont Parking - page 98 — 7a LE PIED A COULISSE GAUCHE, Helge Uhlmann [Bloc 23 - Coulisse]

APREMONT BIZONS (Bois)

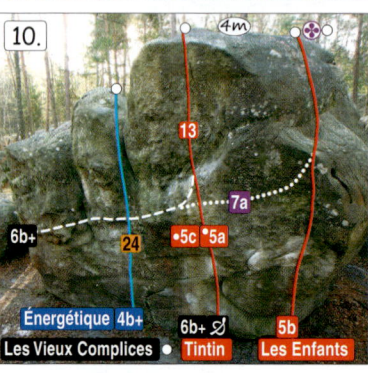

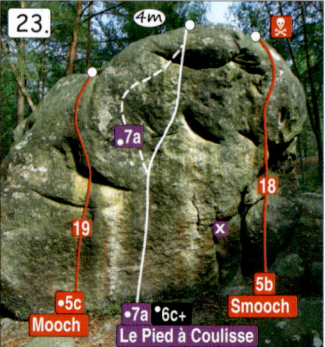

APREMONT BIZONS (Bois)

30. 6a Croque Monsieur >
31. 4a Nectarine
33. 34 4c Chivers
35. 16 6a+ Anti-Gravité
37. 7b Bizon Futé
37. 7c+ Il Était une Fois Bleau / 6c+ Fausse Route >
37. 6b Panama / 6b Madagascar / 36 5b Chi >
38. 33 4c Popeye

40. 5a Château Vert / 41 4c+ Château Rouge
41. 38 5b Malfaire / 7a Malafrat
43. 42 6a Contortion / 5b Le Disco

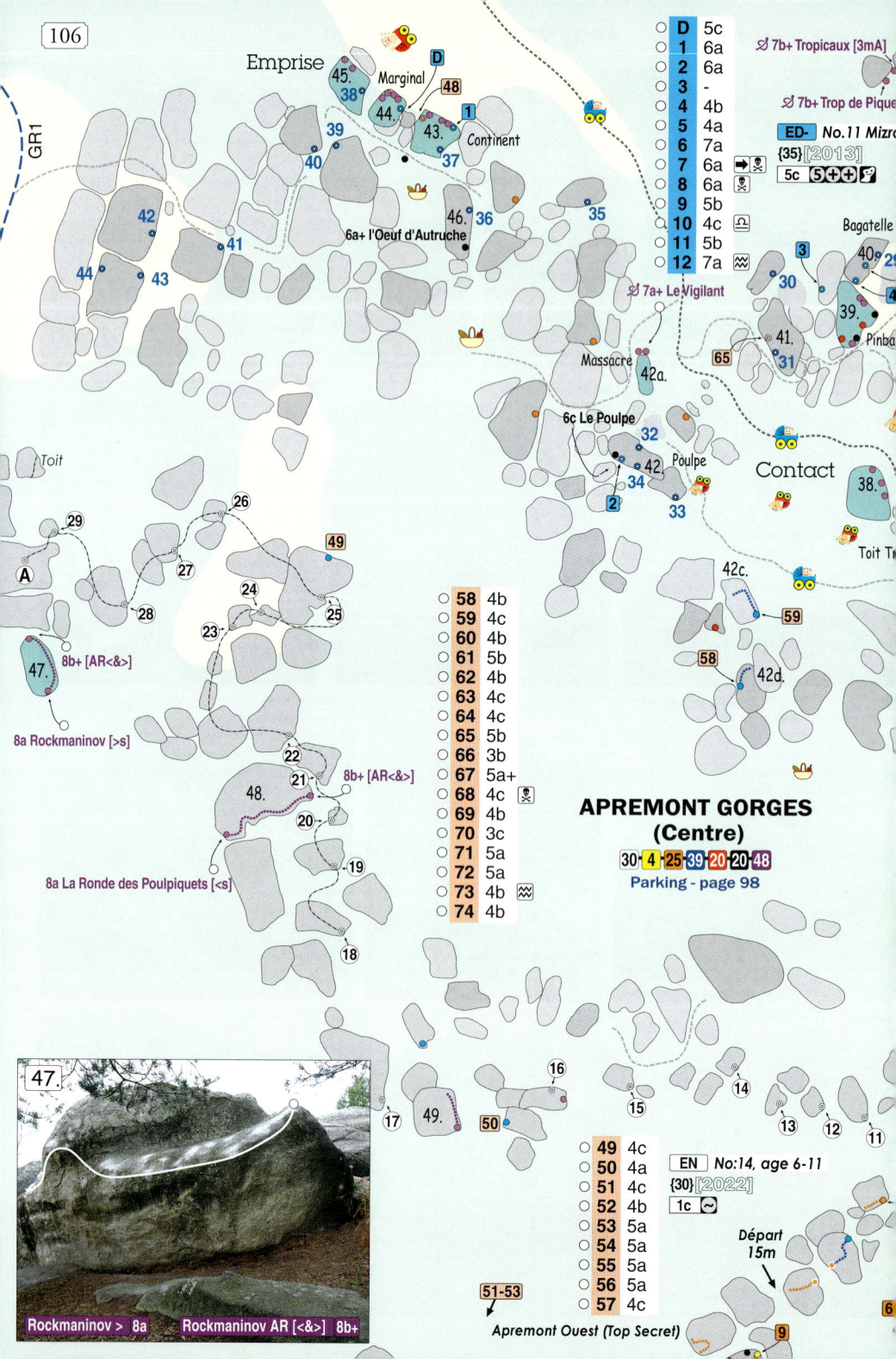

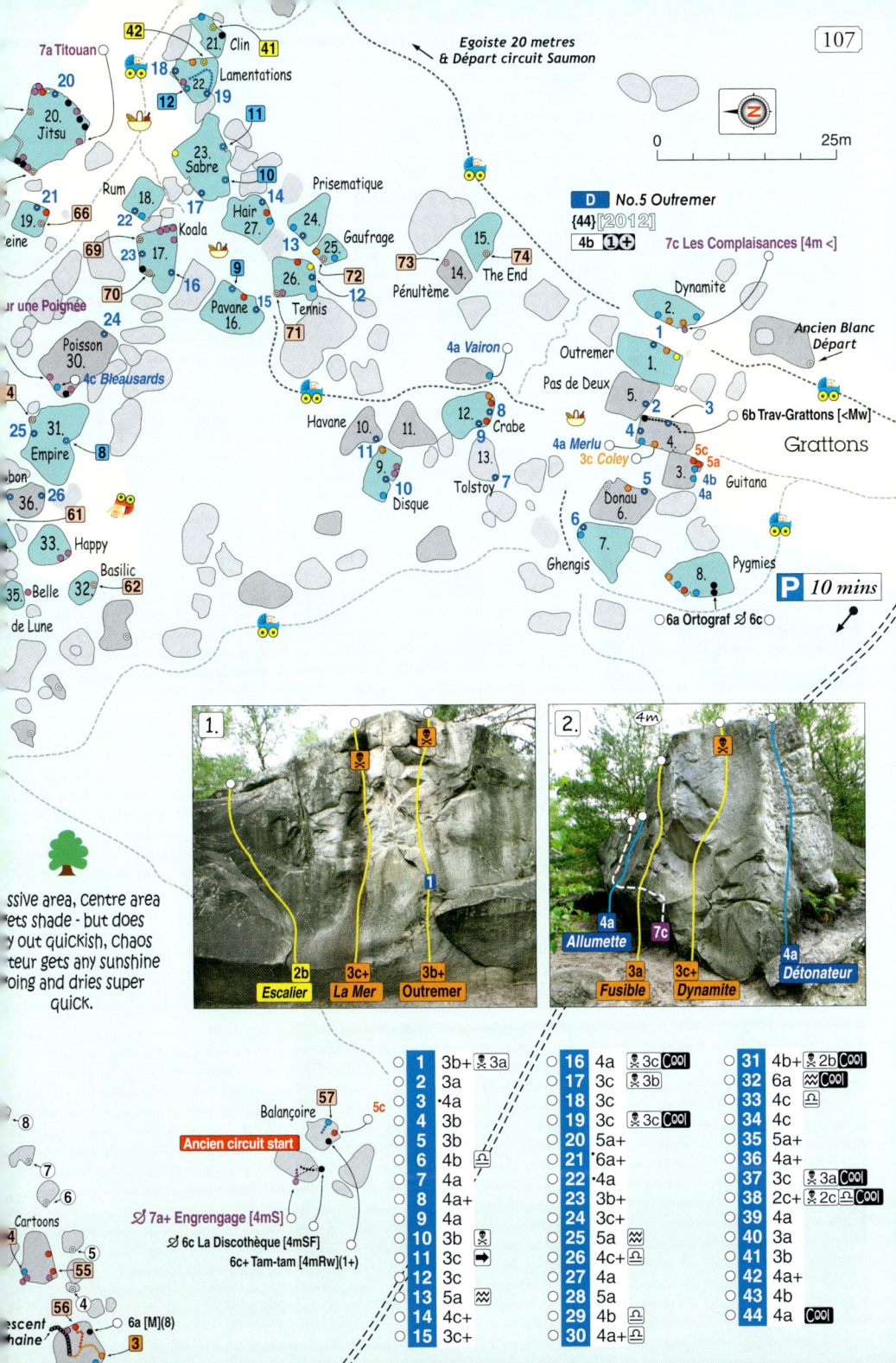

APREMONT GORGES (Centre)

Aerial plan - page 10[6]

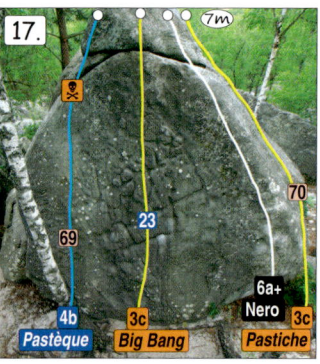

Apremont Parking - page 98 — 4c **LA PROMENADE DE SANTÉ** 59, Valeria Villar [Bloc 42c]

APREMONT GORGES (Centre)

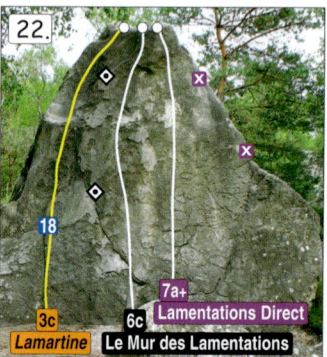

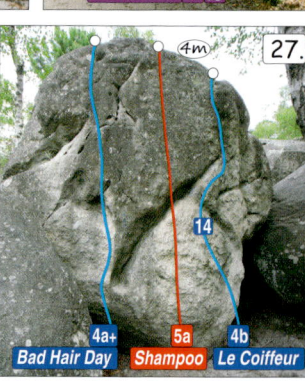

APREMONT GORGES (Centre)

Aerial plan - page 106

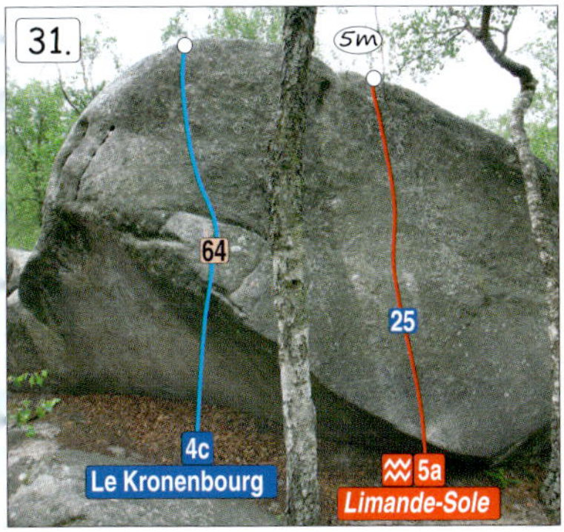

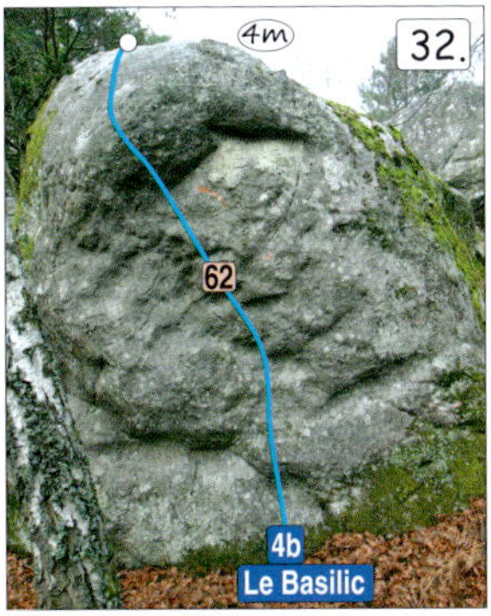

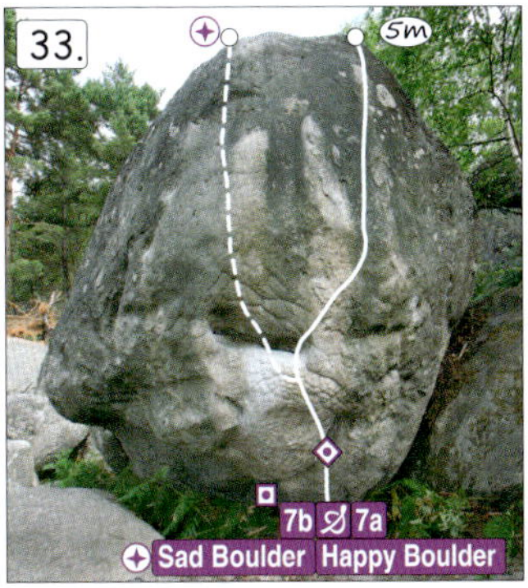

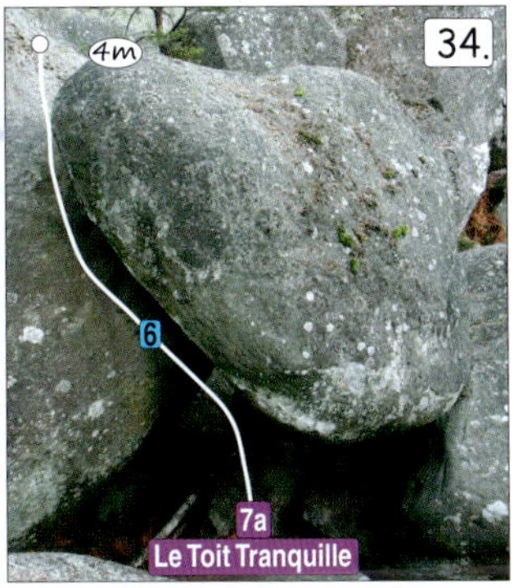

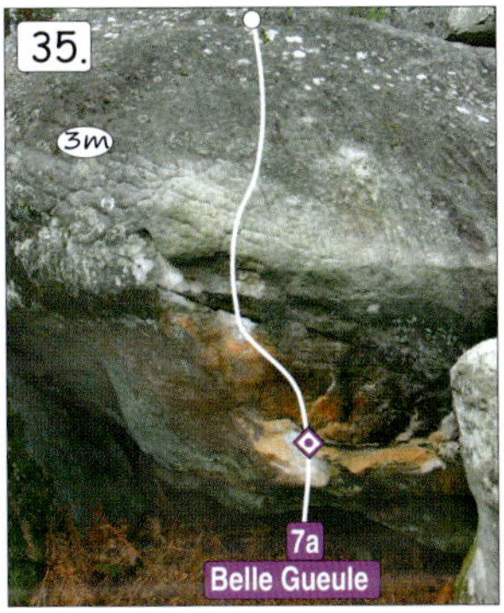

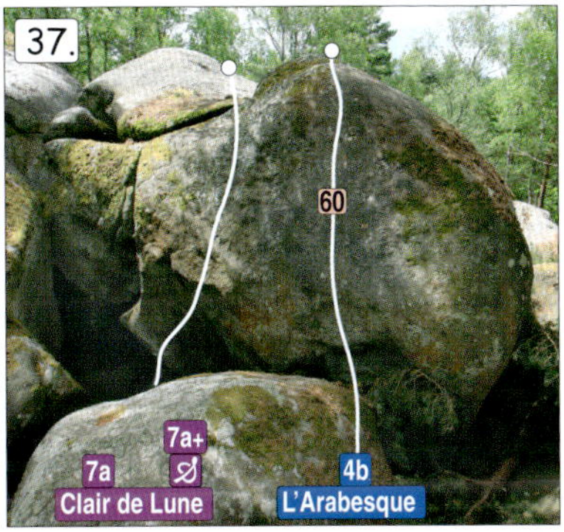

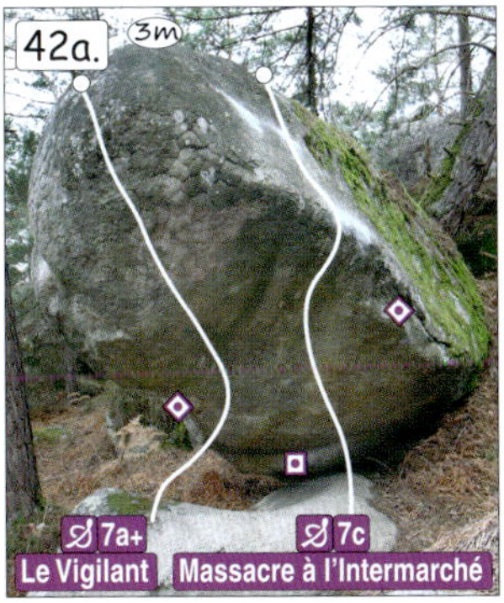

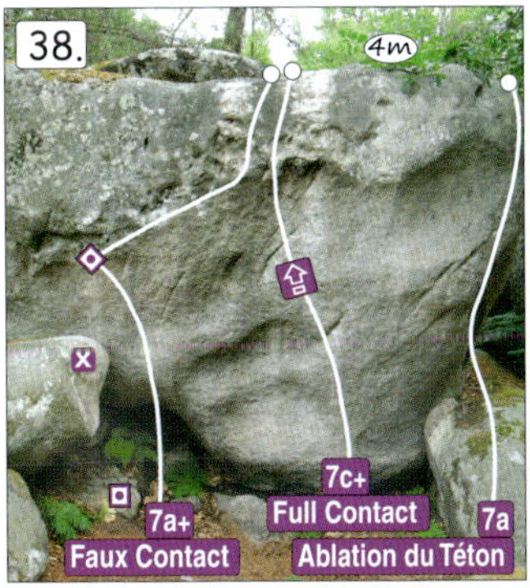

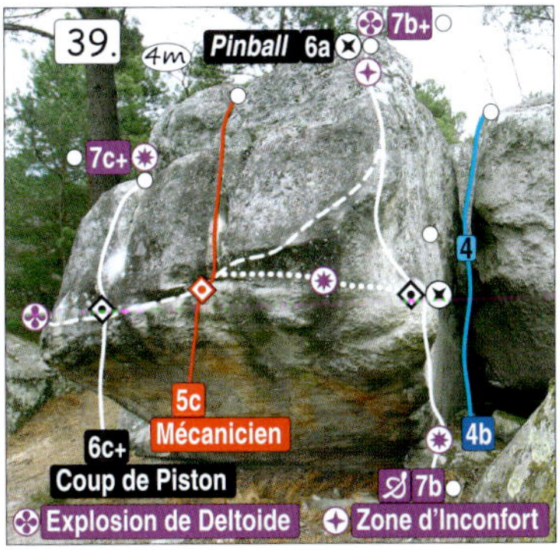

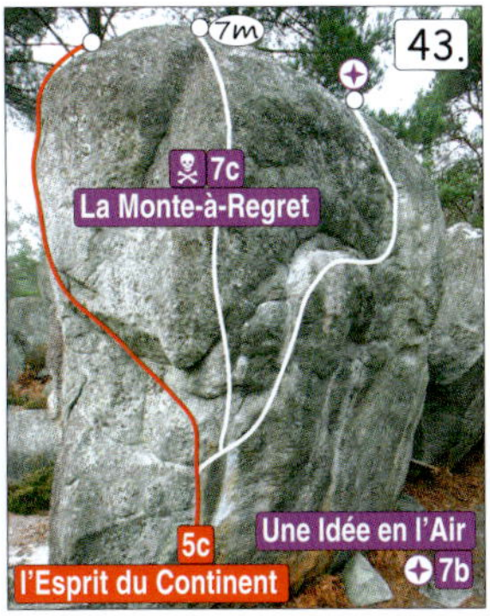

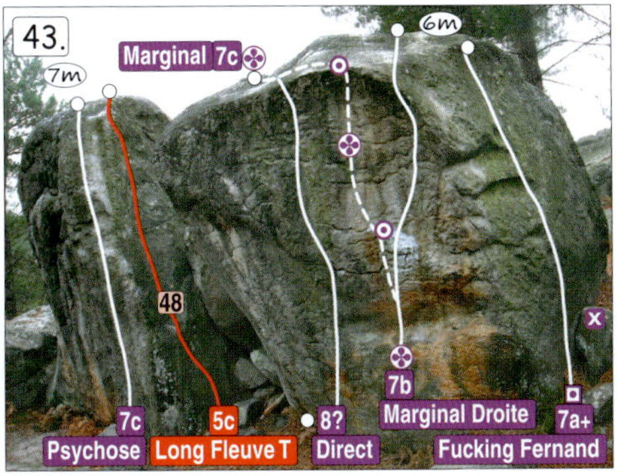

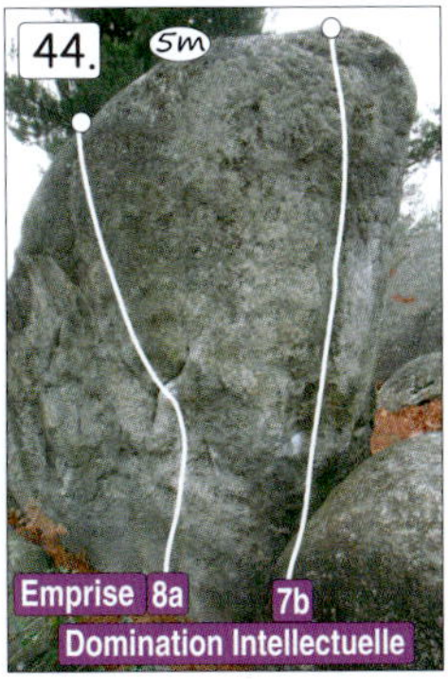

Apremont Parking - page 98

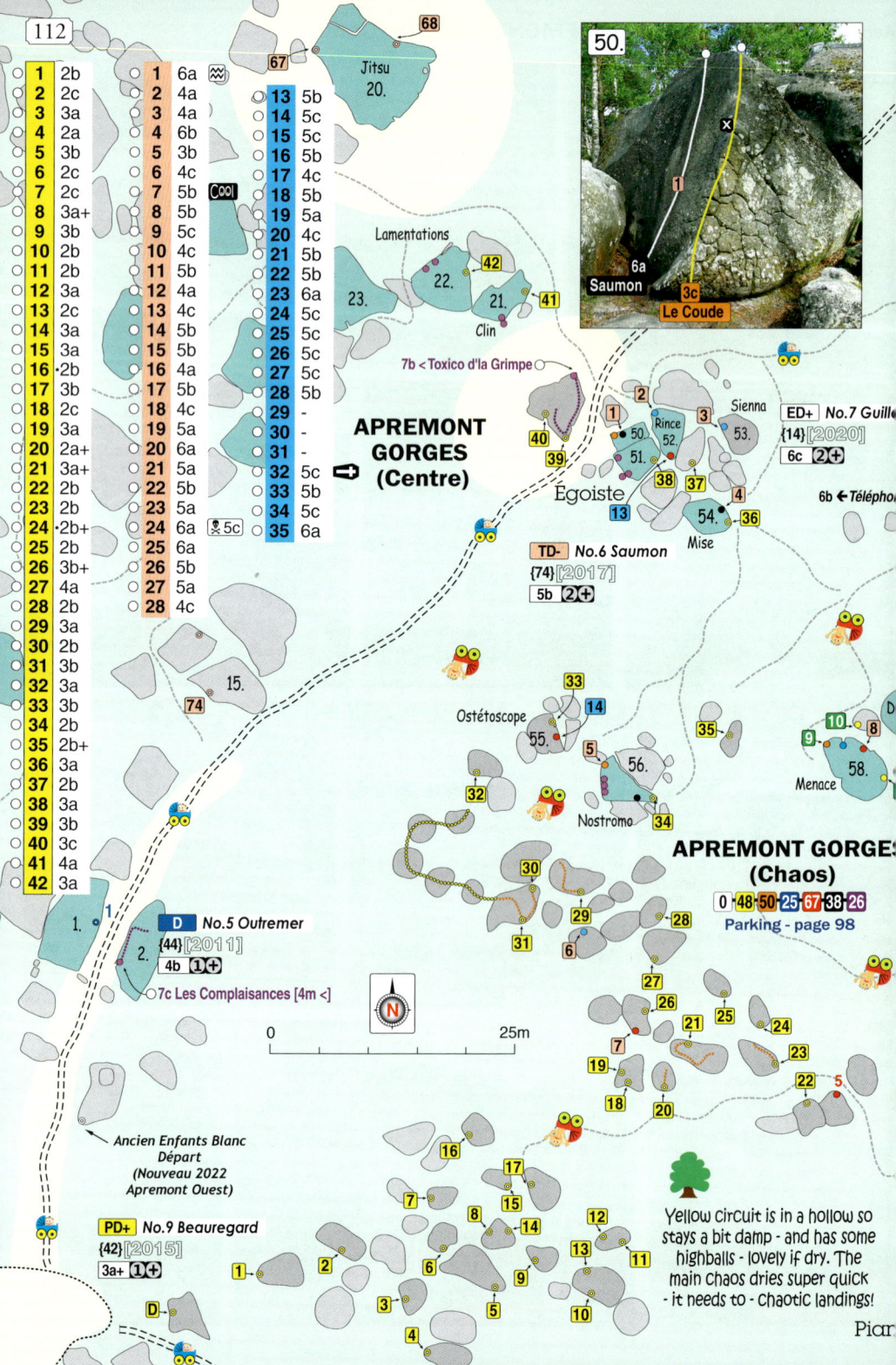

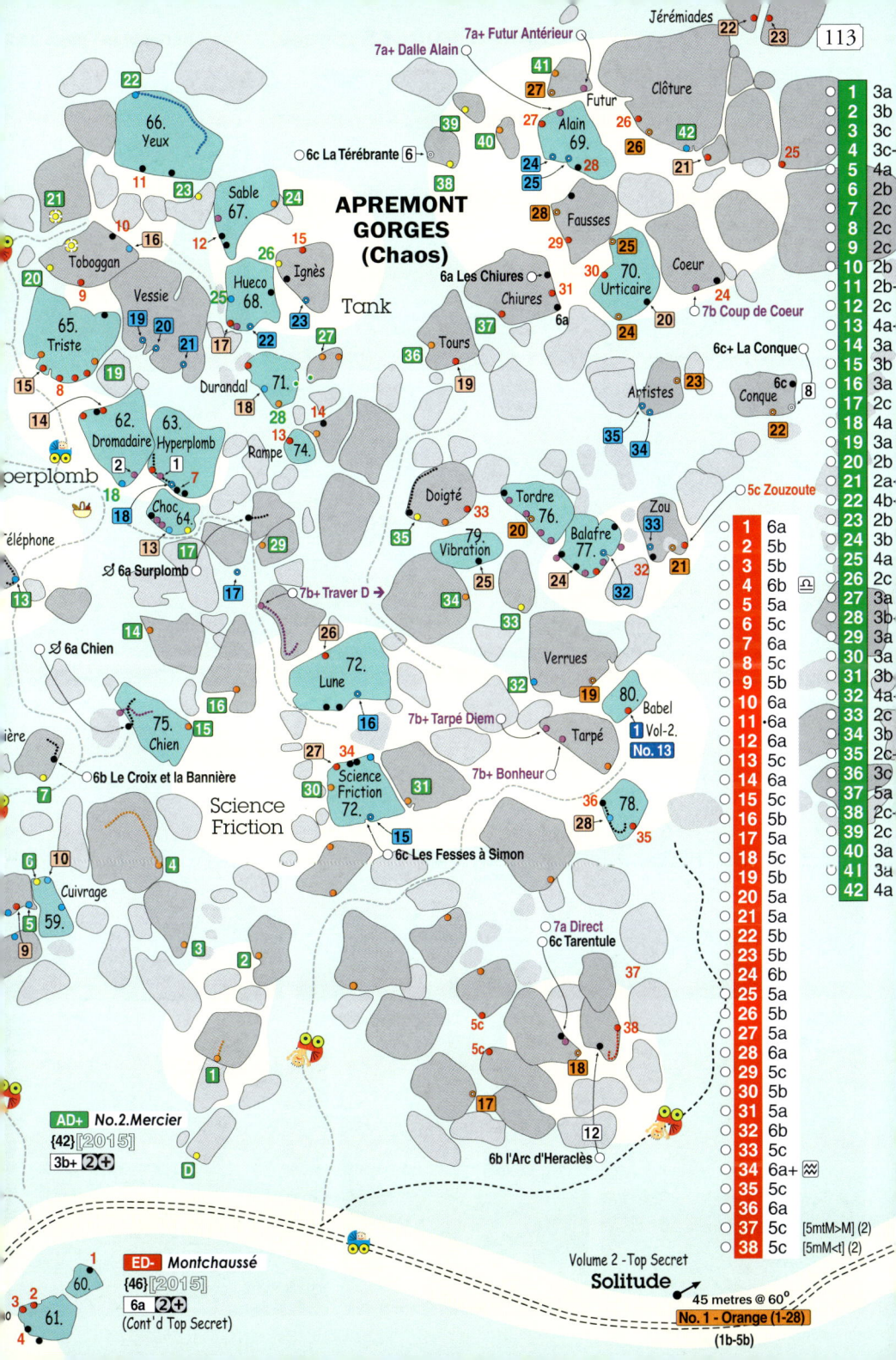

APREMONT GORGES (Chaos)

Aerial plan - page 112

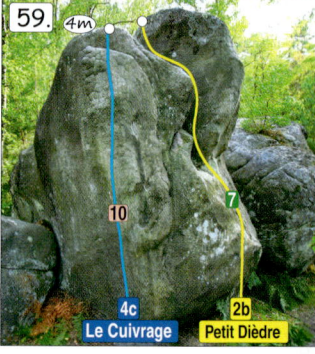

Apremont Parking - page 98

7a LE RÉTABLISSEMENT, *Maki Carmona [Bloc 75 - Chien]* ▶

APREMONT GORGES (Chaos)

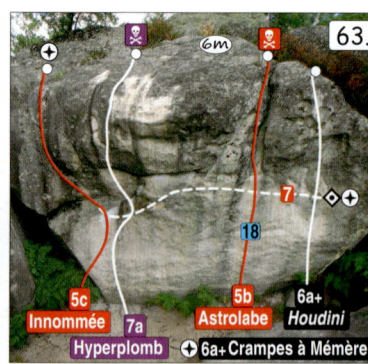

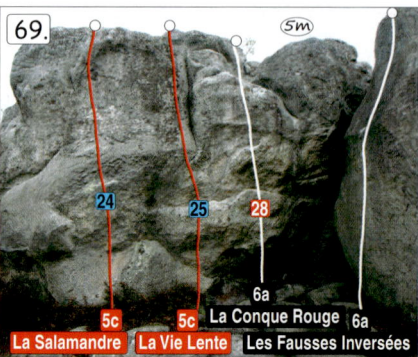

APREMONT GORGES (Chaos)

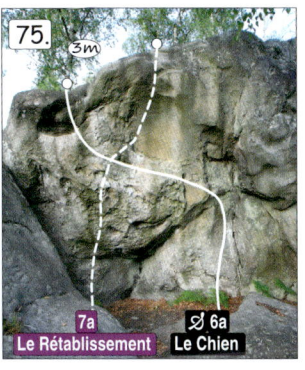

Apremont Parking - page 98

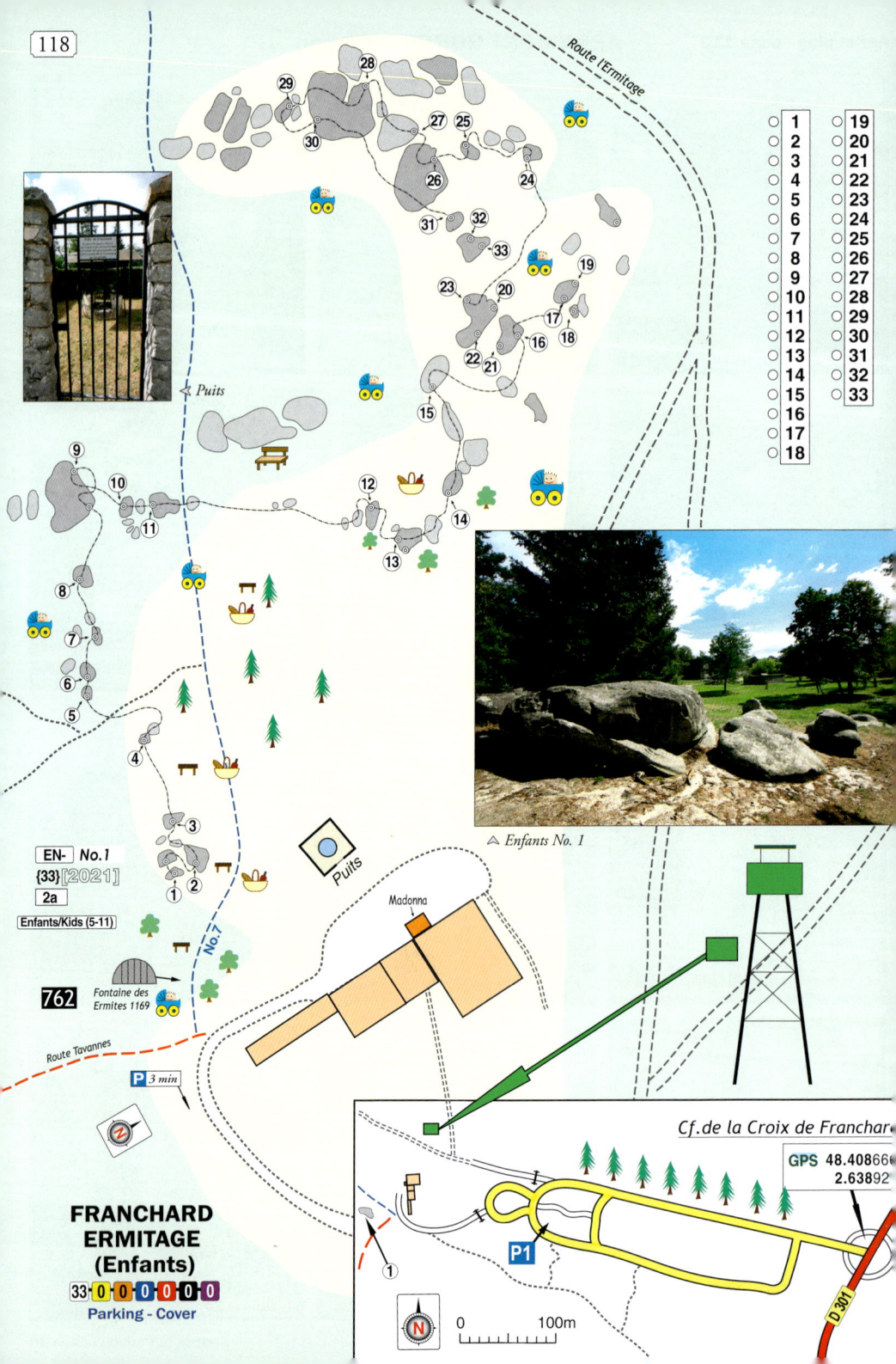

ROCK ON

BULGING WITH CLIMBING GEAR

Many shops claim to be climbing specialists.
At Rock On we sell Climbing/Mountaineering equipment
& Books and absolutely nothing else. NOTHING ELSE.
Now that's specialist.

EVERYTHING FOR THE DEDICATED BOULDERER

Mile End Climbing Wall
Haverfield Road, Bow,
London E3 5BE
Tel: 020-8981 5066

www.rockonclimbing.co.uk

FRANCHARD ISATIS - (Crocodile)

#	Grade	Desc	#	Grade	Desc	#	Grade	Desc	#	Grade	Desc	#	Grade	Desc
1	2a+	[3m M] (1)	16	3c	[3m A:] (2)	16	4c	[3m N] (1)	1	5a	[4m M] (1)	1	6b	[4m M] (1)
2	2c	[2m F] (1)	17	3c	[3m <Mg] (1+)	17	4b	[3m Mi] (1)	2	5a+	[3m G] (1+)	2	5c	[4m M] (1)
3	2b	[4m d] (1+)	18	3a	[5m :A] (1+)	18	5b	[5m dw] (2)	3	5a	[3m Ri] (1+)	3	6a+	[3m >M] (1)
4	3b	[3m M] (1)	19	4a	[3m M] (1)	19	5a+	[3m dw] (1)	4	5a+	[3m M] (1)	4	•6c	[4m M] (1)
5	3a	[3m M] (1)	20	3b	[3m M] (1)	20	•4a	[4mD](2+) [Cool]	5	5a	[3m Fs] (1)	5	5c	[3m :A] (1)
6	3a	[3m G] (1)	21	•4a	[3m M] (1+)	21	4b	[3m >M] (2+)	6	5b+	[4m A] (1)	6	•5a+	[4m Rs] (1)
7	3b	[2m r] (1)	22	4a	[4m dw] (1)	22	5a	[3m Mw] (1)	7	4c	[3m M] (1)	7	6a	[4m :M] (1)
8	3a	[3m :A] (1)	23	3c+	[3m df] (1)	23	5a	[3m Mw] (1)	8	5b	[4m dw] (2)	8	6a	[4m Ms] (1)
9	3c	[2m >M] (1)	24	4a	[4m Mg] (1+)	24	5b	[3m >df] (1)	9	5a	[5mFM](2) 4b	9	6a	[5m Ms] (1)
10	2a	[2m d] (1)	25	4a	[3m M] (1)	25	5a	[4m M] (1)	10	6a	[4m <M] (1+)	10	6a	[3m G] (1)
11	3a+	[2m :A] (1)	26	3c	[3mN](1+) 3c	26	5a	[3m dg] (1)	11	5a	[4m df] (1)	11	5c	[4m A:] (1)
12	2b	[2m Nf] (1)	27	4a	[3m N] (1)	27	•4a	[4m Nc] (1+)	12	5c	[4m A] (1+)	12	5c	[5m Mw] (1)
13	2c	[3m D] (1)	28	3a+	[4m M] (1)	28	4b	[3m M] (1)	13	5b	[4m Mr] (1+)	13	5c+	[5m MA] (1)
14	4a	[3m d] (1)	29	3c+	[4m F] (1+)	29	4a	[3m M] (1)	14	5c	[3m A:] (1+)	14	6b	[4m F] (2+)
15	2b+	[5m df] (1) [Cool]	30	3a+	[3m N] (1)	30	3b	[3m G] (1)	15	5b	[3m Rj] (1)	15	6a	[4m d] (1)
16	2c	[3m M] (1)	31	3c	[2m <M] (1)	31	4b	[3m N:] (1+)	16	•5c	[3m d] (1)	16	6b+	[3m Ms] (1)
17	2a	[3m M] (1)	32	3a	[3m M] (1)	32	4a	[4m d] (1+)	17	5b+	[4m A:] (1)	17	5c	[4m Nc] (1)
18	3a	[4m A:] (1)	33	3b	[4m Mr](2) 3b	33	3c	[4mN] (1)	18	5b	[4m df] (1)	18	6b	[3m Mw] (1)
19	2b+	[3m M] (1)	34	2c	[6m df] (1) [Cool]	34	5a+	[4m Pc] (1)	19	•5c	[4m A: R] (1)	19	6b+	[4m Ri] (1)
20	4a	[4m A:] (1+)	35	3c+	[5m dw] (2) [Cool]	35	5a	[3m M] (1)	20	5a	[3m Nc] (1)	20	6b	[3m Mw] (1)
21	2b	[2m M] (1)	36	3c	[4m M] (1)	36	4b	[4m F:] (1)	21	4b	[4m d] (1+)	21	6a	[3m R] (2-)
22	3a	[2m Fr] (1+)	37	4a	[3m M] (1)	37	3b	[4m :A] (1)	22	5a	[4m Mg] (2)	22	6a	[4m R] (2)
23	2c	[3m d] (1)	38	4b	[4m ds](2) [Cool]	38	4b	[3m M] (1)	23	5b	[5m M](2) 4b	23	5c	[4m Mi] (2)
24	3b	[3m d] (1)	39	•3b	[3m M] (1)	39	4c	[3m M>g] (1+)	24	5b	[4m M] (2+)	24	6a+	[5m dw] (2)
						40	5a	[3m A:] (1+)	25	4c	[3m F] (1+)	25	6a	[4m d] (1)
						41	4c	[6m df] (2) [Cool]	26	5b	[3m Mr] (1+)	26	5c	[5m dg] (2)
						42	4a	[3m M] (1+)	27	5a+	[4m :A](2+) [Cool]	27	6b+	[3m <M] (2)
						43	5a	[4m Mr] (1)	28	6a+	[4m dw] (1)	28	6a	[3m AR] (1)
						44	4b	[3m N] (1+)	29	5c	[4m A<d] (2)	29	6a	[5m M] (2)

Franchard - Isatis & Cuisinière Parking

Motorhomes: No overnight parking in any of the forest parkings. Fines !!!

Attention !!! Voiture "Vol" - Car Break in

150 metres no parking zone

6 km — Fontainebleau — D 409

5 km — Arbonne

P2 — Route de l'Ermitage — 761 — 767

2.2m — Route de Cul de Chaudron — Route de Loup

P1 Isatis-Cuisinière
GPS 48.411261
2.598482

Cf. de la Plaine de Macherin

Cf. des 3 Frères

R. d. Buttes de Fontainebleau — Route de Chatelain

P3

Route Belair

Cuisinière Amédée Vol 2. (Top Secret)

P1: 14min
P3: 7min

Cf-Renardeau

Cuisinière Centre — page 144
Cuisinière Est — page 146

<12 min> Route de l'Isatis

765

P1: 2'15"min

766

page 142

764

Isatis Crocodile page 121

Franchard Sablons Vol 2. (Top Secret)

Isatis Angle Ben page 123

Franchard-Haute Plaines Vol 2. (Top Secret)

Isatis Memel page 125

Isatis Iceberg page 140

Route des Gorges de Franchard

Hale Bopp (Top Secret)

Route Amédée

Cuisinière Crête Sud Vol 2. (Top Secret)

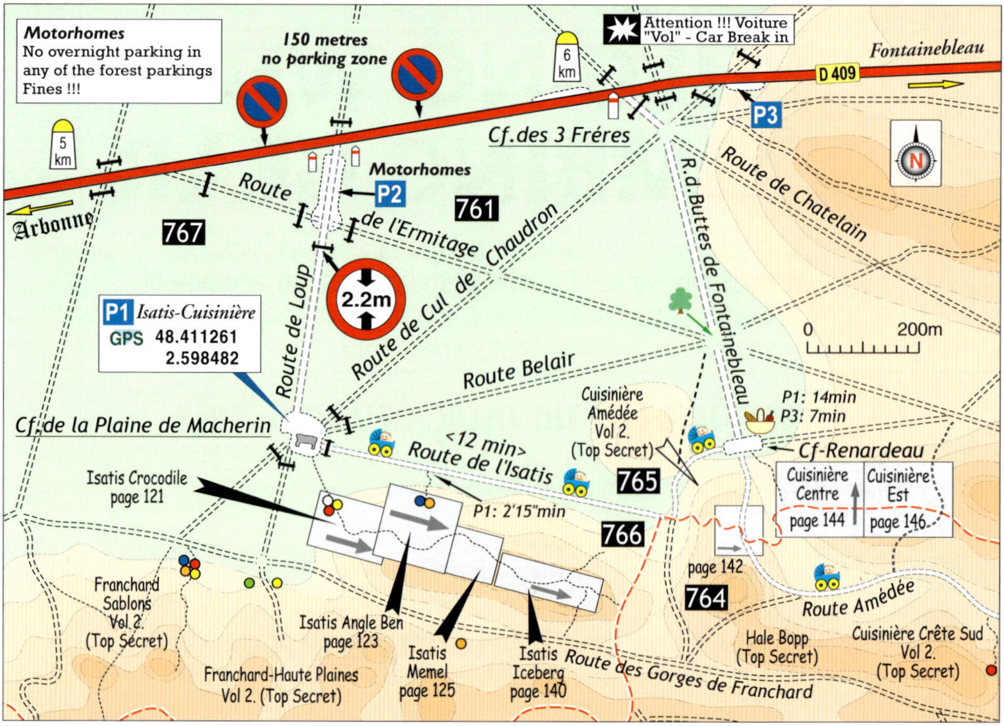

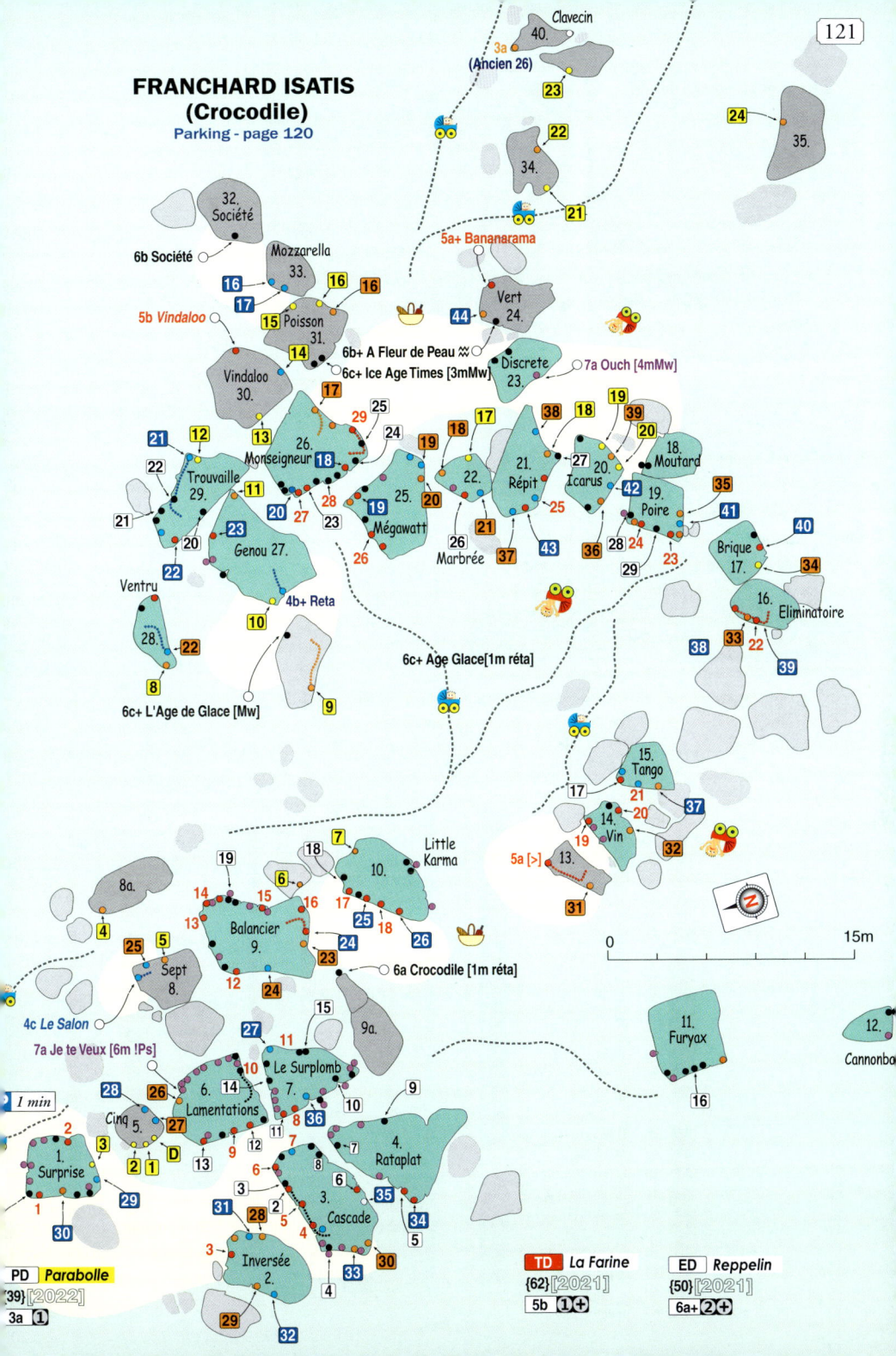

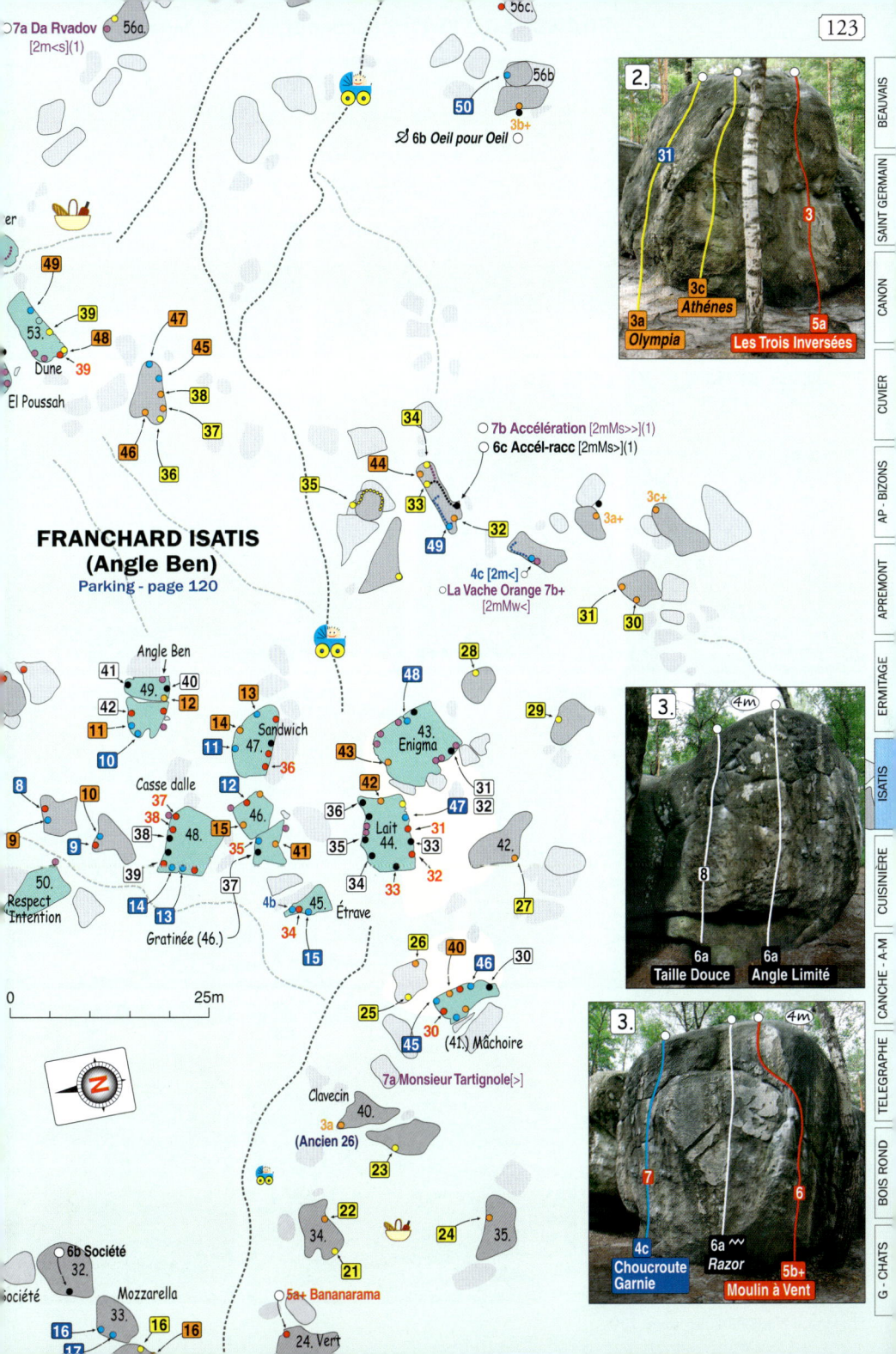

FRANCHARD ISATIS (Crocodile)

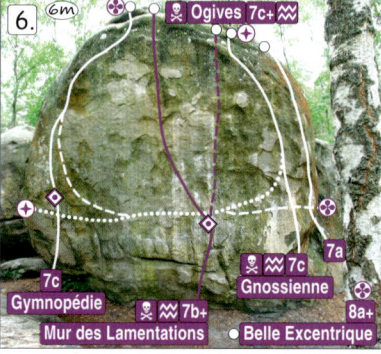

FRANCHARD ISATIS (Crocodile)

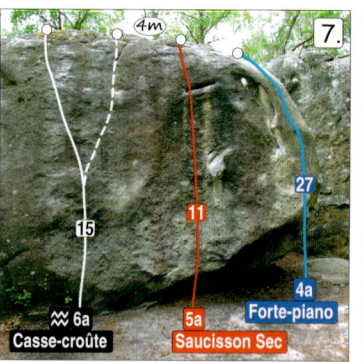

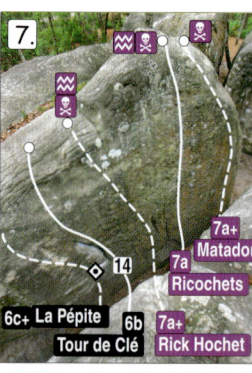

FRANCHARD ISATIS (Crocodile)

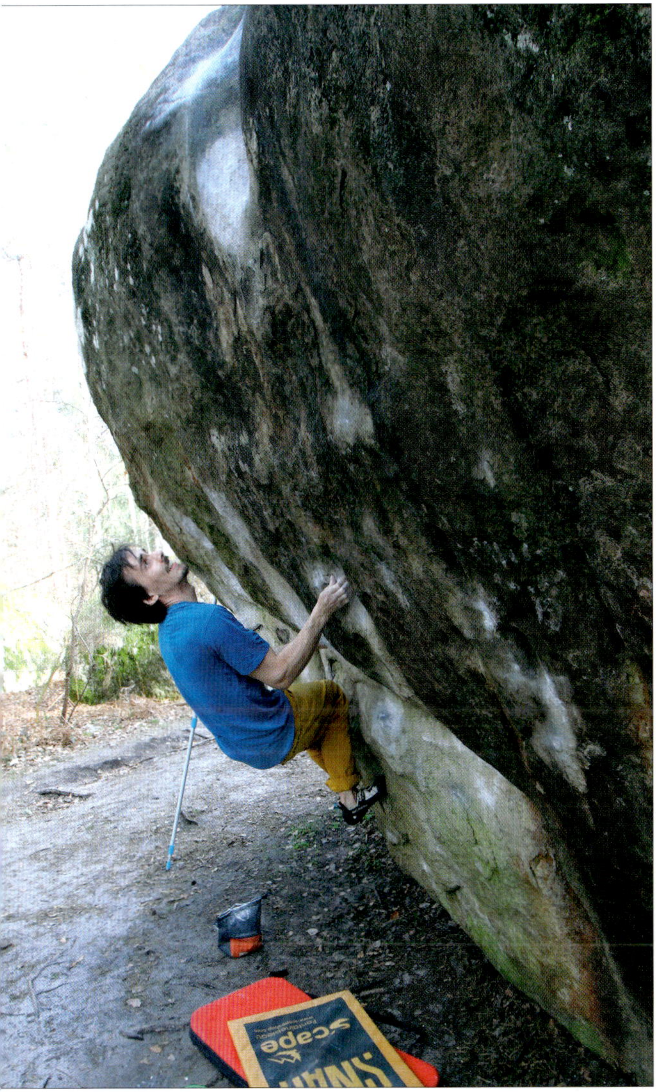

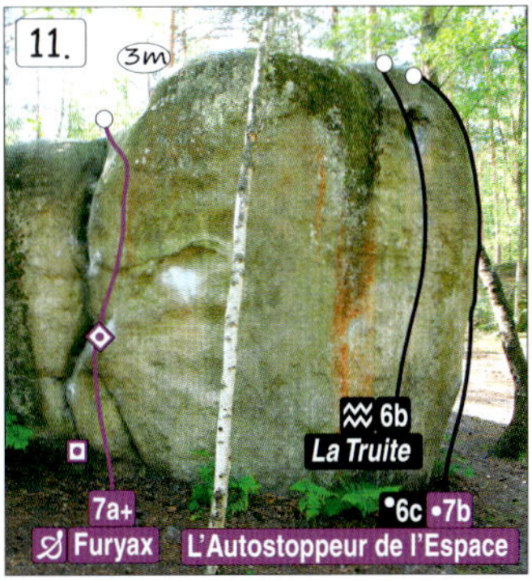
11.
3m
6b
La Truite
•6c •7b
7a+
Furyax
L'Autostoppeur de l'Espace

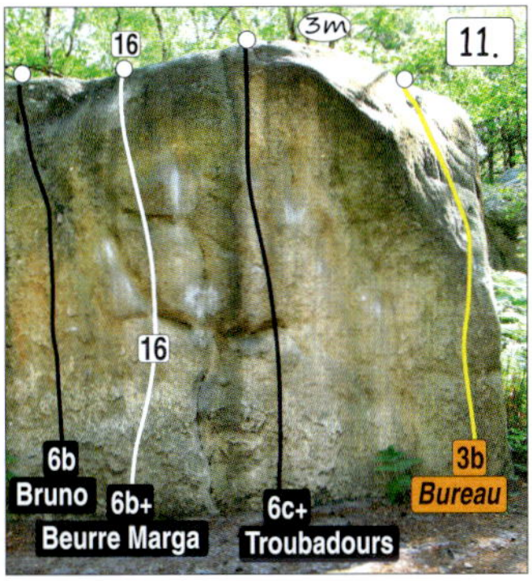
16
3m
11.
16
6b
Bruno
6b+
Beurre Marga
6c+
Troubadours
3b
Bureau

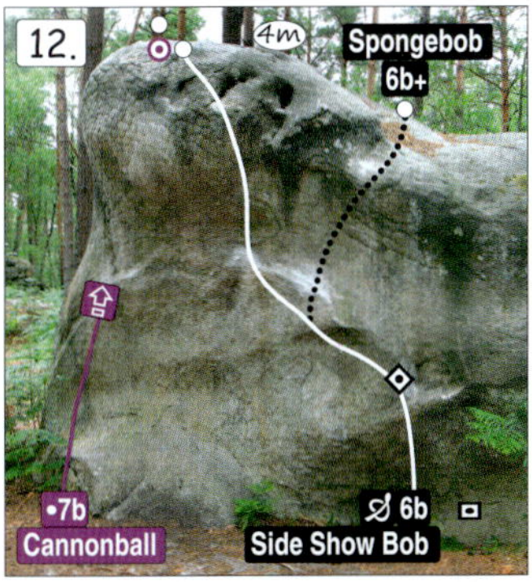
12.
4m
Spongebob
6b+
•7b
Cannonball
6b
Side Show Bob

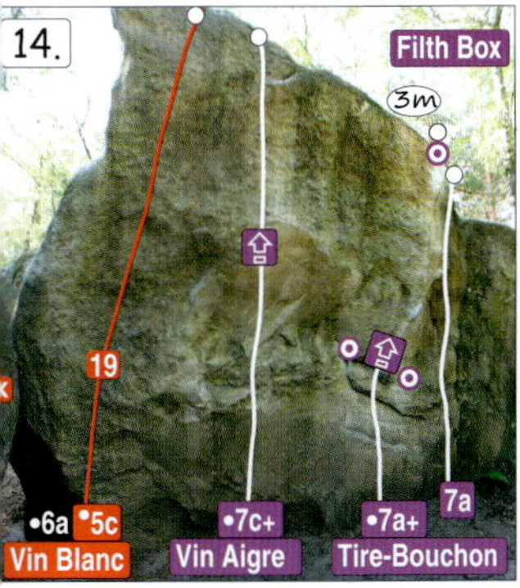
14.
Filth Box
3m
19
•6a •5c
Vin Blanc
•7c+
Vin Aigre
•7a+
7a
Tire-Bouchon

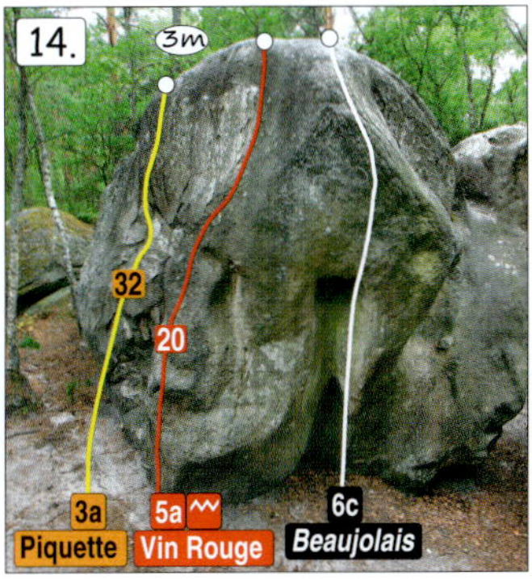
14.
3m
32
20
3a
Piquette
5a
Vin Rouge
6c
Beaujolais

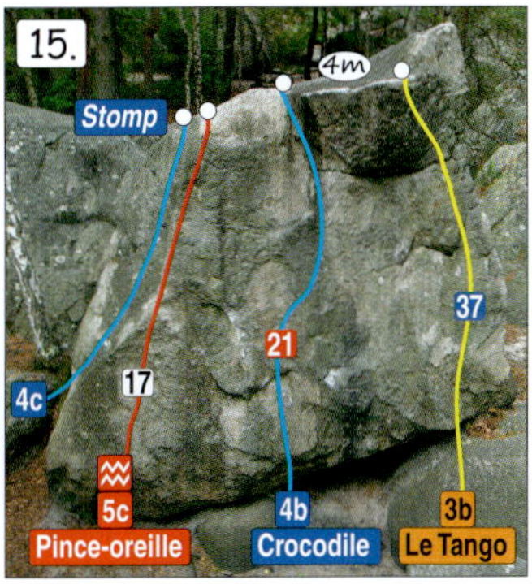
15.
4m
Stomp
4c
17
21
37
5c
Pince-oreille
4b
Crocodile
3b
Le Tango

7b+ SURPRISE, *Corentin Psomas* *[Bloc 1 - Surprise]*

FRANCHARD ISATIS (Crocodile)

Aerial plan - page 12

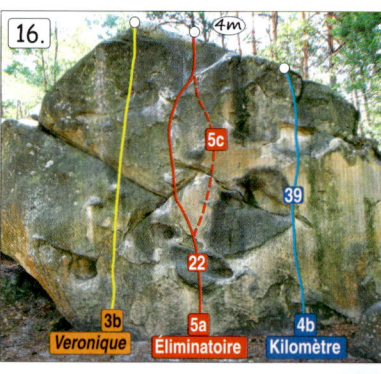

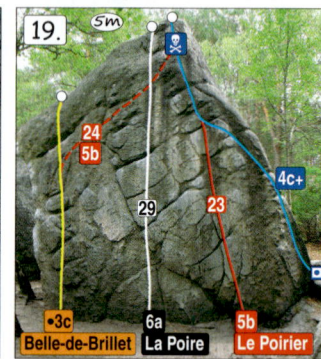

Franchard Isatis Parking - page 120

6a LA POIRE 29, *Murray Freestone [Bloc 19 - Poire]*

FRANCHARD ISATIS (Crocodile)

Aerial plan - page 121

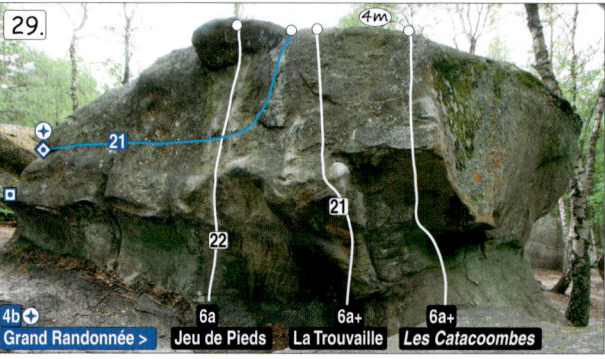
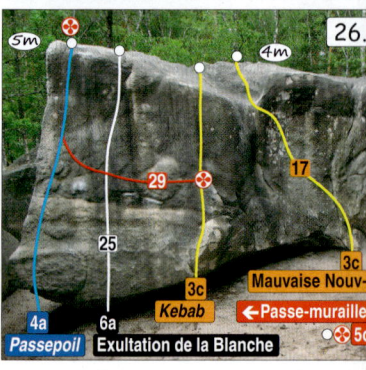

6a CASSE-CROUTE 15 , Najlaa Halfi [Bloc 7 - Surplomb]

FRANCHARD ISATIS (Angle Ben)

Aerial plan - page 123

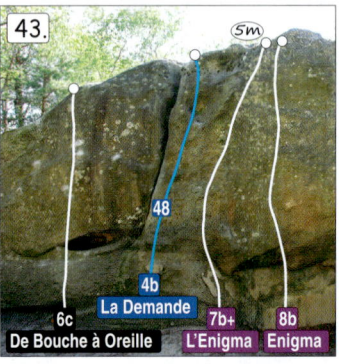

6b+ L'OPPO-EXPO, Andreas Quiroz [Bloc 43 - Enigma]

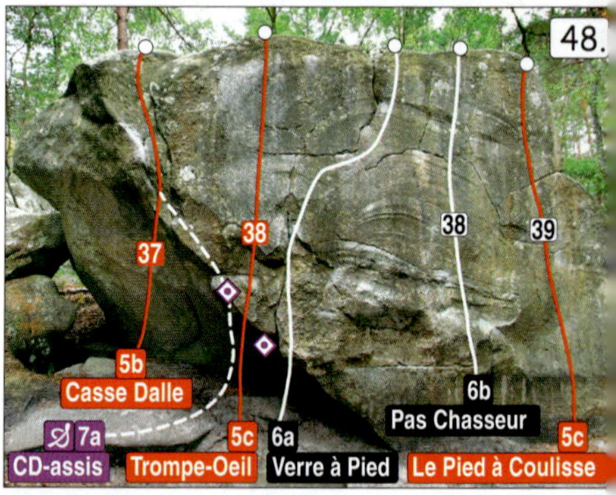

FRANCHARD ISATIS (Angle Ben)

Aerial plan - page 123

Franchard Isatis Parking - page 120

7a NEZZUNDORMA, Mariona Bosch [Bloc 46 - Nezzu]

FRANCHARD ISATIS (Angle Ben)

Aerial plan - page 123

Franchard Isatis Parking - page 120

FRANCHARD ISATIS (Memel)

FRANCHARD ISATIS (Memel)

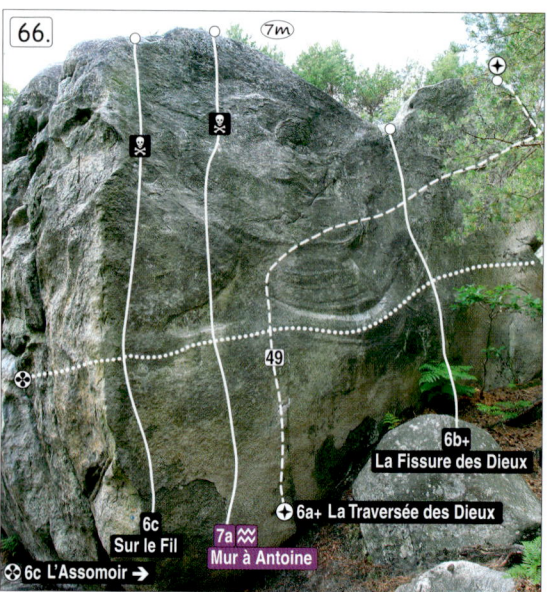

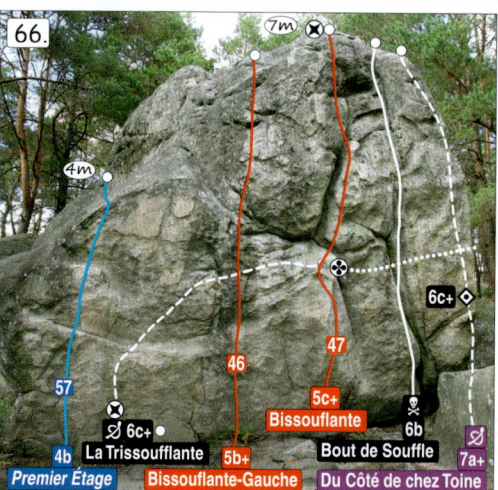

Franchard Isatis Parking - page 120

7a+ L'ULTIME SECRET, Irvin Guinot [Bloc 64 - Dru] ▶

FRANCHARD ISATIS - FOND (Iceberg)

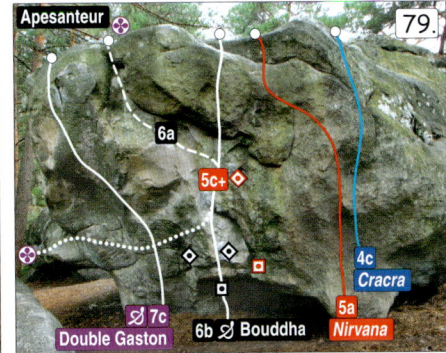

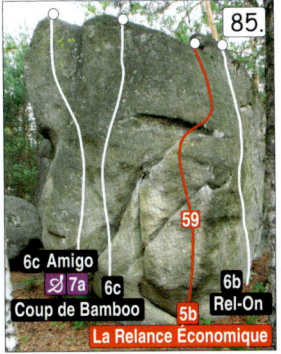

Franchard Isatis Parking - page 120

FRANCHARD CUISINIÈRE (Amédée - Noir circuit-TOP SECRET)

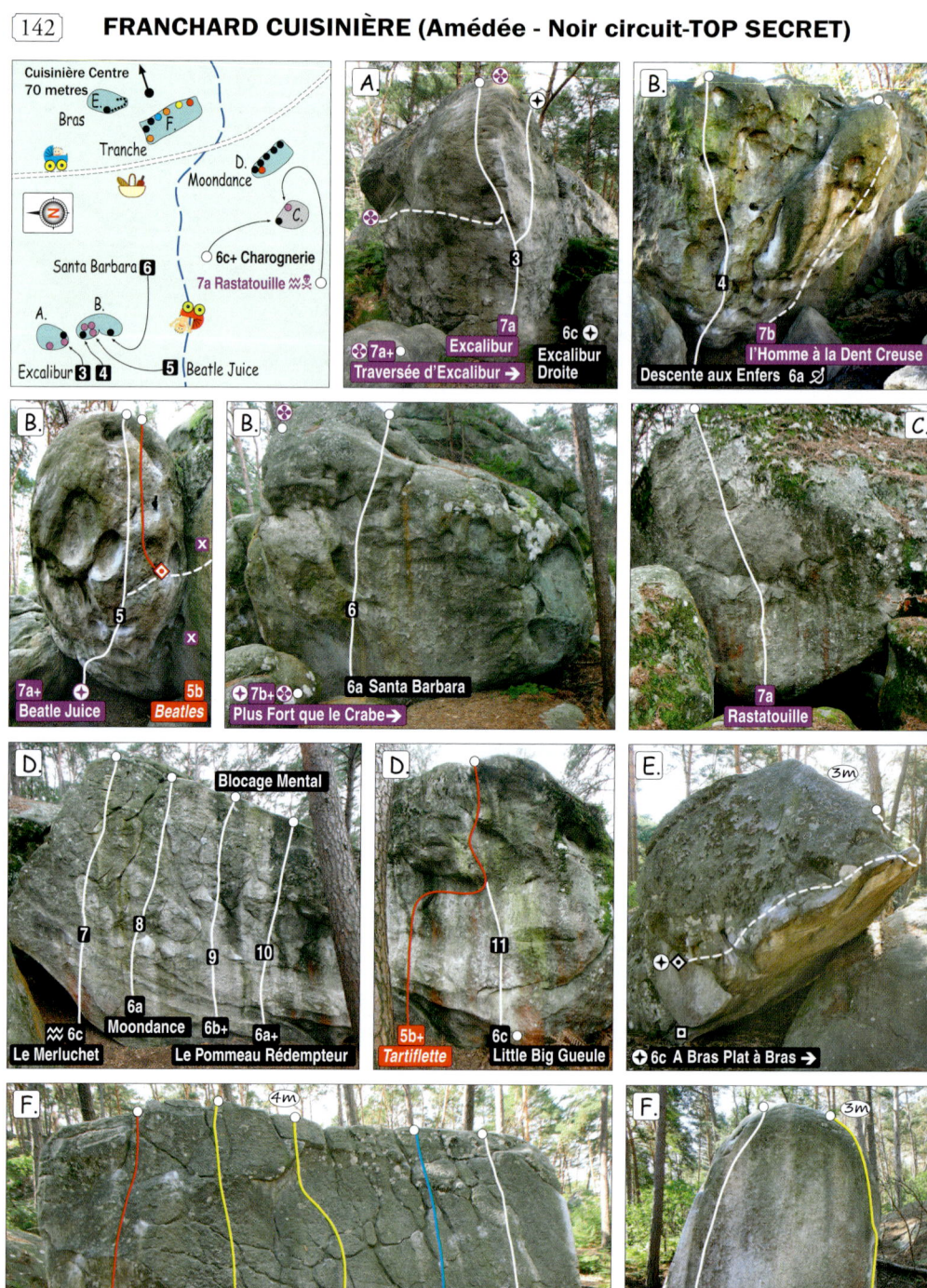

Cuisinière Parking - page 120

FONTAINEBLEAU - 100% Technique & Tips - rock preservation

Fontainebleau has a huge history of Bouldering, and as such - keeps it grading policy very strict and conservative. There is certainly no grade inflation, there never has been, and its unlikely to ever happen. All 35,000 problems are graded by local climbers, with fairness being the key. Most climbers visiting Font for the first time, get completely shut down with problems at their normal grade. The list below is a fun way to look at the percentage elements for success at Font, even with big power - its only 35%. Take note of all the other parts, it should help you unlock a great many problems.

1. Power (35% element of Font climbing). Crash pads: when your power runs out, you need one. Top-tip, create a very good flat and level, landing zone. Link up with others and use some of the smaller pads to fill in the gaps, then use a big flat one as the final top landing zone. If doing easier circuits on your own, use a smaller flexi folding double or triple style. This style is also usually more friable, so treat them carefully. Never drag pads from problem to problem, bad erosion.

2. Footware (Foot friction 20% element) Mini door-mats: Some people like bare feet, others loose shoes, others tight shoes. It's your choice, but what is imperative - is that they are meticulously clean. Your foot friction is hugely important at Font. Experts will sit on the crash pad, and clean their shoes until the rubber goes a dark black for best friction, and then step very carefully straight onto a door mat to stay clean. The mini door-mat is an essential part of the kit at Font, since any loose sand falls into the bristles (unlike on a pad). You place it at the start zone, which is often a different place to the fall zone - where the pads are.

3. Hand Friction: (15%) Most climbers are used to chalk (Light Mag Carb). It certainly works very well at Font to dry up any moisture in the hands. However, the best tip is to be smart, choose the right location for the ambient temperature: shady on hot days, cool but not cold; and pick out dry rock that has really good air flow - windy if its rained recently. Then you hardly ever dip your hand, because you don't feel you need to.

4. Rock Friction: (15%) This is where you definitely need a pof. The "most useful part of the pof," is to swish the tail over the rock prior to climbing. This effortlessly cleans any loose sand from the holds, and enables you to attain perfect friction for both hands and feet. Make one yourself. Get a square 1.2m piece of cotton, then from climbing shop or website - Colophony Resin (crushed crystals 500g). Place a big fist sized amount in the centre of the rag, then tie up with cord. The resin is distilled from Pine trees, a perfectly natural substance that breaks down in daylight, smells beautiful - like the forest too, and gives a tackyness to the fingers. It wears off the rock instantly and does not polish at all. Note: polished holds are simply solid quartz, which get further polished by tiny quartz crystals (sand), and unfortunately by any climbers "not" cleaning their feet first.

5. Flexibility: (10%) Sure there are some problems with big holds where you don't need flexi, but then why come to Font. Surely climbing at Font is all about climbing strange shapes that require good to excellent flexibility, stretch out before and after, its really worth it.

6. Intelligence: (5%) Simply bashing away at the rock does not pay any dividends at Font, except wear out your skin, and leaves you deflated. Be ingenious, crafty and skillfull. That's the key to having fun.

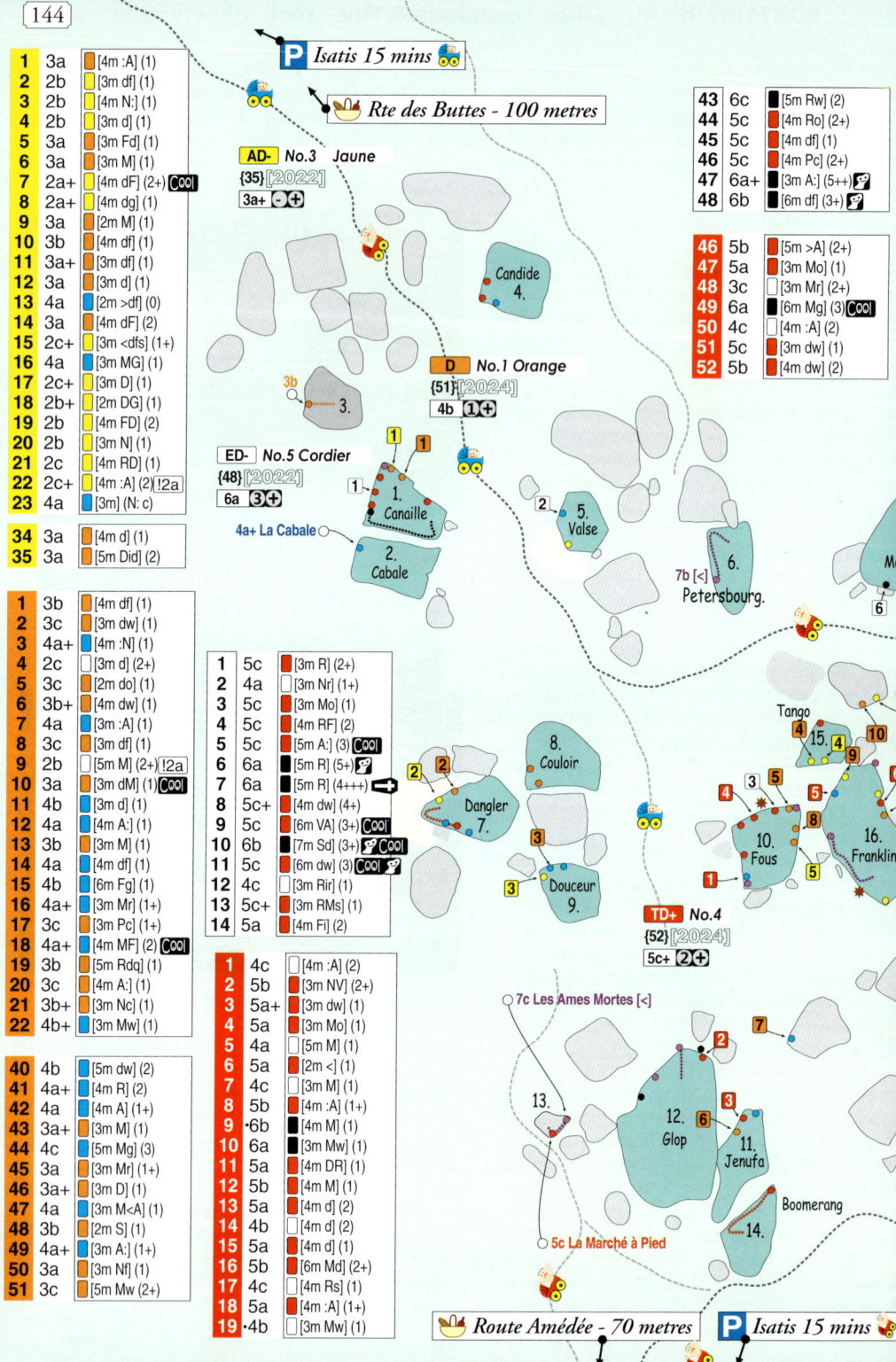

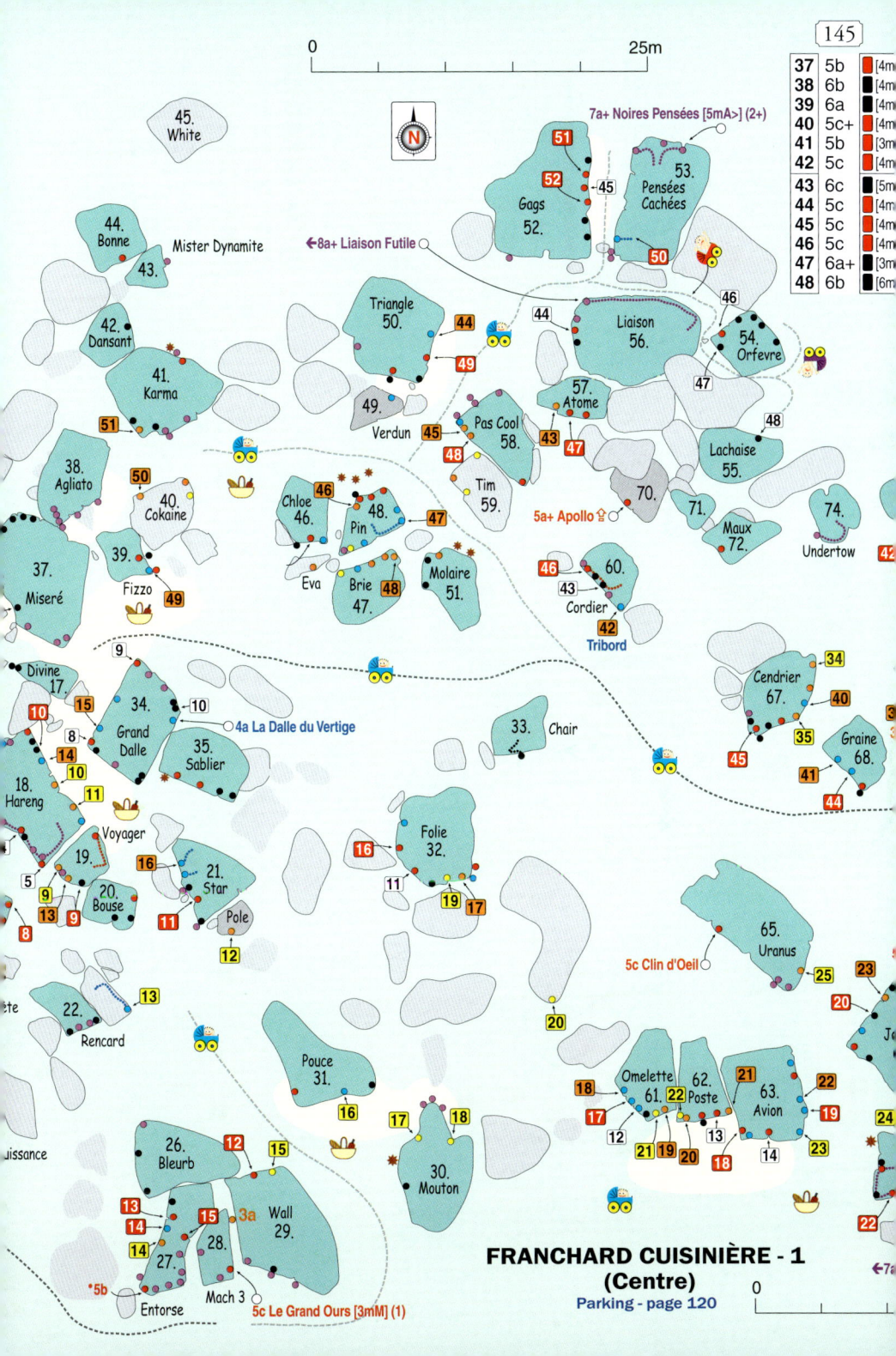

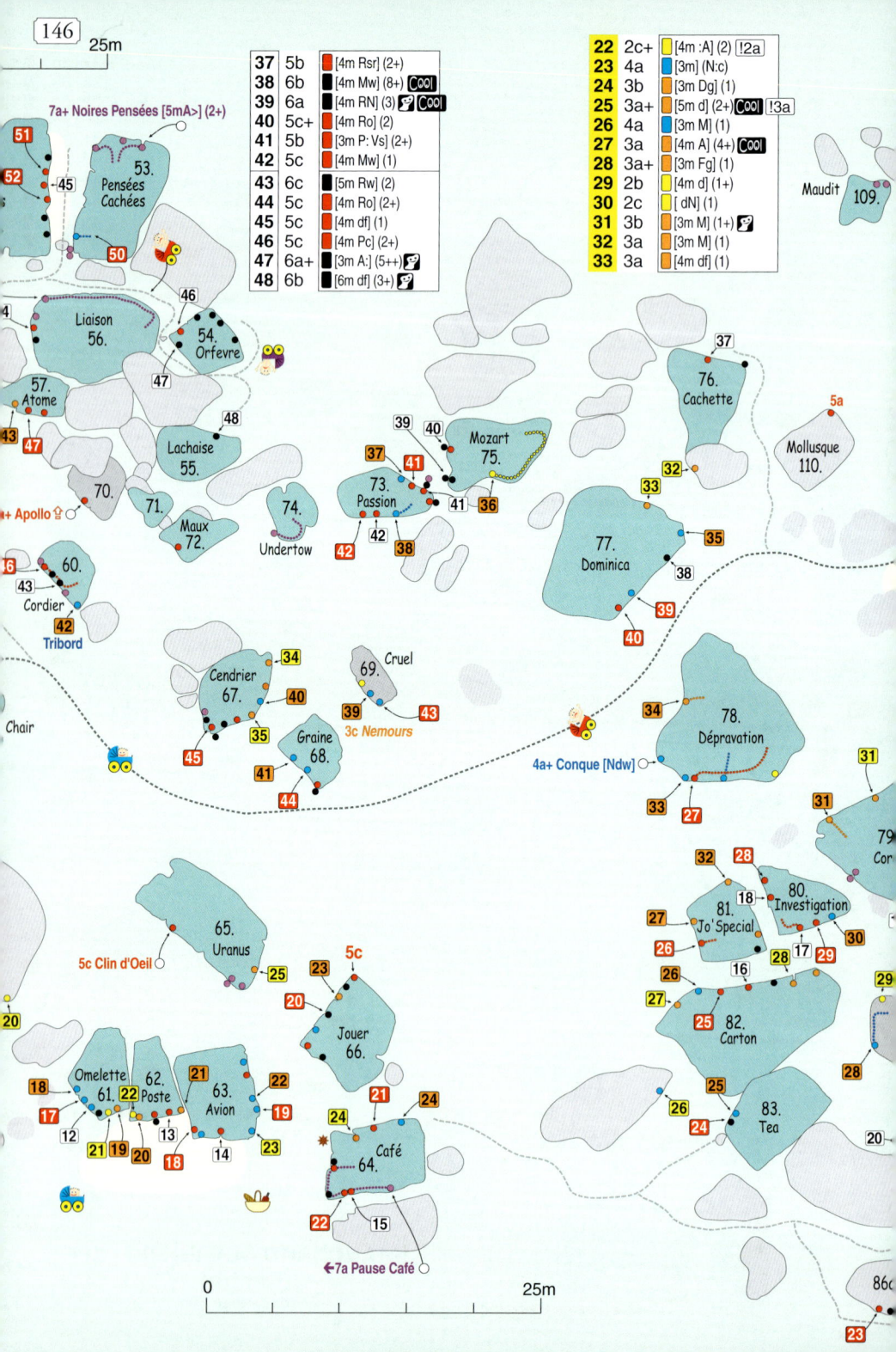

FRANCHARD CUISINIÈRE

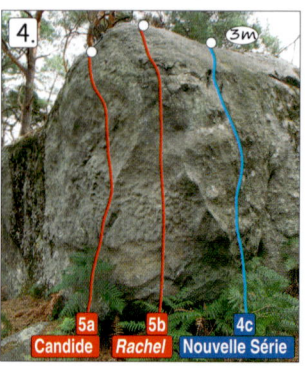

Cuisinière Parking - page 120

FRANCHARD CUISINIÈRE

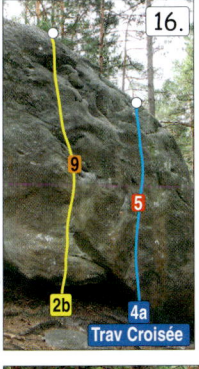

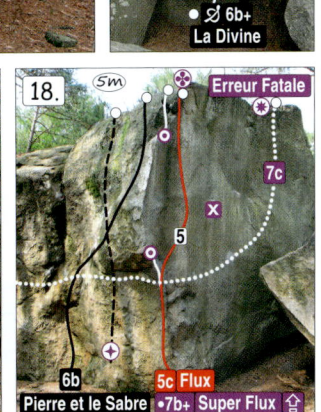

FRANCHARD CUISINIÈRE

Aerial plan - page 144

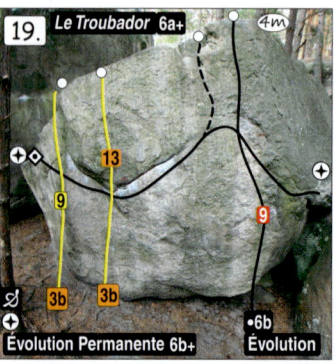

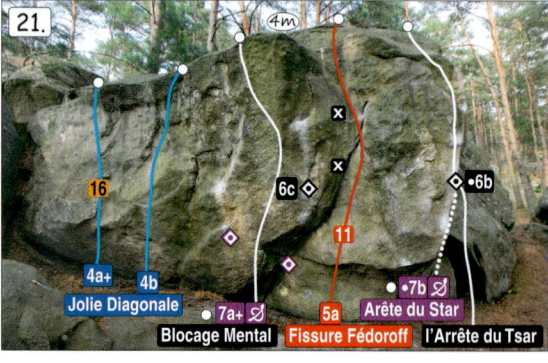
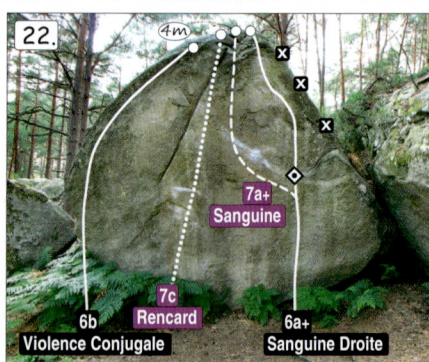

Cuisinière Parking - page 120

6b LA SUPERBE, Ben Moon [Bloc 25. - Jouissance] ▷

FRANCHARD CUISINIÈRE

Aerial plan - page 144

26. 7b Le Bleurb

26. 6b+ Le Souffre-Douleur / 6b Matière Grisée

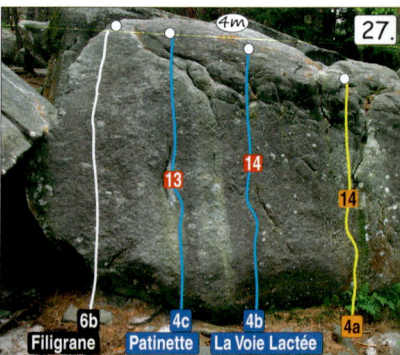
27. 6b Filigrane / 4c 13 Patinette / 4b 14 La Voie Lactée / 4a 14

27. 7a+ Impulsion / 5b Impulsion du Moment / 7c Crash Test / 7b+ Double Entorse

27. 7a+ Entorse / 7a Rétrofriction / 5a 15 Soupière

28. 7a+ L'Impasse du Hasard / 7a Mach 3

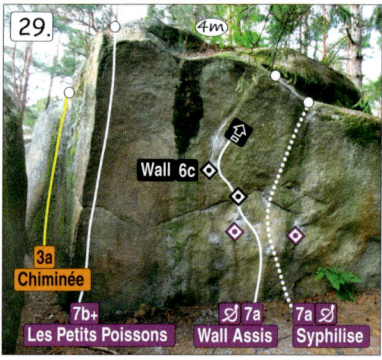
29. 3a Chiminée / 7b+ Les Petits Poissons / 6c Wall / 7a Wall Assis / 7a Syphilise

7b Cinq et Demie / Le Mouton à 5 Pattes 7a

30. 7a Le Mouton à 6 Pattes / 2c+ 17 Poignées de Valise

31. 5c Coup de Pouce

31. 4a 16 La Tempête

30. 6c Le Mouton

Cuisinière Parking - page 120   5b LA FOLIE DOUCE 16, Clelia & Stephane [Bloc 32. - Folie]

FRANCHARD CUISINIÈRE

FRANCHARD CUISINIÈRE

FRANCHARD CUISINIÈRE (Centre)

Aerial plan - page 144

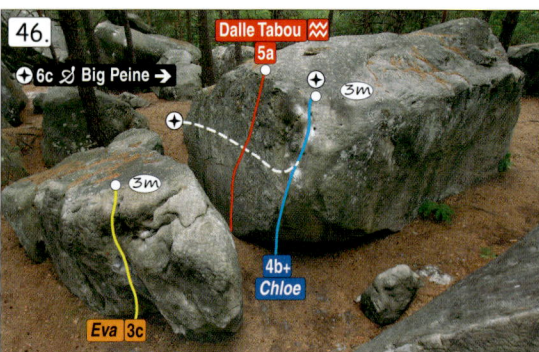

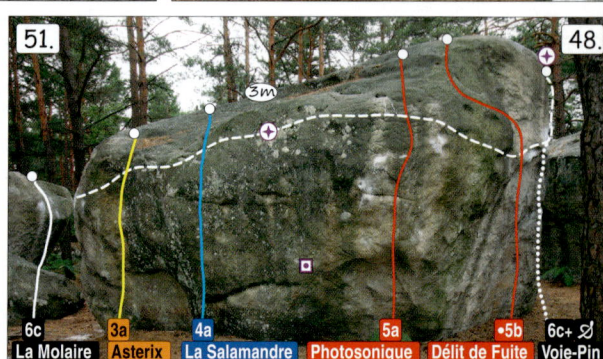

Cuisinière Parking - page 120

5c LE ROUGE VIF, *Blanka Sebulveda [Bloc 66. - Jouer]* ≫

FRANCHARD CUISINIÈRE (Centre)

Aerial plan - page 144

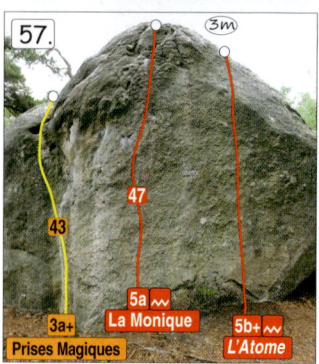

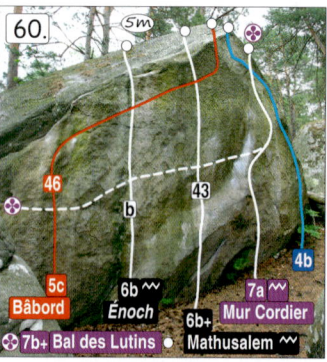
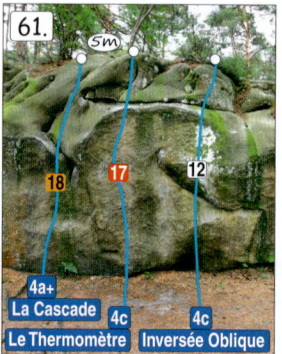

Cuisinière Parking - page 120

7b+ ECLIPSE, Alinoé Kasprzak [Bloc 53. - Pensées Cachées]

FRANCHARD CUISINIÈRE - 2 (Est)

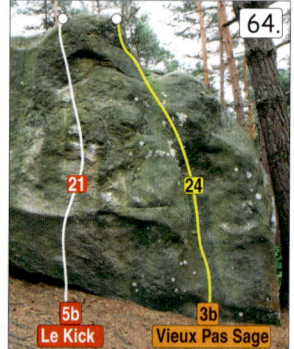
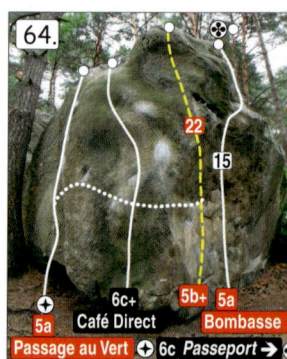

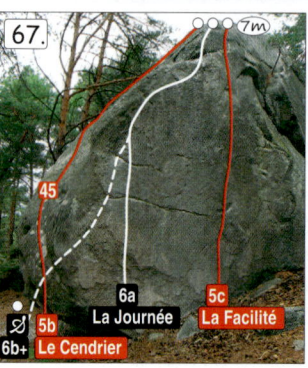
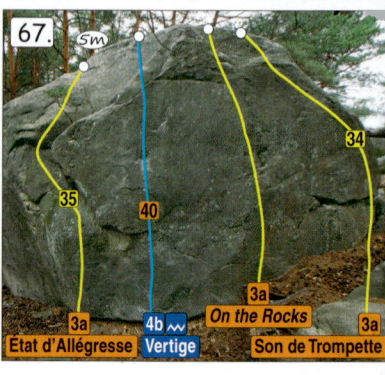

FRANCHARD CUISINIÈRE - 2 (Est)

Cuisinière Parking - page 120

FRANCHARD CUISINIÈRE - 2 (Est)

Aerial plan - page 146

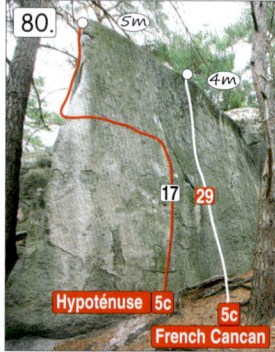
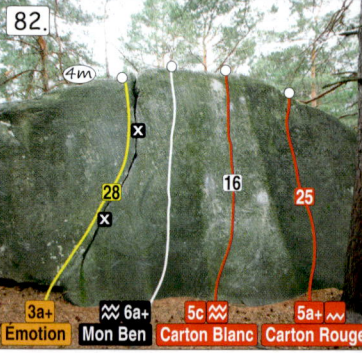

Cuisinière Parking - page 120

5c CARTON BLANC 16, Martyn Samuel [Bloc 82 - Carton]

FRANCHARD CUISINIÈRE - 2 (Est)

Aerial plan - page 146

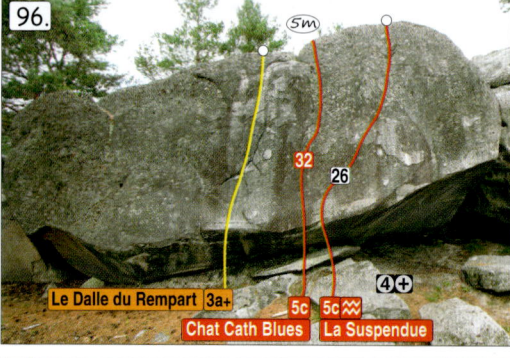

Cuisinière Parking - page 120

FRANCHARD CUISINIÈRE - 2 (Est)

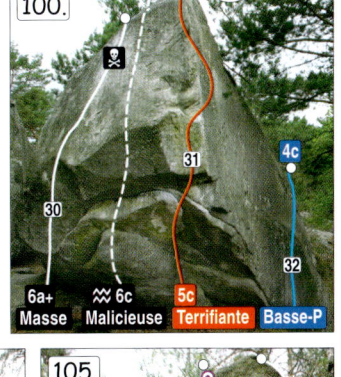

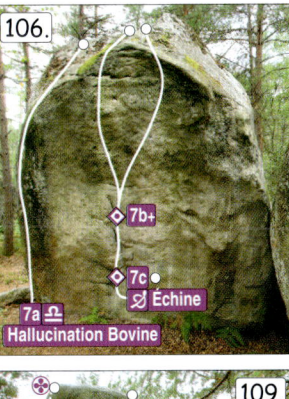

Cuisinière Parking - page 120

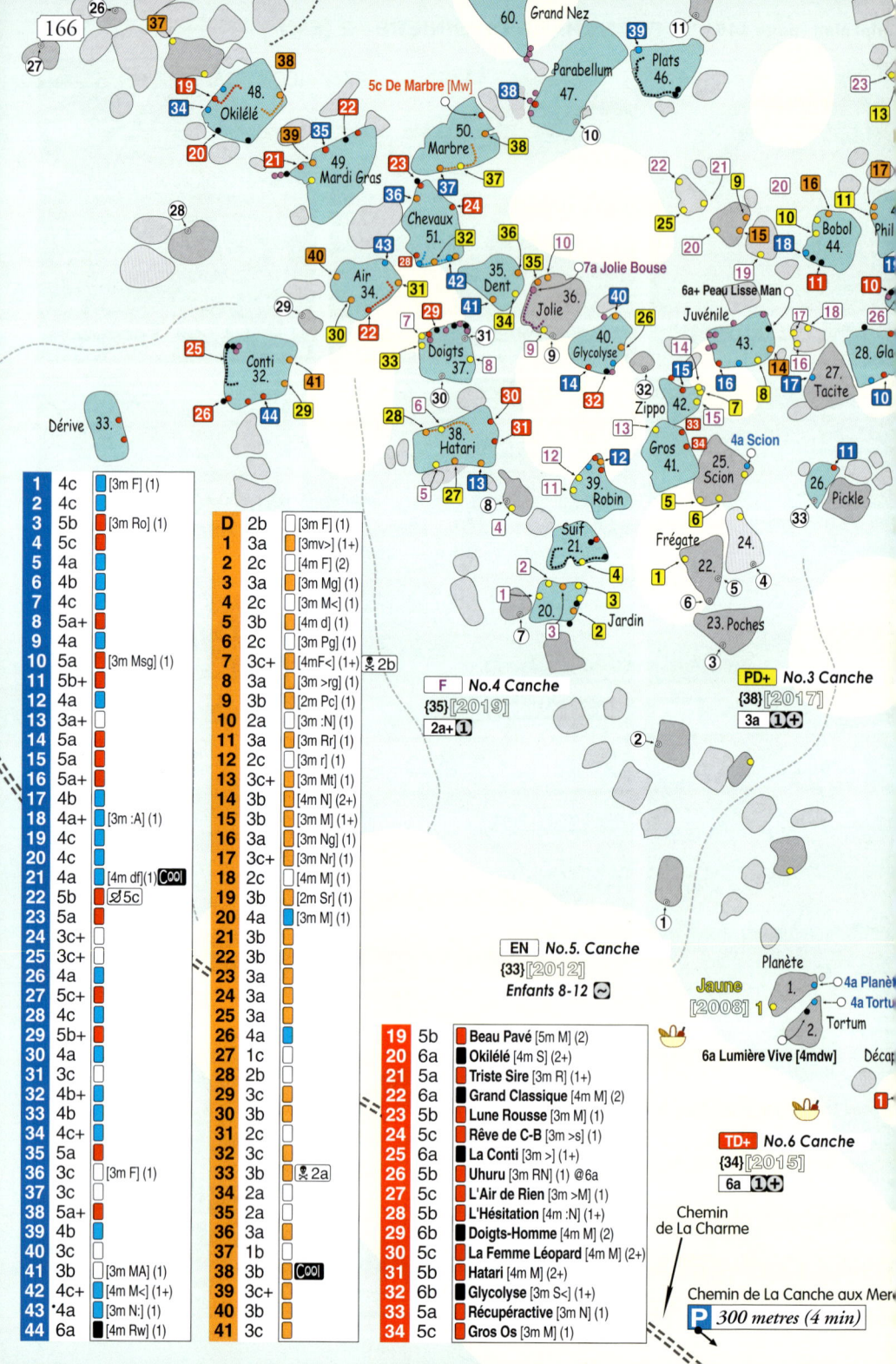

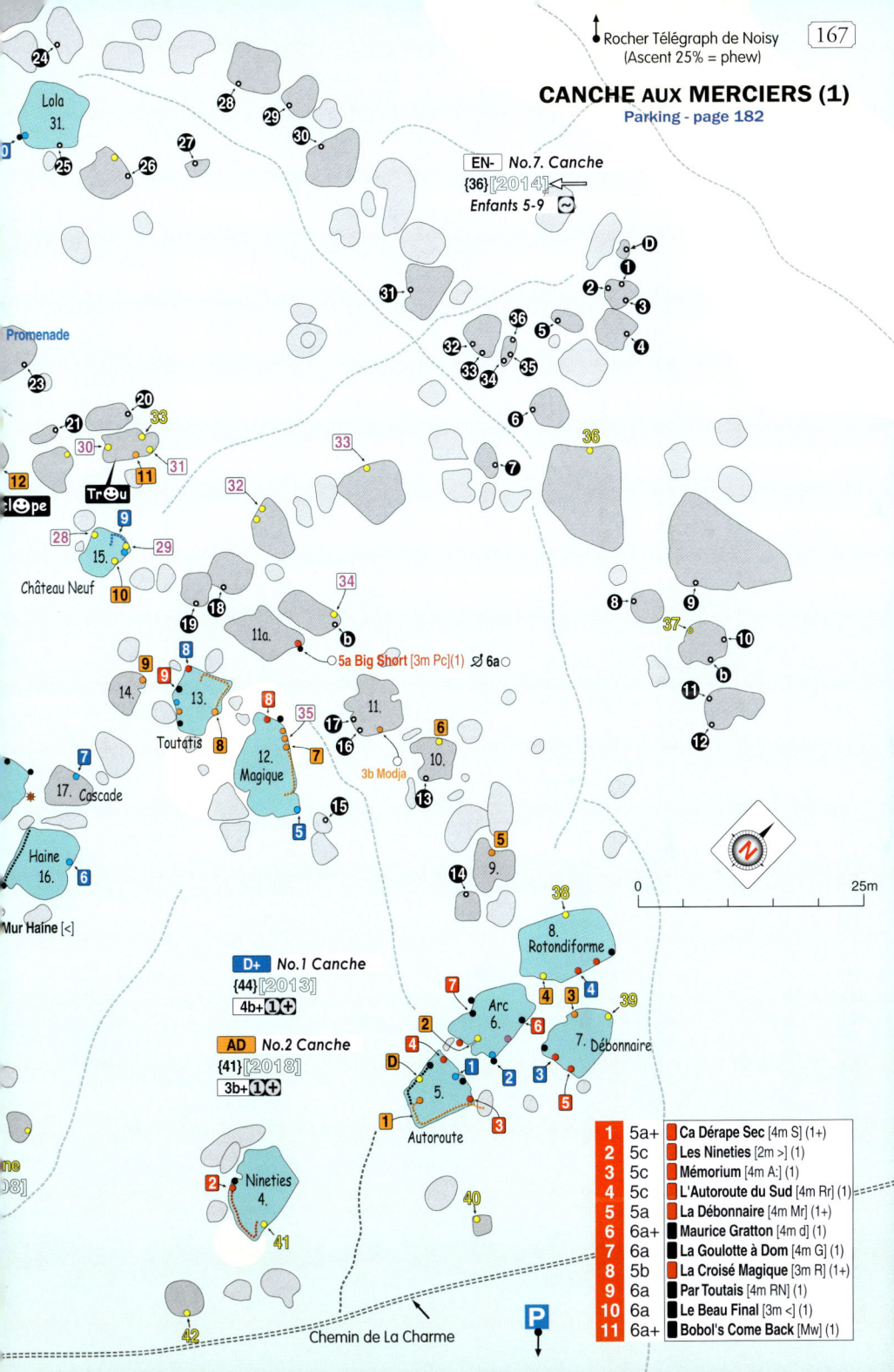

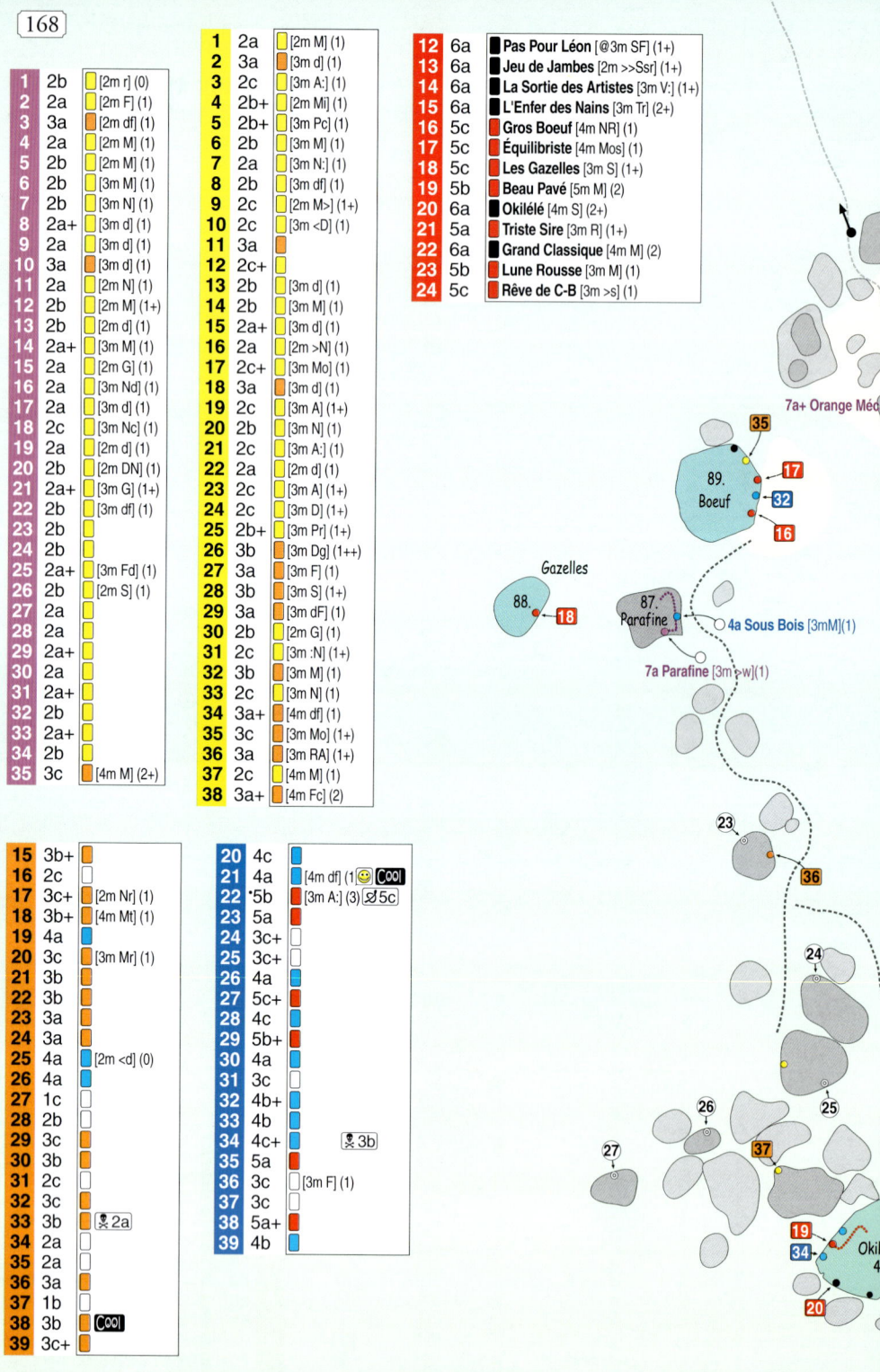

CANCHE AUX MERCIERS (2)
Parking - page 182

0 — 25m

- 32
- 85. Soleil
- 30, 31, 29, 20, 21
- 84a.
- 84.
- 6c Le Fond du Baril
- 30, 29, 28, 27
- 79. Égomoije
- 19, 28
- 6b Naissance [<]
- 78. Naissance
- 80. Seance
- 18
- 81. Heister
- 4c Ganser [Mw]
- 27
- 5a Stratosphérique
- 82. Piscine
- 83. Fond
- 77. Stratosphéric
- 76. Toit
- 17, 26
- 72. Nadine
- Clementine
- 75.
- 5c Jus de Clementine
- 6b+ Planorme Dauphin
- 74.
- 6b+ Le Dauphin
- 16
- 73. Loir
- 7a+ Quel Talon [Ss]
- 25
- 6b+ Le Loir [>]
- 15
- 70. Mali
- 14
- 7c L'Or et l'Ail [<]
- 68. Vents
- 69. Larmes
- 6b+ Apéri-Bloc [>]
- 24
- 6b Larmes à L'Oeil
- 21, 67. Rat, 23, 20, 17
- 7c Épaulard [>]
- 25, 15, 24
- 6c Deep Grès [>]
- 71. Penchee
- Franky
- 62.
- 63. Nains
- 26, 21
- 20, 19, 22, 23
- 13
- 33
- 61. Racine
- 7a+ Racine Carrée [>]
- 12
- 64. Artists
- 14
- 19, 16
- 6c Le Planiforme
- 21
- 65. Coin
- 66. Jambes
- 13, 22, 18
- 7b+ Rage Dedans
- 3c Lepricorn
- 15, 24
- 60. Grand Nez
- 22
- 11, 23
- 39
- 46. Plats
- 24
- 5c De Marbre [Mw]
- 47. Parabellum
- 38
- 50. Marbre
- 38, 37, 36, 23, 24
- 51. Chevaux
- 10
- Gras
- 22, 21, 25, 15
- 23, 13, 24, 14
- 30. Hydes
- 17, 16
- 44. Bobol
- 45. Philatélie
- 31. Lola
- 20, 25

169

CANCHE AUX MERCIERS

Aerial plan - page 166

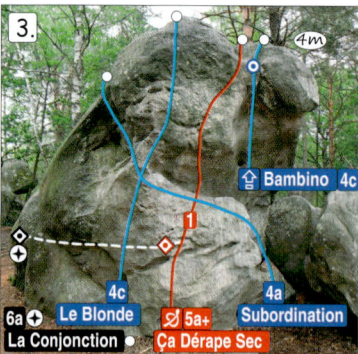

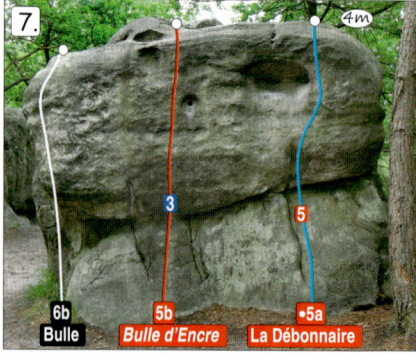

Canche-aux-Merciers Parking - page 182

3a DERAPAGE CONTROLE 18 , Heike den Blaauwen [Bloc 67, Rat]

CANCHE AUX MERCIERS

CANCHE AUX MERCIERS

28.
- 4b Sorbetière
- 4c Boule de Glace
- 3c+ Glace au Chocolat

28.
- 5c Morphoillogique
- 5c Epice
- ←Pixel 6c+

29.
- Exploreur 7a+
- ←Le Beau Final 6a

30.
- 6a La Dalle aux Hydes

31.
- 4c Lola
- Le Dictat de Lola 6a

32.
- 6a La Conti →
- 6c Chasseur d'Ombre →

32.
- 7a Double Face →
- 7b+ Super-Conti →
- 5b / 6a Uhuru

32.
- 5a Oxygène
- 5c Le Ballon

33.
- 5c La Dérive
- Les Croix des Croisés

34.
- 5c L'Air de Rien →

35.
- 3b Le Dent

Canche-aux-Merciers Parking - page 182

CANCHE AUX MERCIERS

Aerial plan - page 166-169

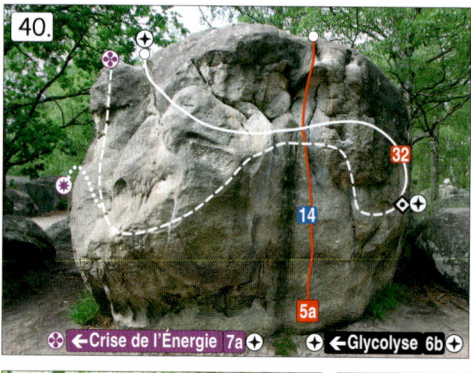

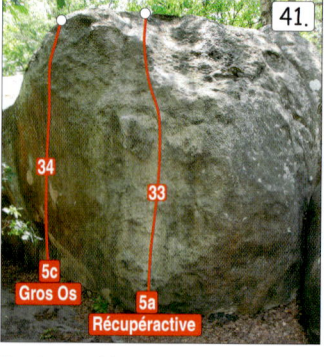
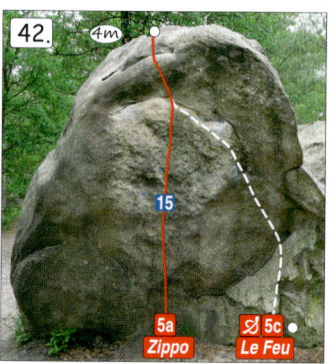
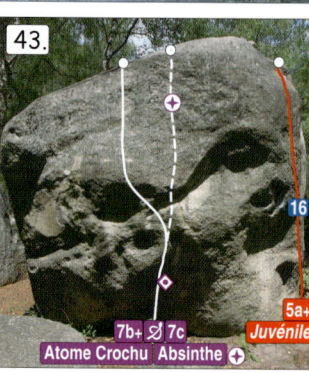

Canche-aux-Merciers Parking - page 182

7a RADIO CROCHET, *Chad Foti [Bloc 49, Mardi Gras]* ▷

CANCHE AUX MERCIERS

Aerial plan - page 166-169

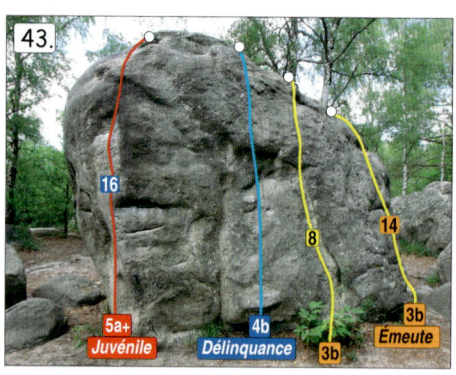
43. 16 — 5a+ Juvénile | 4b Délinquance | 8 — 3b Émeute | 14

43. 7a Kéo | 7a+ Perte de Contrôle | Dérapage 7b | Trace de Pneus +

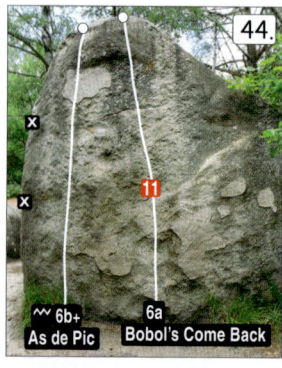
44. 6b+ As de Pic | 11 — 6a Bobol's Come Back

45. 19 — 4c Philatélie | 12 — 2c+

45. 5b La Limace | 6a+ Le Conque

46. 39 — 4b La Bateleuse

46. 6c+ P-Plats AR | Les Petits Plats 6b+

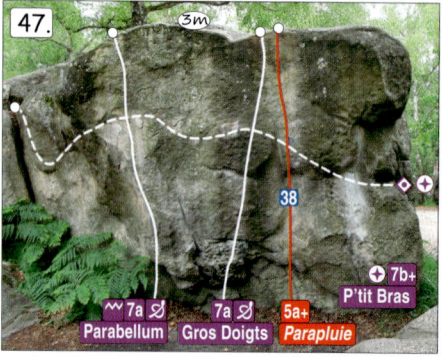
47. 7a Parabellum | 7a Gros Doigts | 38 — 5a+ Parapluie | 7b+ P'tit Bras

48. 19 — 5b Beast Beau Pavé | 34 — 4c+ Beauty | 20 — 6a Okilélé

48. 6a+ Boule de Nerfs

CANCHE AUX MERCIERS

Canche-aux-Merciers Parking - page 182

CANCHE AUX MERCIERS

Aerial plan - page 166-169

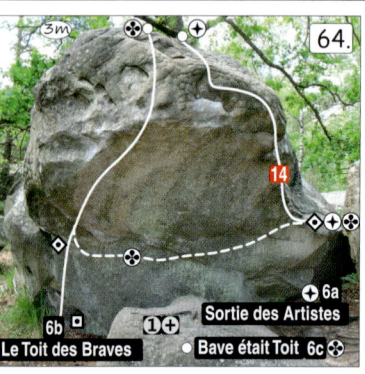

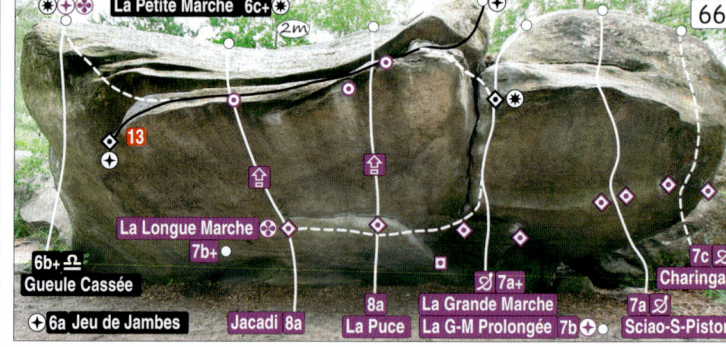

CANCHE AUX MERCIERS

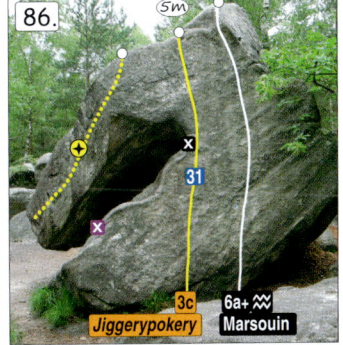
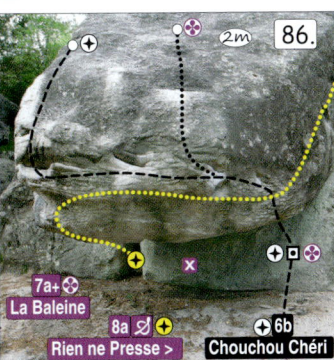

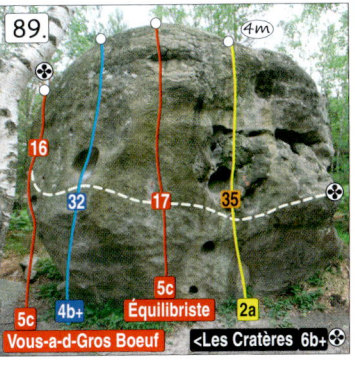

Canche-aux-Merciers Parking - page 182

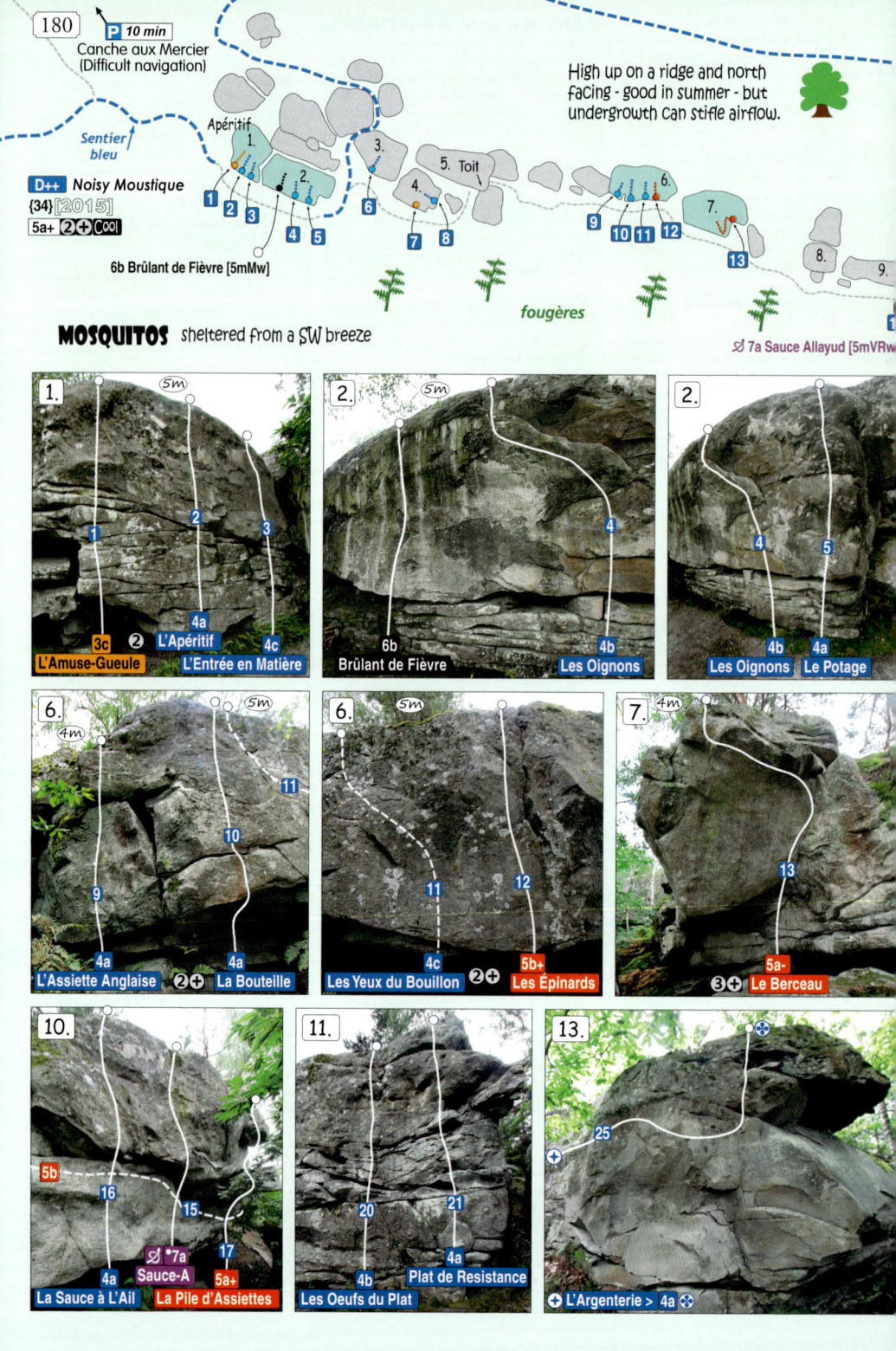

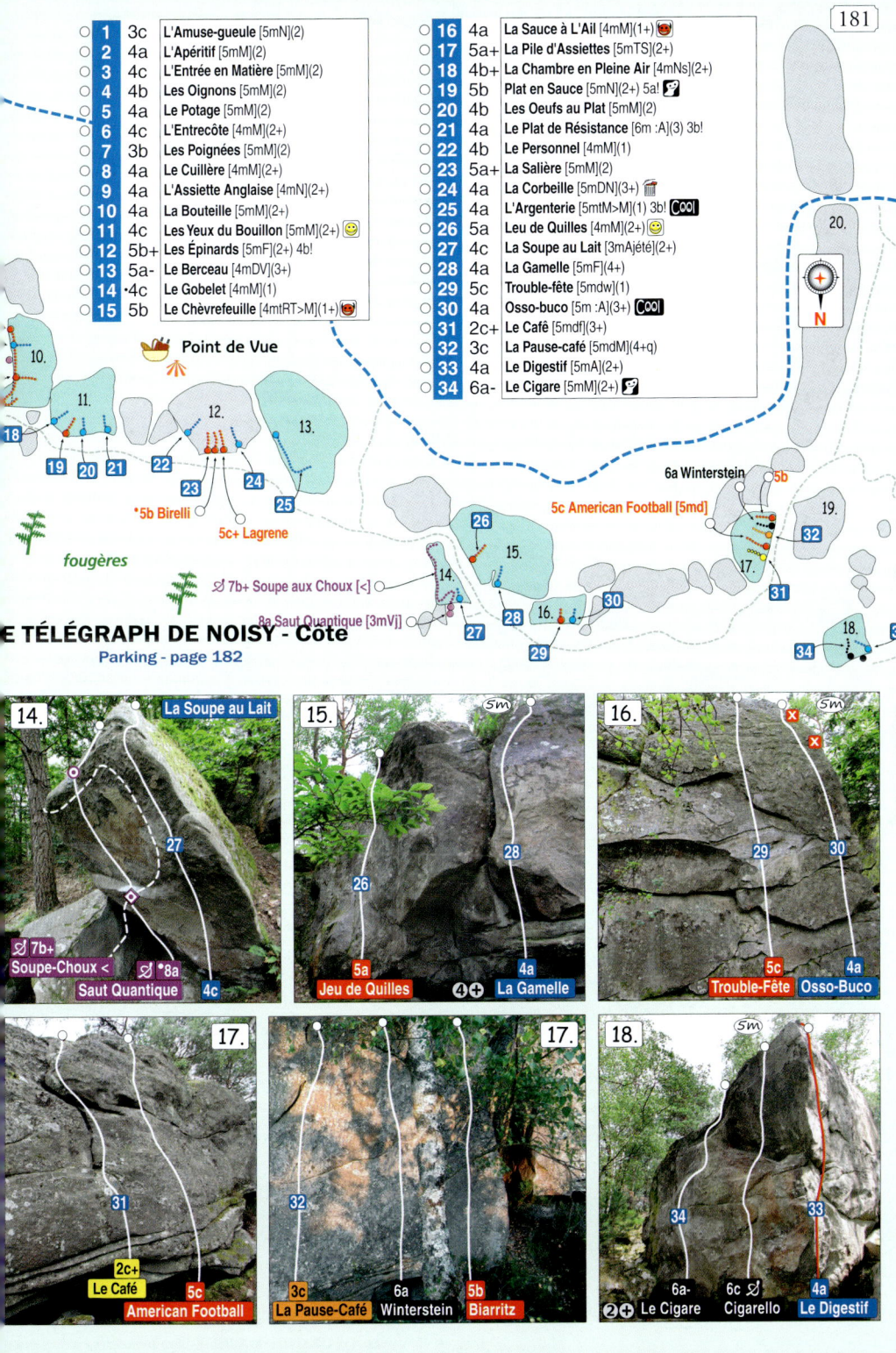

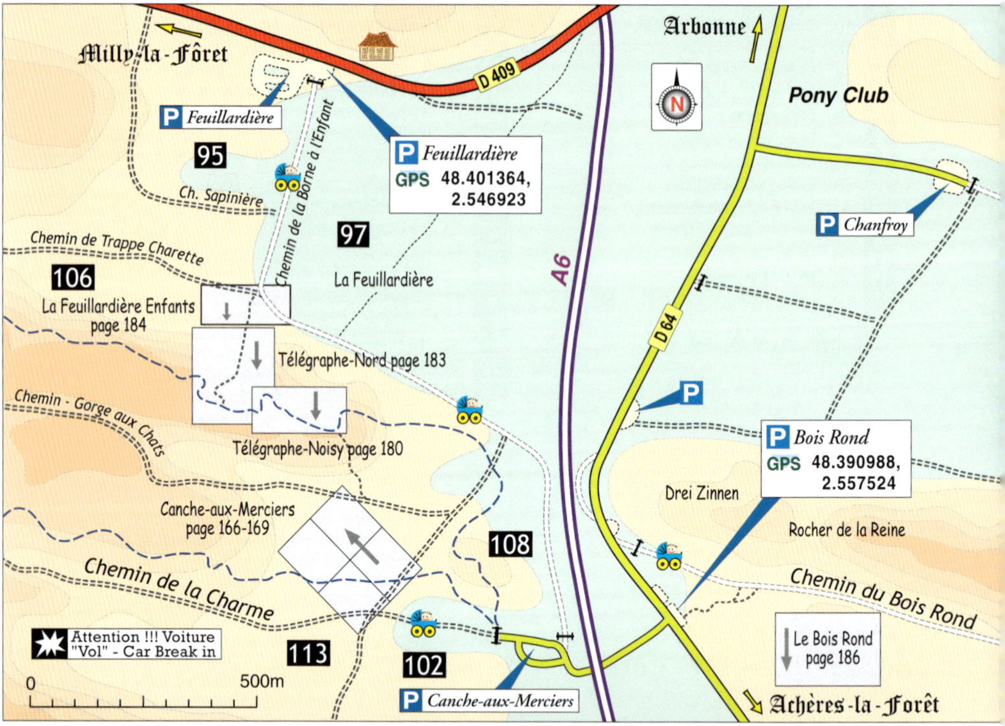

182 | Parking - CANCHE-AUX-MERCIERS/TÉLÉGRAPHE/BOIS ROND

7a+ LA GRANDE MARCHE, Alex Brandt [Bloc 66 - Jambes]

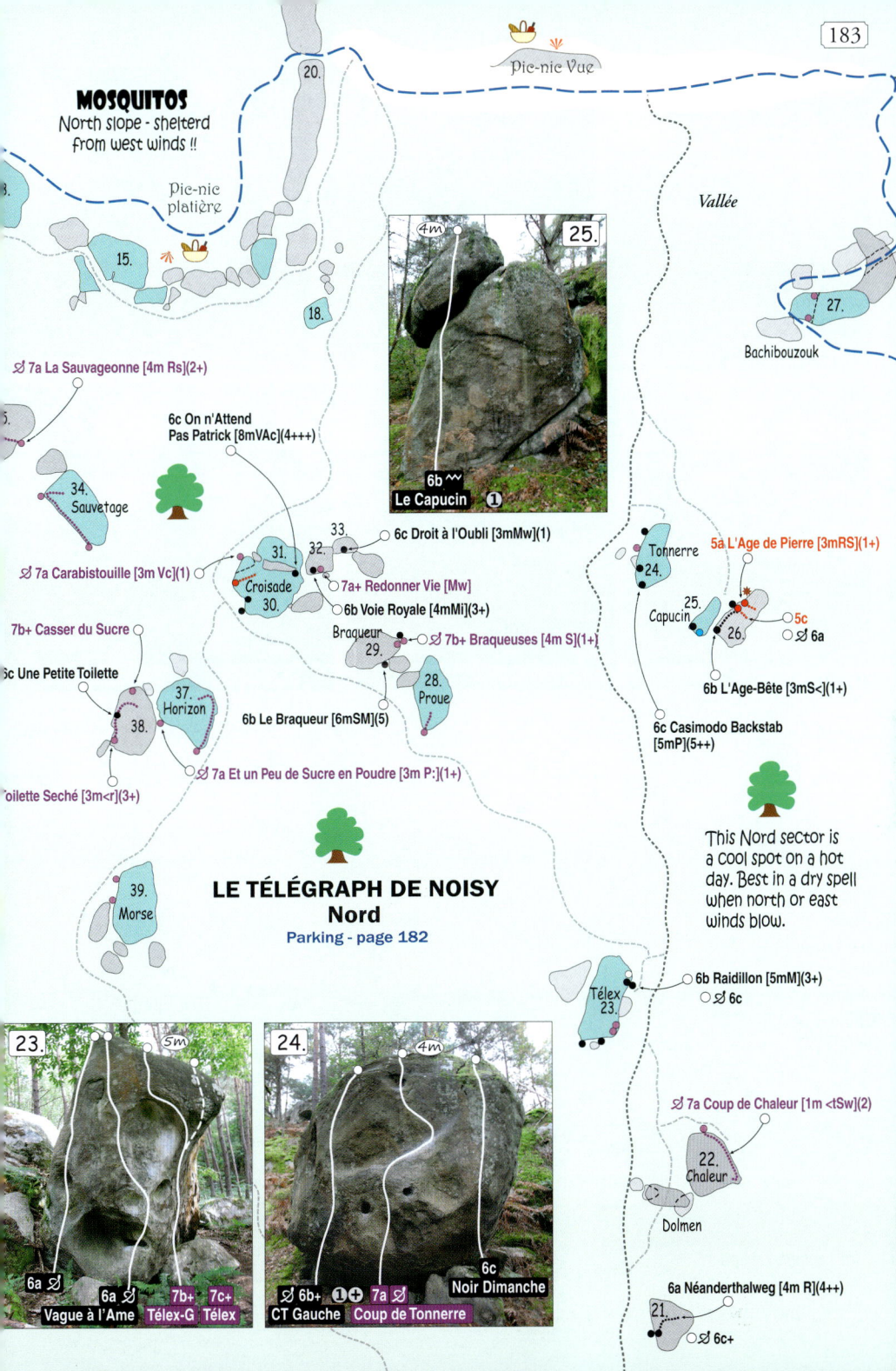

MOSQUITOS
North slope - sheltered from west winds !!

Pic-nic platière

Pic-nic Vue

Vallée

Bachibouzouk

25.
4m
6b
Le Capucin ①

🌿 7a La Sauvageonne [4m Rs](2+)

34. Sauvetage

6c On n'Attend Pas Patrick [8mVAc](4+++)

🌿 7a Carabistouille [3m Vc](1)

7b+ Casser du Sucre

6c Une Petite Toilette

37. Horizon

38.

Toilette Seché [3m<r](3+)

31. Croisade
30.
32.
33.
6c Droit à l'Oubli [3mMw](1)
7a+ Redonner Vie [Mw]
6b Voie Royale [4mMi](3+)

Braqueur
29.
🌿 7b+ Braqueuses [4m S](1+)

28. Proue

6b Le Braqueur [6mSM](5)

🌿 7a Et un Peu de Sucre en Poudre [3m P:](1+)

Tonnerre
24.

5a L'Age de Pierre [3mRS](1+)
Capucin 25.
26.
5c
○ 🌿 6a

6b L'Age-Bête [3mS<](1+)

6c Casimodo Backstab [5mP](5++)

This Nord sector is a cool spot on a hot day. Best in a dry spell when north or east winds blow.

39. Morse

LE TÉLÉGRAPH DE NOISY
Nord
Parking - page 182

Télex 23.
6b Raidillon [5mM](3+)
○ 🌿 6c

23.
5m
6a 🌿 | 6a 🌿 | 7b+ | 7c+
Vague à l'Ame | Télex-G | Télex

24.
4m
🌿 6b+ ①❷ | 7a 🌿 | 6c Noir Dimanche
CT Gauche | Coup de Tonnerre

🌿 7a Coup de Chaleur [1m <tSw](2)

22. Chaleur

Dolmen

6a Néanderthalweg [4m R](4++)
21.
○ 🌿 6c+

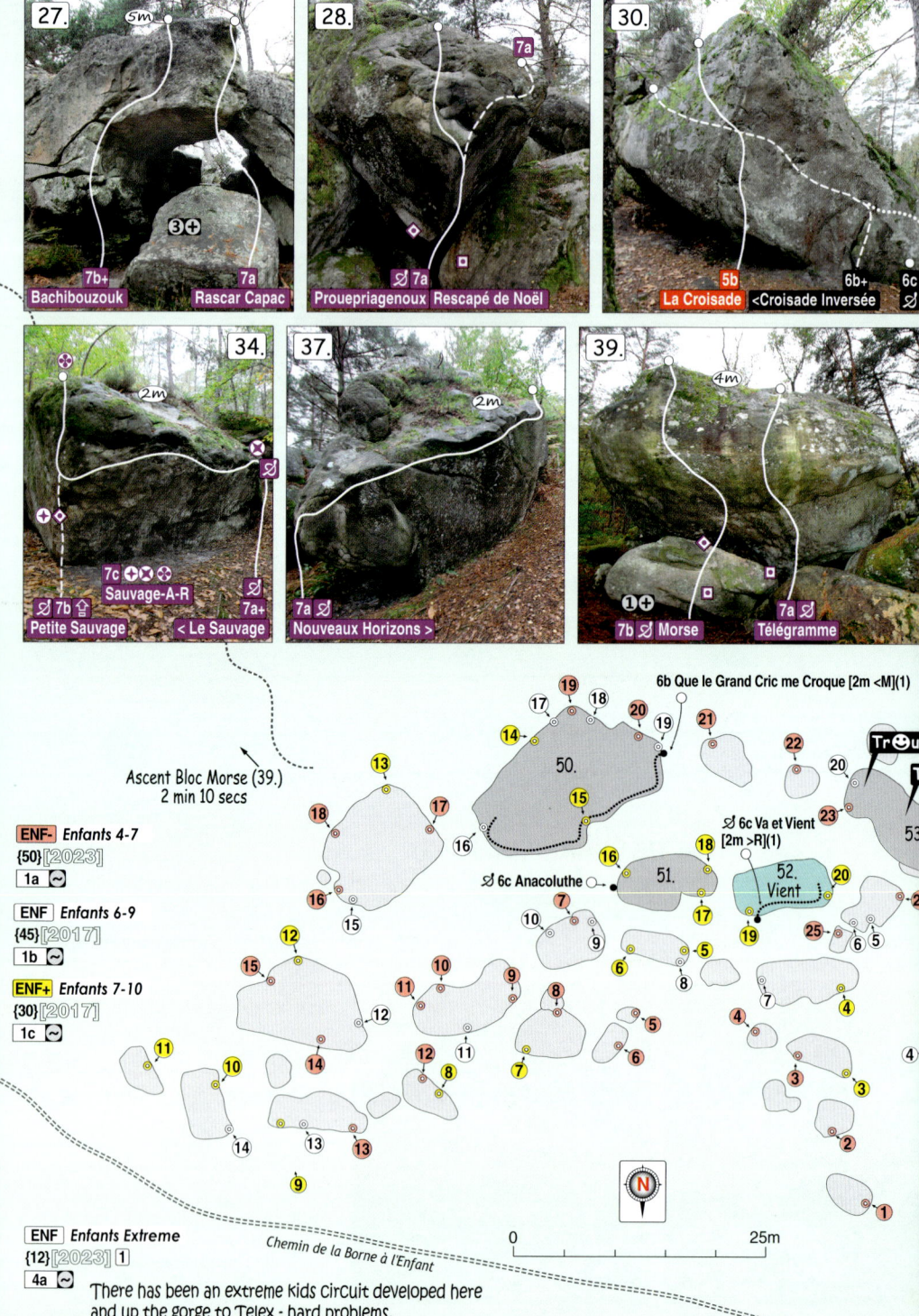

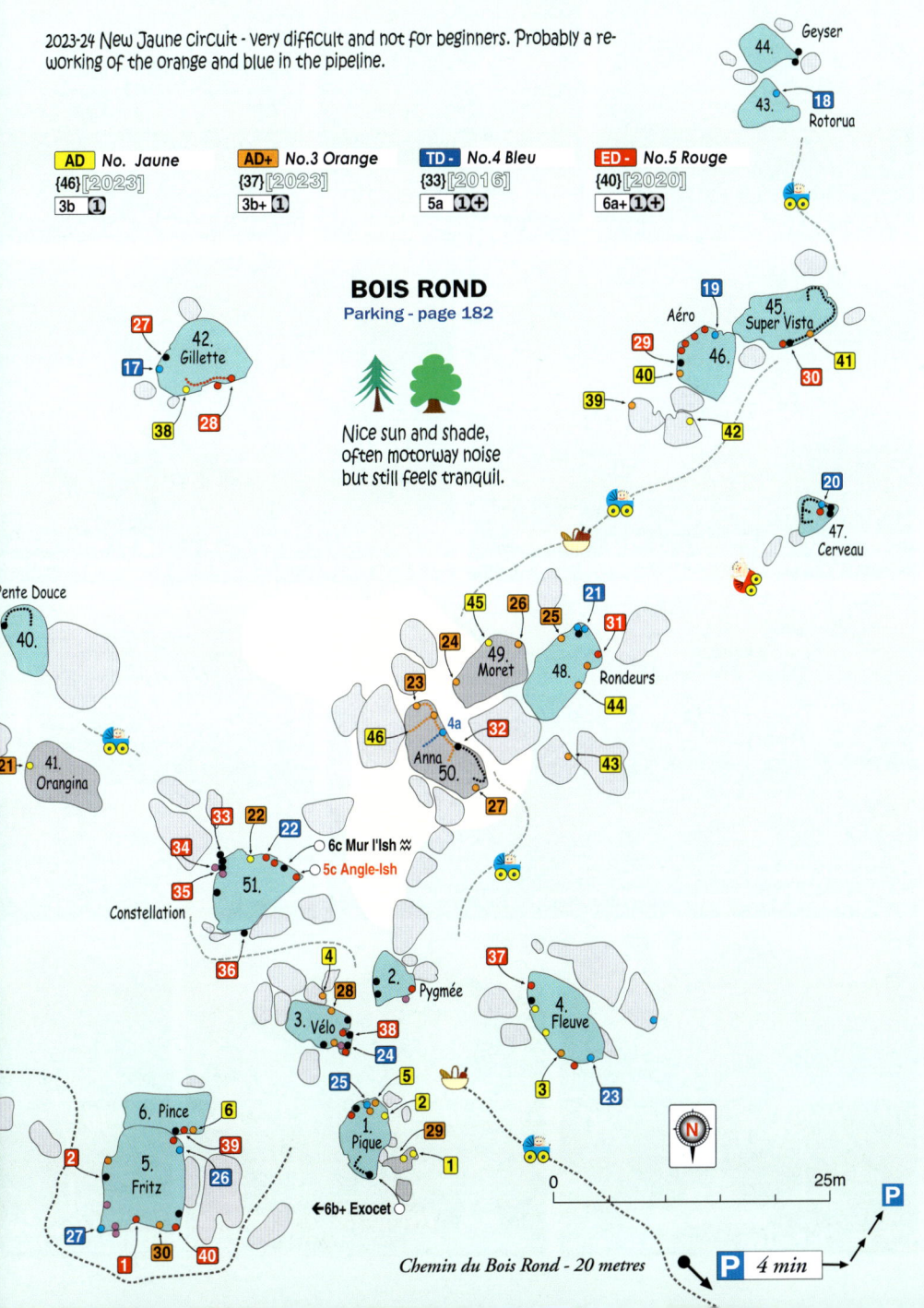

BOIS ROND

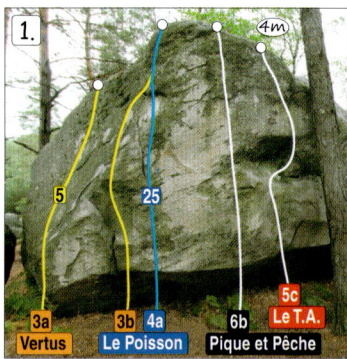

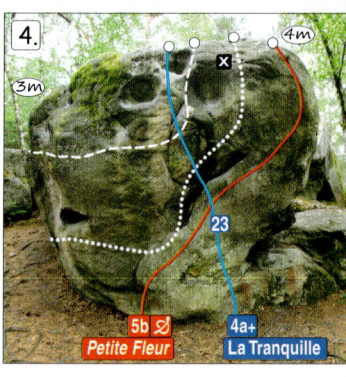

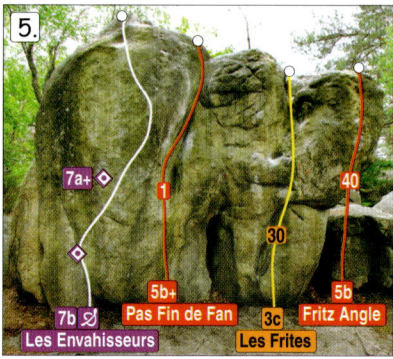

Circuits: Bois Rond - 2024

#	Yellow			#	Orange			#	Orange			#	Blue			#	Red		
1	2b+	[4m P] (2+)		D	2c							D	·4a			1	5b+		
2	2c	[3m j] (1)		1	3a	[3m So] (1+)						1	5a+	[3m Rr] (1+)	🐻	2	6b		
3	3b	[3m R] (1) 🐻		2	4a							2	6a	[5m df] (1) 😊		3	6a		
4	3a+	[3m P] (1)		3	4c	[4m Mw] (2+)						3	4c	[3m Mw] (1)		4	6a	⤴
5	3a	[4m df] (1)	!2b	4	4a							4	·4a	[3m Mr] (3)		5	6b+		
6	·3a+	[3m rf] (1)		5	3b							5	4b			6	6a	≋
7	3b	[4m df] (1) 😊		6	3a	💀 2c						6	·4c			7	6a+	≋
8	2c	[4m df] (1)		7	3a							7	4c			8	6a		
9	·3b	[3m d] (1)		8	4a							8	5a+		💀	9	6a	💀
10	3c	[4m df] (1)		9	3b	💀 2c						9	5b+			10	5c		
11	·3a	[4m O] (1)		10	2b+							10	·4a			11	·6a+		
12	3c	[3m Mi] (1)		11	4a							11	5a			12	6a+	→
13	3a	[3m A:] (1)		12	3b							12	4b			13	5a	≋
14	·3b	[3m d] (1)		13	3a							13	4c			14	6b		
15	3c	[3m R] (1) 🐻		14	2c							14	·4a			15	5c		
16	2c	[3m Ror] (1) 😊		15	3b							15	4a			16	5c	⌬6a+
17	3a	[3m Mo] (1)		16	2b							16	4c			17	5c		
18	3c	[3m A:] (1)		17	3a+							17	4b+			18	6b	⤴
19	3b	[3m Pc] (1)		18	2c+							18	·4c			19	6a+	≋
20	3c	[2m dr] (1)		19	3b							19	4c+			20	6a+	≋
21	3a	[3m N] (1)		20	3b							20	4b+	⌬5a		21	5b		
22	2b	[3m N] (1)		21	2c							21	4a			22	·6a		
23	3a-	[4m df] (1) Cool		22	2b+							22	·5b+			23	6b	↪
24	3a+	[3m D] (1) 😊		23	3c							23	4a+			24	5c	⌬6c
25	3a+	[2m >df] (1)		24	3a+							24	·4a			25	6a		
26	3b	[2m N:] (1)		25	3a+							25	4a			26	5c	⤴
27	2b	[4m dA] (1)		26	3a+							26	4c+			27	6b	≋
28	3b	[2m >P] (1)		27	3c+							27	4c			28	5c		
29	2c	[3m A] (1)		28	3b+	[3m A: r] (1+) Cool						28	5b			29	6c	↪
30	·3c	[3m Mo] (1)		29	2c							29	5a			30	6b+	↪
31	·2c	[3m R>] (1+)		30	3c	💀 3a						30	5a			31	5b		
32	2b+	[3m A:] (1)		31	4a+	[4m df] (1)						31	5c			32	6a+	↪
33	2c	[4m df] (1)		32	4a+							32	4a			33	6a+		
34	·2b	[3m G] (1)		33	3b							33	5b			34	6c	⤴
35	2c	[3m N>G] (1+) Cool		34	3b											35	7a	⌬7a+
36	3a	[3m Ri] (1)		35	3a+											36	6b	⌬
37	·3c	[2m VA:] (1) 🐻		36	3b+	↪										37	5c+	⤴
38	2c	[2m r] (1)		37	3b											38	6a	↪
39	3a	[3m N:] (1)														39	5b		
40	3a	[3m M<o] (1)														40	5b		
41	·3c	[3m M] (1)																	
42	2c	[2m NV] (1) 🐻																	
43	3a	[3m rd] (1) 😊																	
44	3a	[3m Mr] (1) r3a																	
45	2b+	[3m N] (1+) Cool																	
46	3a	[3m M] (1+)																	

Le Baume du T-Rex
pour les doigts

△ **7a+ REMPART**, *Jo Montchaussé [Bloc 49 - Constellation]*

△ **7a+ BANDE PASSANTE**, *Jo Montchaussé [Bloc 35 - Passante]*

BOIS ROND

Aerial plan - page 186

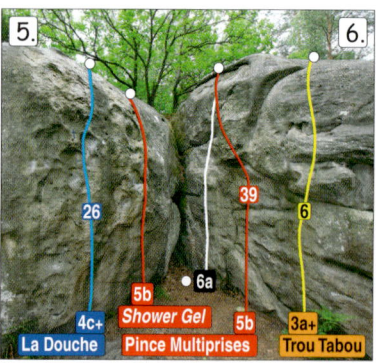

Bois Rond Parking - page 182   4b LA GRATOUILLE [3], Johanna Wehkamp [Bloc 19 - Glasnost]

BOIS ROND

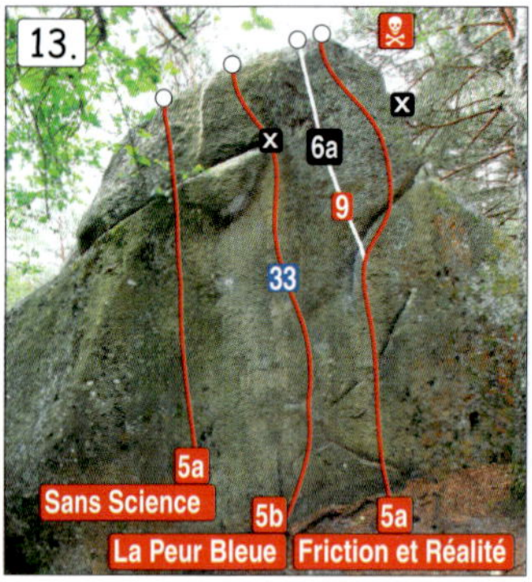

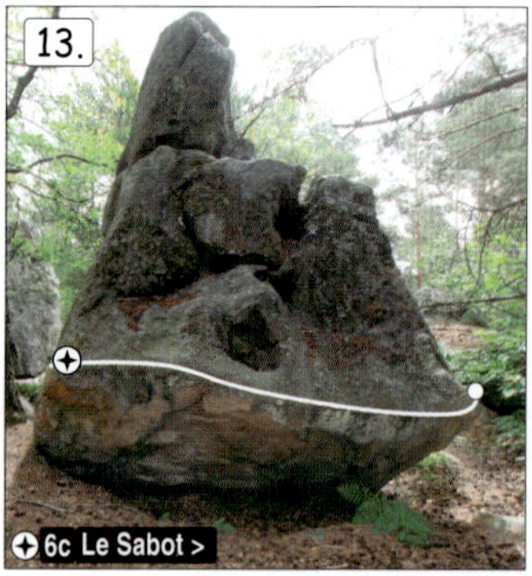

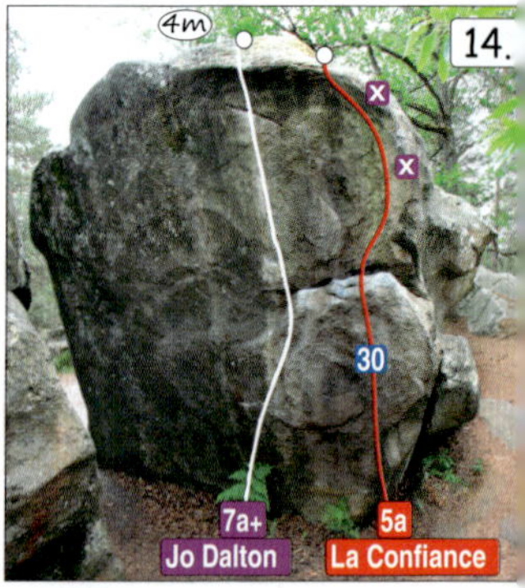

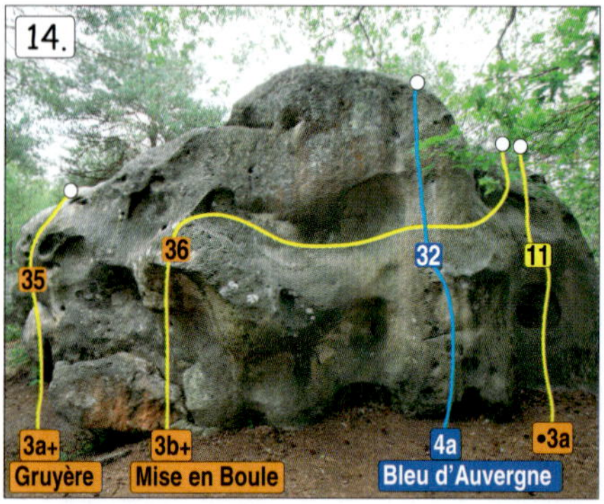

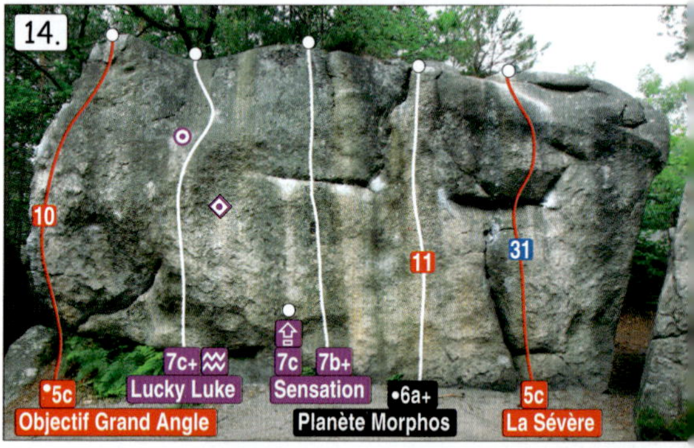

5c L'APPUI ET LE BOTTANT 17, *Nuria Brockfeld [Bloc 24 - Bottant]*

BOIS ROND

BOIS ROND

195

Bois Rond Parking - page 182

BOIS ROND

34.
35.
26
36
35
13
5c Razorback
7a+ Bande Passante
3a
2c
4c
La Smirsch
3a+
La Mise en Pli

35.
18
2c+
Feuille de Chou

36.
22
15
4a
Chute d'Eau
•7a+ •7b
Spider Bloc
•6a
6a
Le Meilleur des Mondes
l'Épais Rond

36.
5a+
•4c •5c
Cirrus
6b
Spinatus
6b
Dr Nimbus

36.
23
La Théorie des Nuages 6b

37.
24
5c
25
7a
Toubib or not Toubib
6c
Le Poussée Occulte
6a
Opposition Systématique

37.
5m
14
19
•4a
Hallelujah
4a
Moses
3b
Virage

37.
5m
19
16
3b
Virage
4c
Mur Jéricho
5a
Gaza

40.
6a+
Pente Douce

42.
4m
17
27
6b
Gillette Pare Dalle
4b+ 4a
Le Grelot

42.
Voyage Centre Terre 5c
3m
38
28
2c
Standstart is Easy
5b+
Sitstart is Best

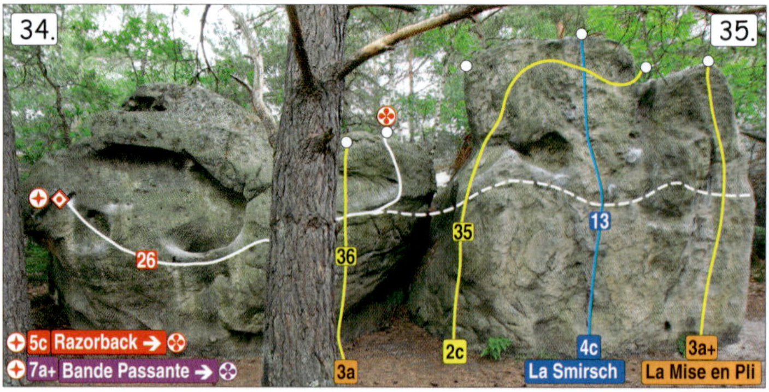

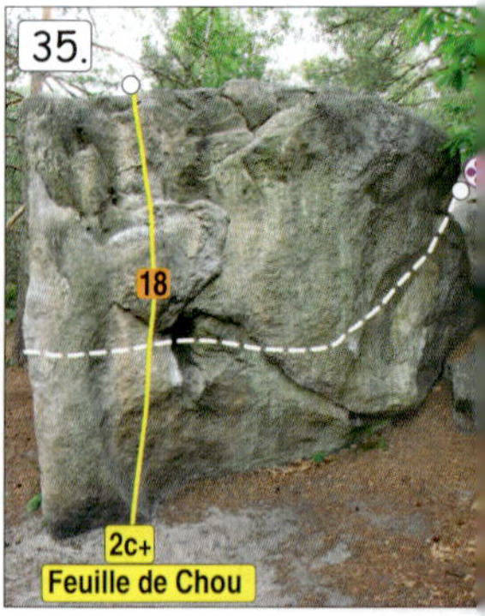

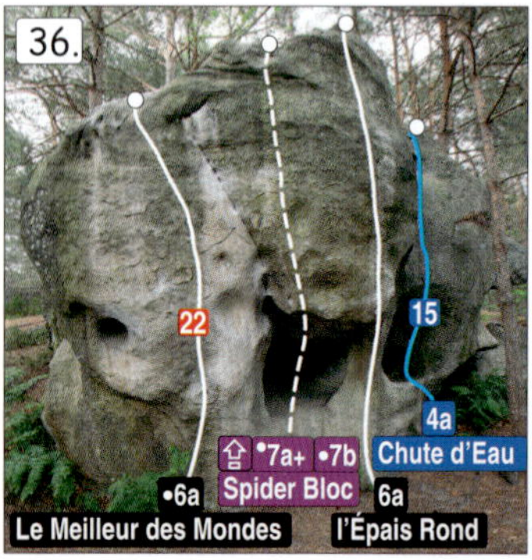

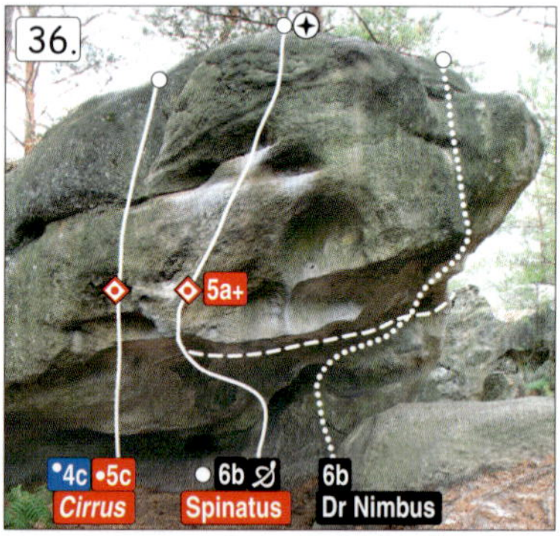

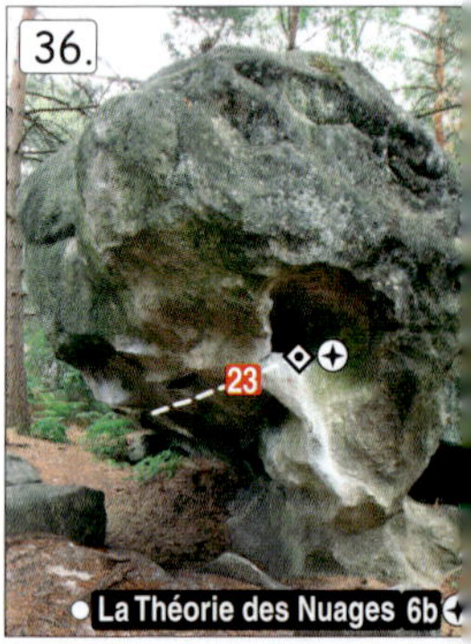

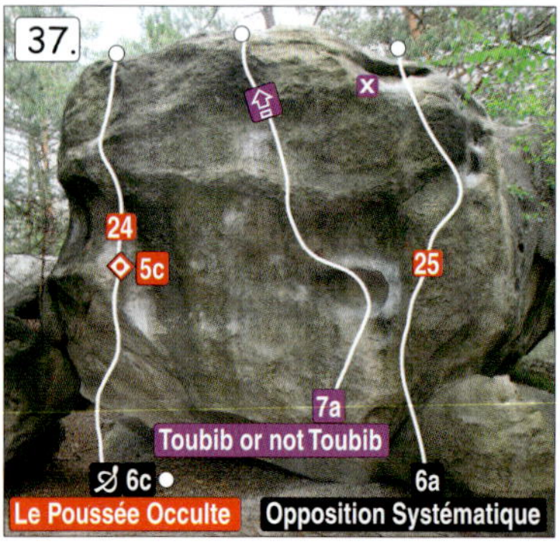

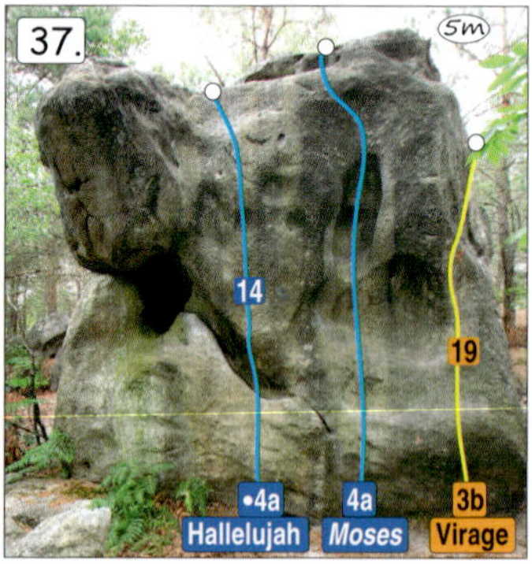

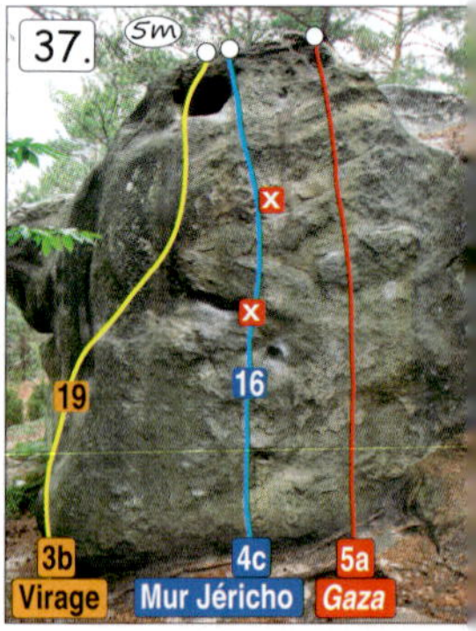

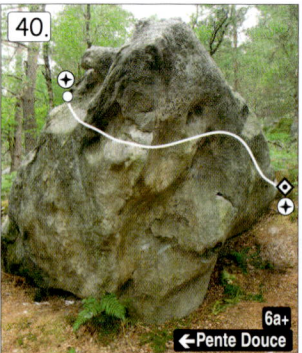

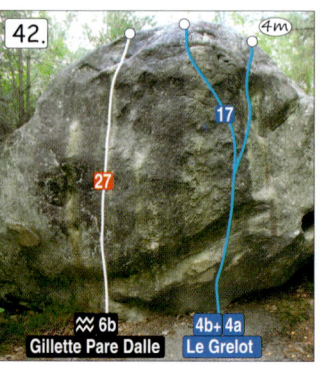

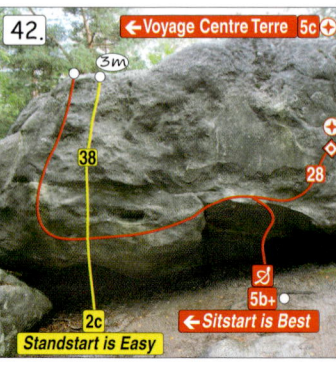

BOIS ROND

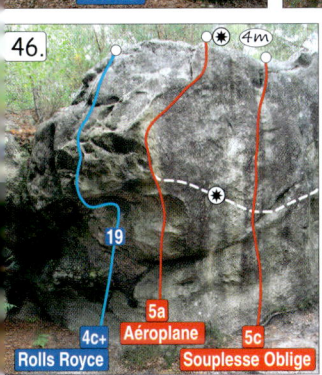

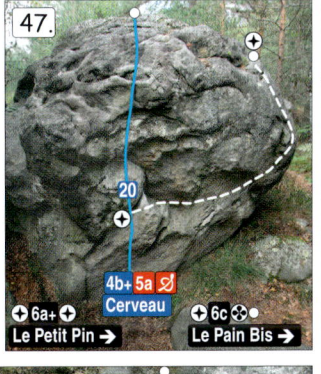

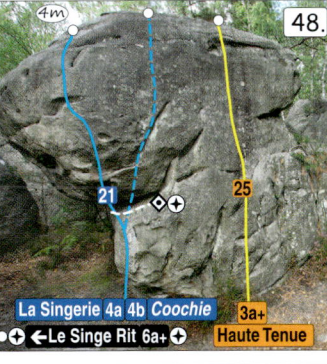

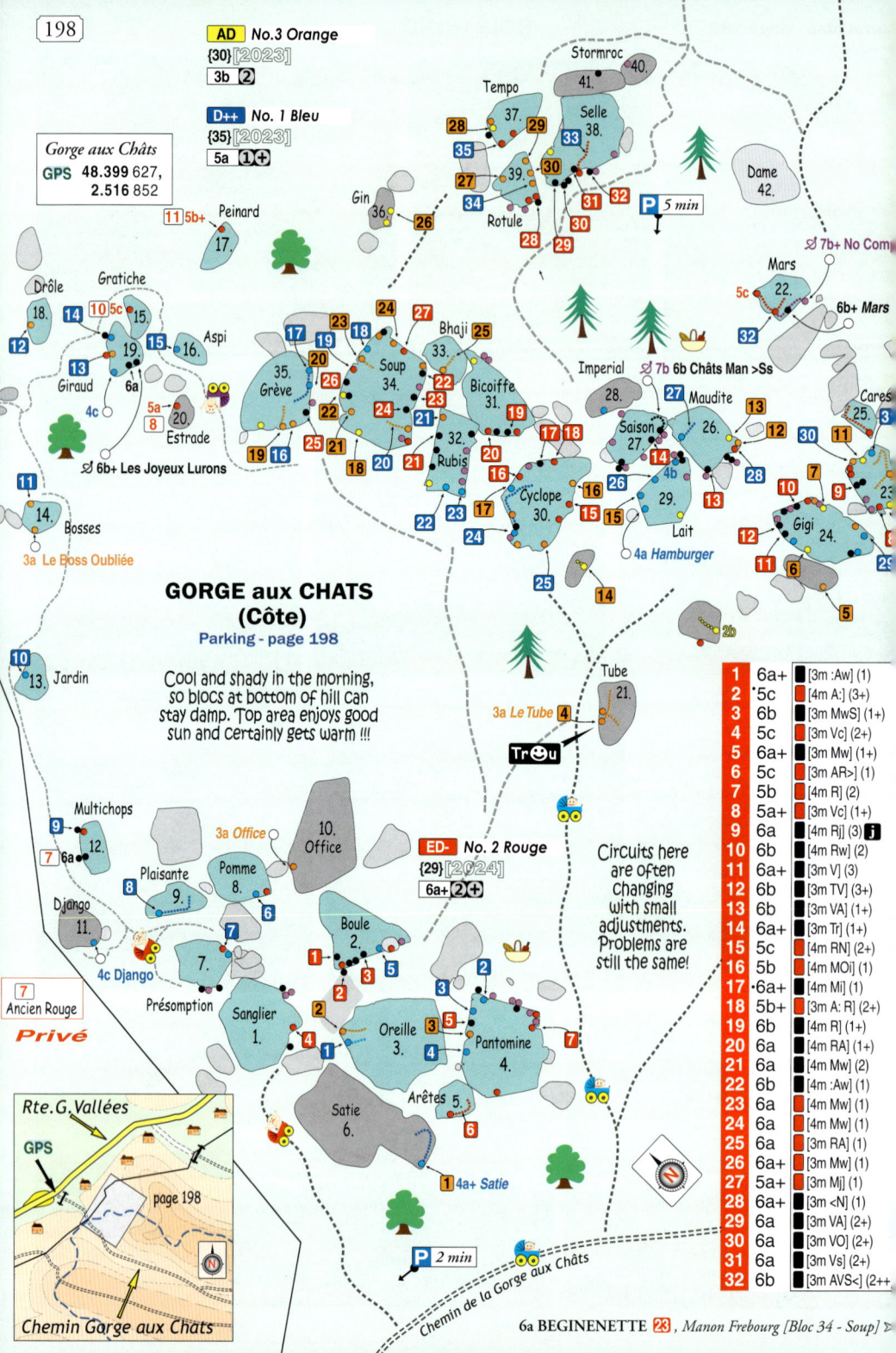

Grade	Info
4a+	[3m A>M] (1)
3b	[4m N] (1)
3a	[4m F] (2+)
3a	[2m r] (1)
3a	[3m Md] (1)
2c	[3m Si] (1+)
2b	[4m M] (1)
2c	[4m C] (1+)
3b	[3m >N] (1+)
3a	[3m d] (1)
2c	[4m Gr] (1) Cool
3a+	[3m N] (1)
2c	[3m F] (1)
2b+	[3m M] (-)
4a	[2m NR] (1+)
3a	[3m Sr] (1)
4b	[4m Mi] (1)
2b+	[2m M] (1)
3a+	[5m df] (2)
4a	[4m DF] (1+)
3c	[3m M] (1)
3c	[3m dF] (1)
3c	[3m :N] (1)
2c	[5m df] (2)
3b	[3m dw] (1)
2b	[2m M] (1)
3a	[3m Ms] (1)
2c	[4m MA] (2)
3a	[4m :N] (2)
3c	[3m df] (1)
4a	[4m Ms] (1)
4a	[2m Fr] (1)
4a	[3m M] (1)
4c	[4m Moc] (1+)
4c	[3m MgS] (1+)
4a	[3m Rr] (1+)
5a	[4m dg] (1+)
4a	[3m A>M] (1+)
5c	[3m Vr] (1+)
4a	[3m M] (1)
3c	[5m MN] (1)
3b+	[3m M] (1) !3b
5a	[4m Vd] (2+)
4c	[3m Vr] (1+)
4c	[4m dN] (1+) !3b
4a	[5m dc] (1)
4c	[4m Vr] (1+)
4c	[3m M] (1)
5a	[3m Mw] (1)
3c	[4m A:] (2)
3a+	[5m A:] (2)
4a+	[4m S] (3+)
4c	[4m VA] (1+)
4b	[M<Rm] (1+)
3b+	[3m Vr] (2+)
4b	[4m M] (1)
4a	[5m F] (2+) !2b
5c	[3m RPs] (2)
4a	[2m dw] (1)
3c	[4m :A] (2+)
4b	[4m GP] (2+) Cool
5a	[3m VR] (2+)
5a	[@3m VS] (3)
3c	[4m d] (1)
5a+	[4m AR] (1+)

GORGE aux CHÂTS

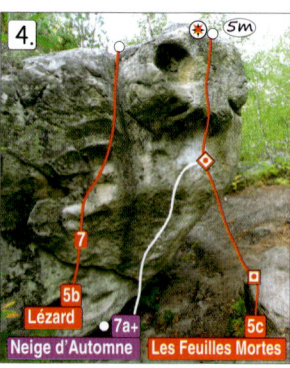

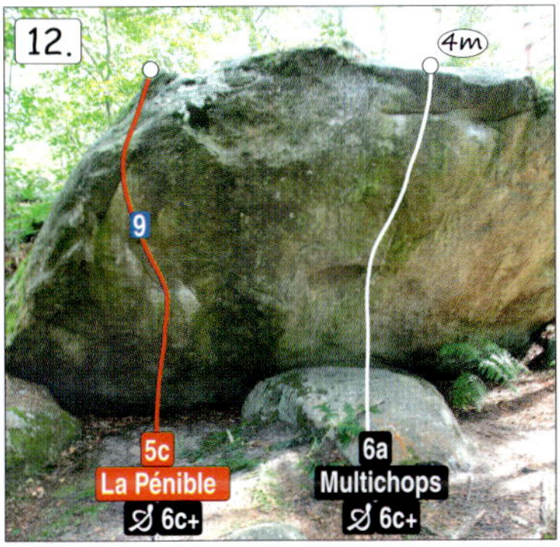

GORGE aux CHÂTS

Aerial plan - page 198 — 201

7. 7a+ Présomption d'Innocence — 4m — Les Mains Pleines 6c+ — 6b+ Gaggia

7. 4m — 7 — La Dalle Gauche 4a+ — La Dalle Bleu 5a

8. 3m — 6 — Le Passe-Plats 4a — Le Terrorist 5a

9. 3m — 8 — La Plaisante 4a

12. 4m — 9 — La Pénible 5c 6c+ — Multichops 6a 6c+

13. 3m — 10 — Vue Sur Jardin 4a

14. 5m — 3b — 11 — Champs de Bosses 3c

15. 5m — Le Gratiche et la Cuisse 5c

16. 5m — 3b — 15 — La Dalle Aspi 4c

17. Peinard 5b+

18. 4m — 12 — Drôle de Sable 3b

19. 6m — 3b — 14 — 13 — Tendance 6a 4c — Belle Saison 5a 3a

22. 4m — Décevante 5a — 32 — 32 — Campagnol 5c 15 — No Comply 7b+

Gorge aux Châts Parking - page 198

GORGE aux CHÂTS

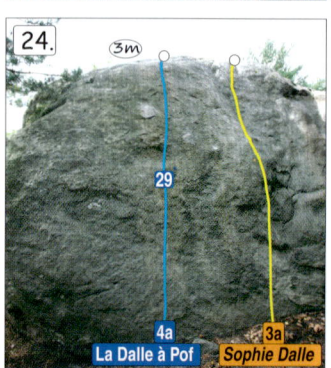

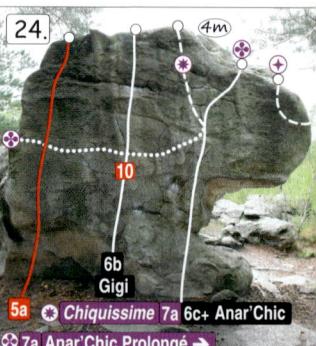

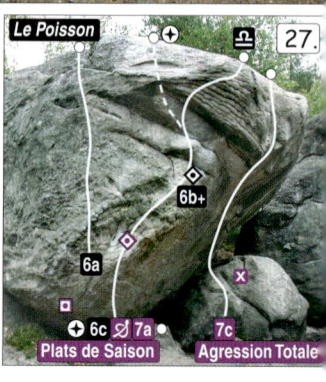

GORGE aux CHÂTS

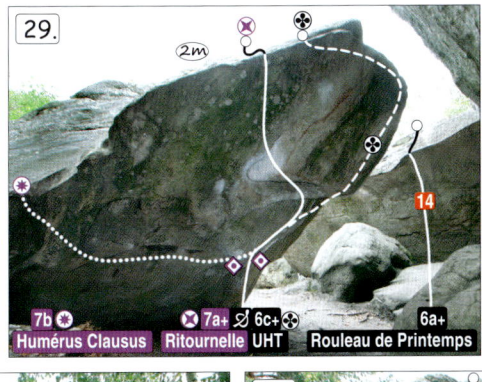

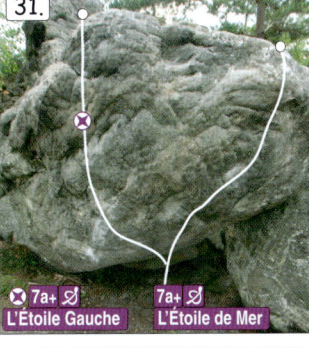

GORGE aux CHÂTS

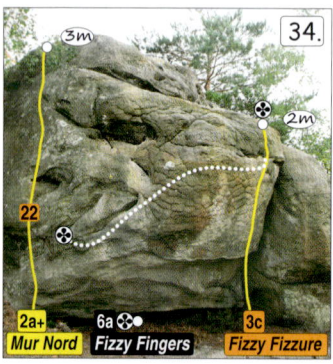
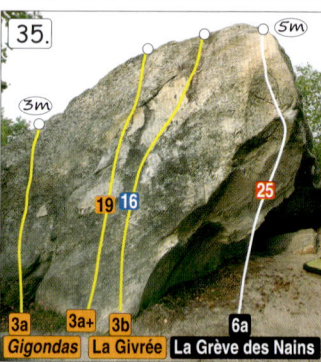
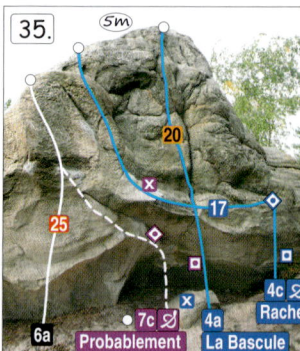

Gorge aux Châts Parking - page 198   6a CERF-VOLANT 17 , Marc'o Montchaussé [Bloc 30 - Cyclop]

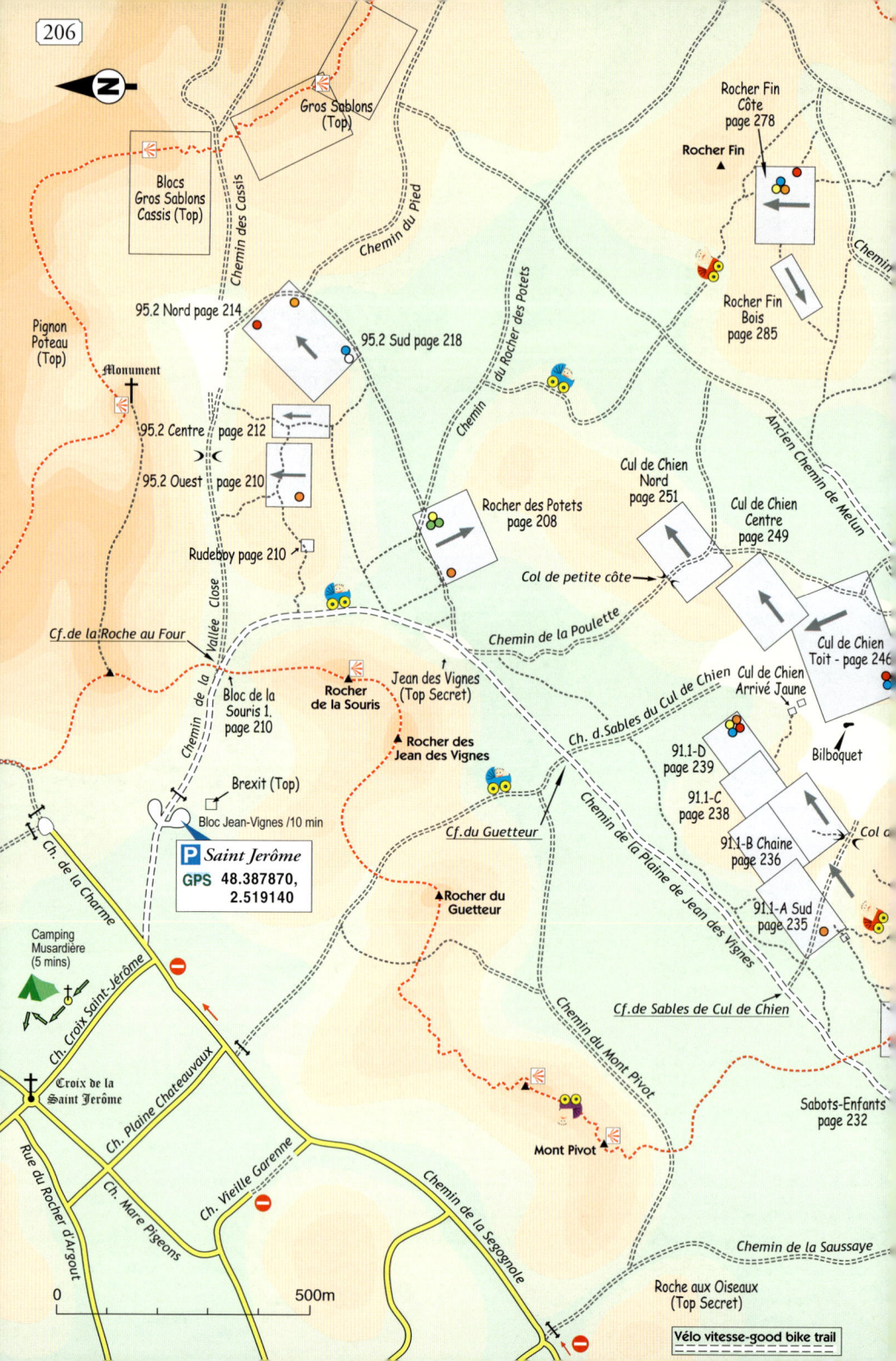

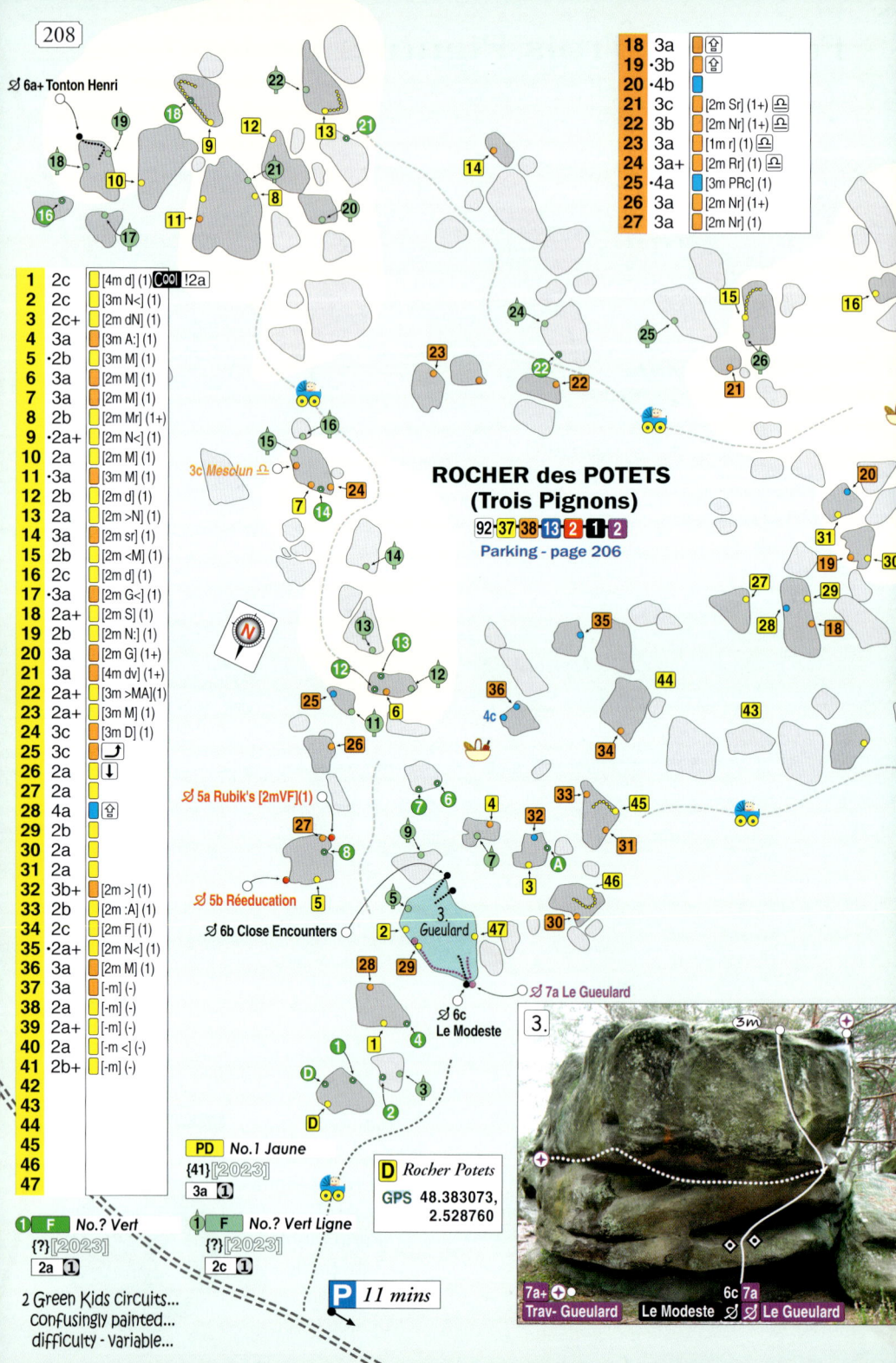

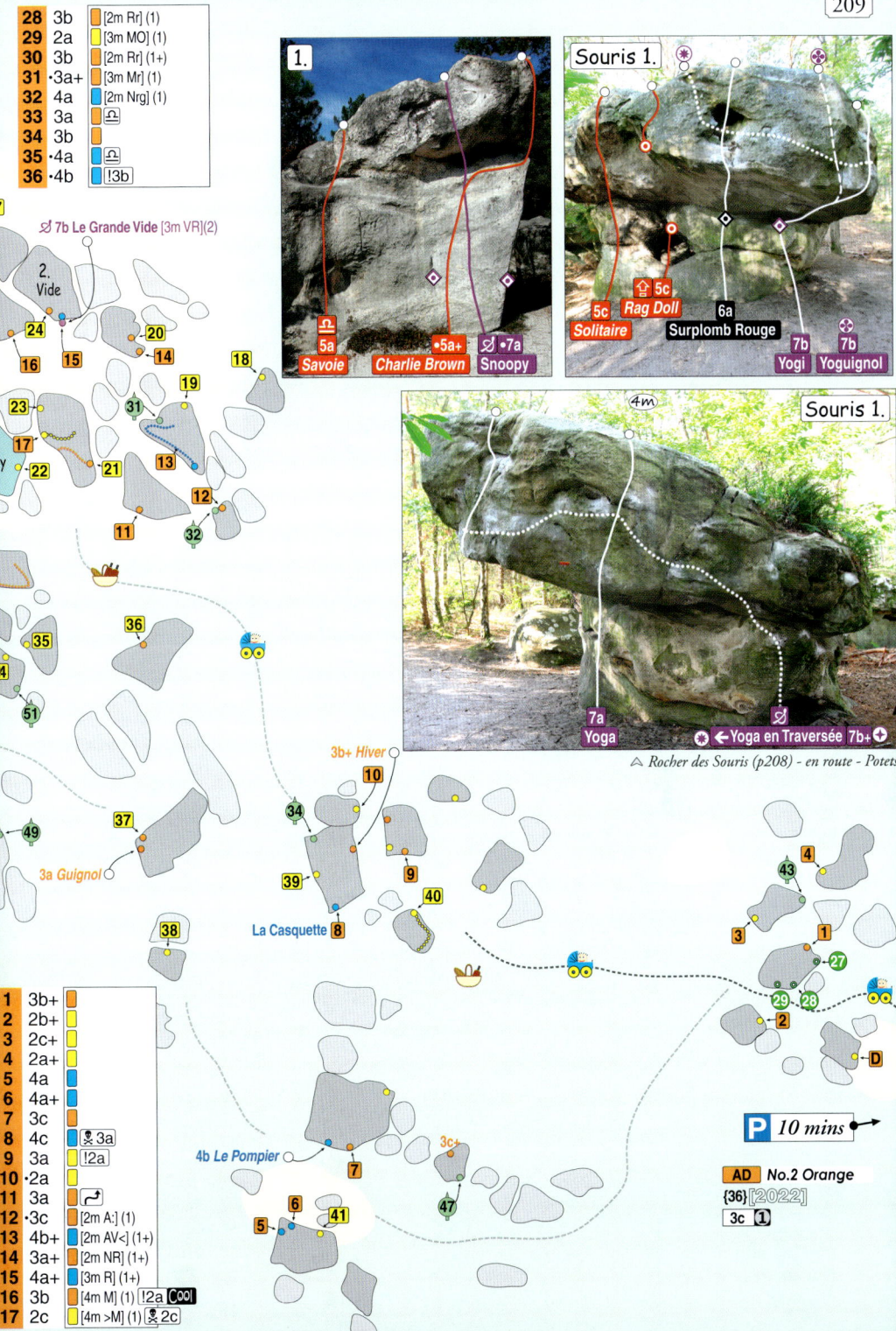

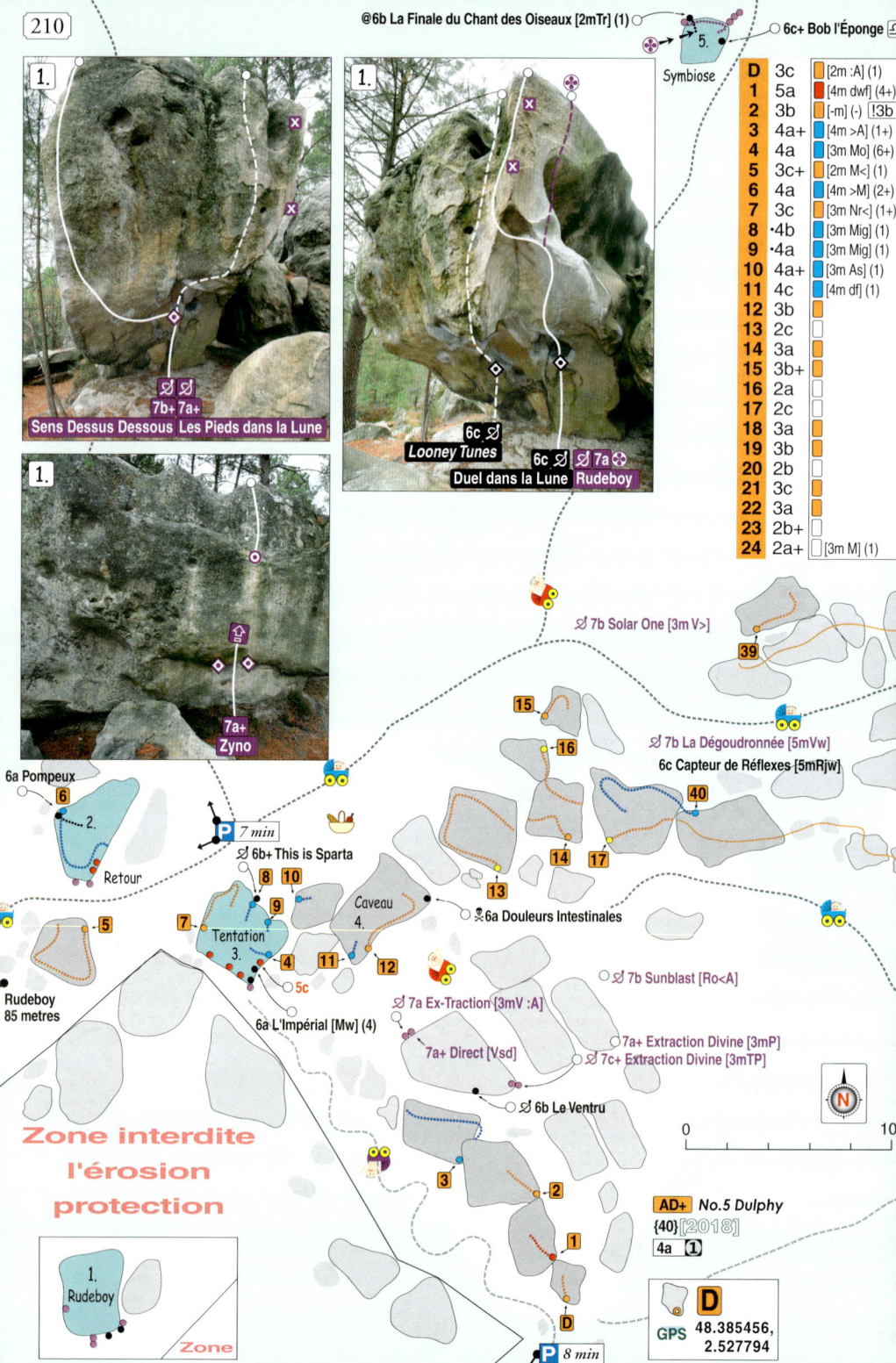

95.2 A-OUEST - Orange
(Trois Pignons)

Parking - page 206

25	3b	[3m R] (1)
26	3c	[3m NRr] (1)
27	4a	[2m >Ms] (1)
28	2c	[3m >Ms] (1)
29	•3a	[3m F] (2)
30	2a	
31	4a	
32	3b	
33	3c+	
34	3b+	
35	2b	
36	3b	
37	3a	
38	3c	
39	3a	
40	4a	

No trees, very popular area.
A lot of traffic.. so slippery,
many problems upgraded - 2023.

95.2 - Centre

95.2 - Centre

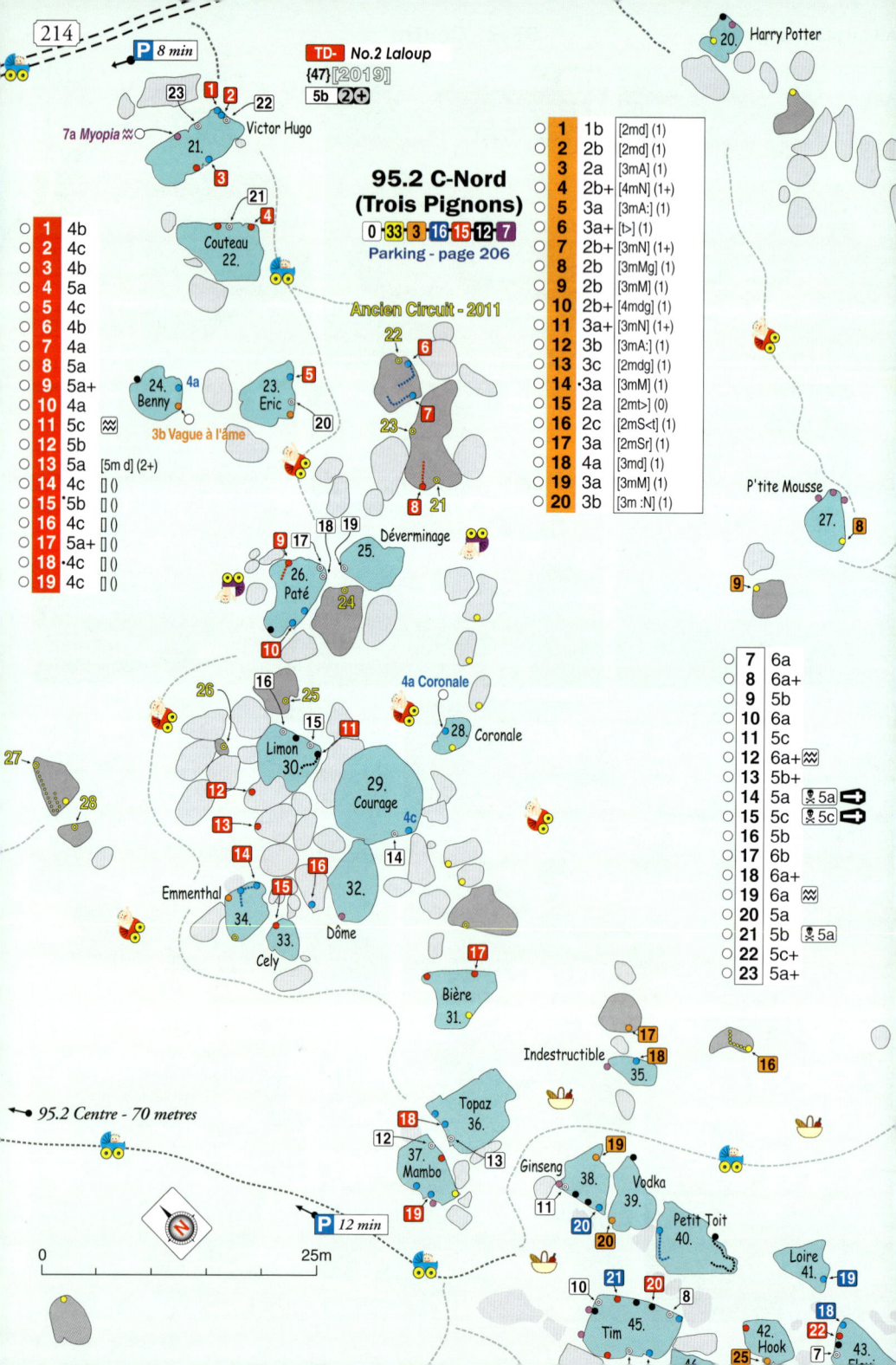

95.2 - Nord

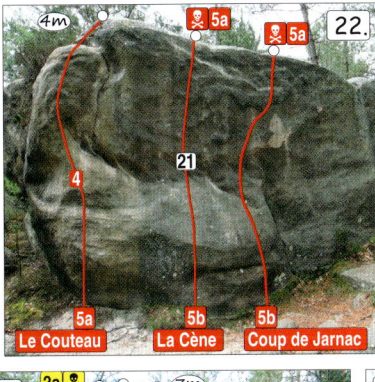

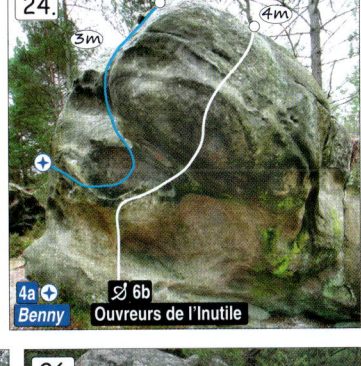

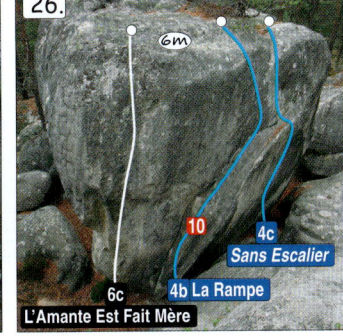

95.2 Parking - page 206

95.2 - Nord

△ **5b EDAM**, Ursula Balderson [Bloc 46 - Edam]

Aerial plan - page 214   **95.2 - Nord**   217

95.2 Parking - page 206

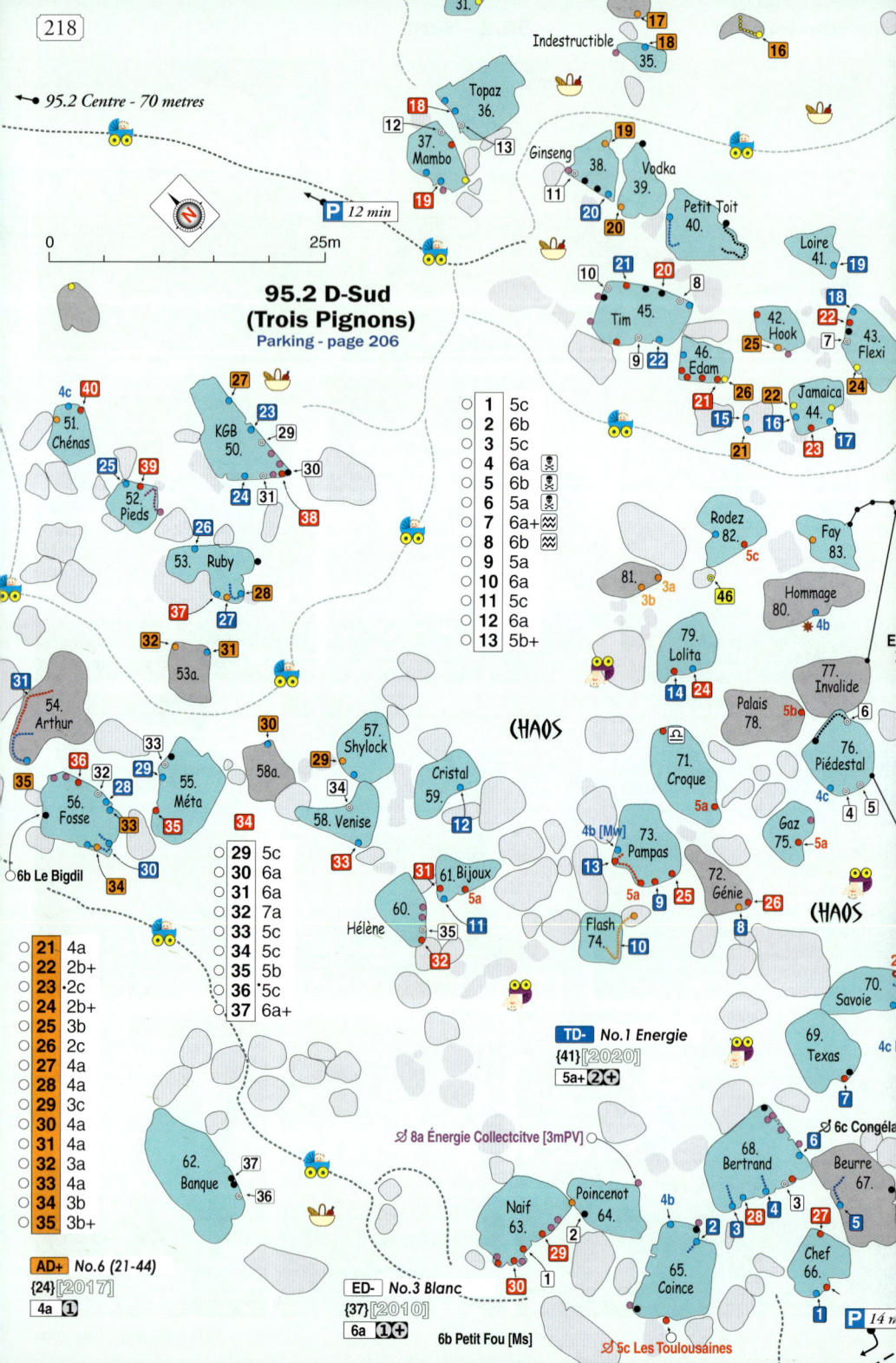

95.2 - Sud

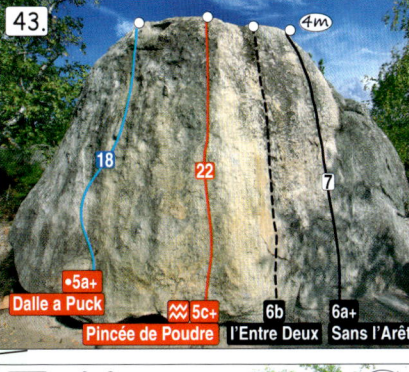
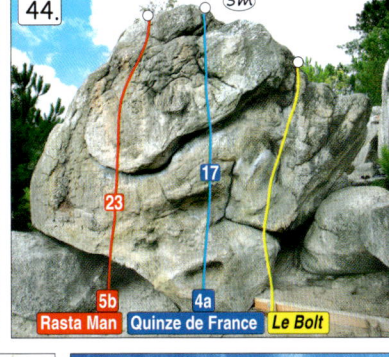

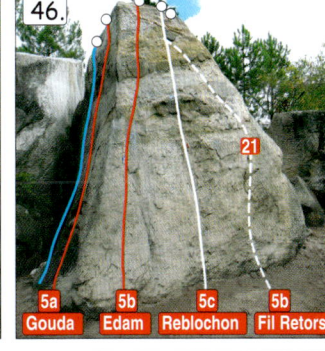
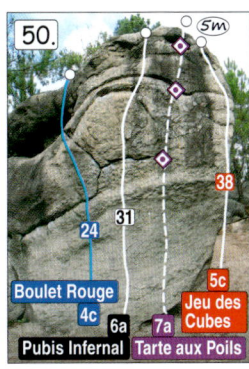

95.2 Parking - page 206

95.2 - Sud

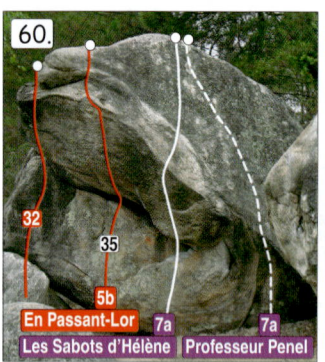

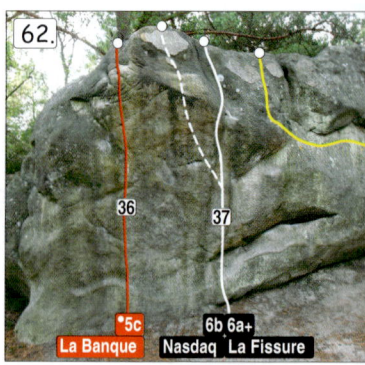

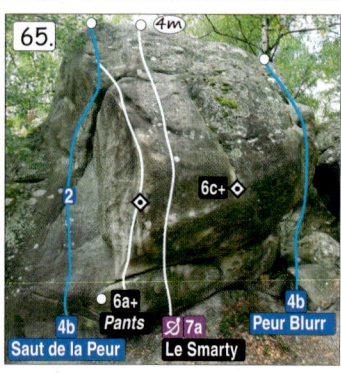

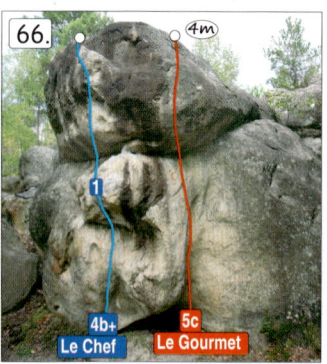
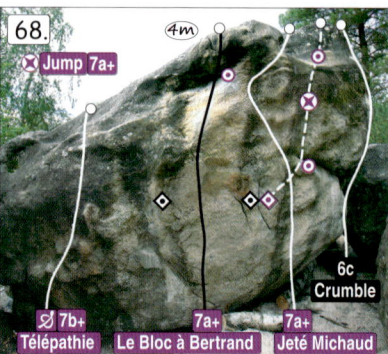

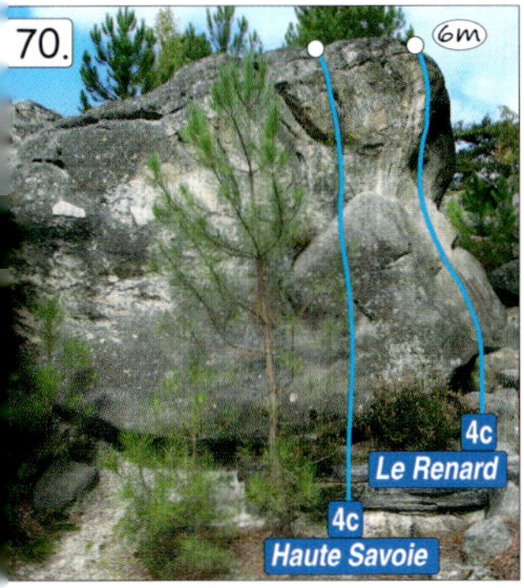
70.
6m
4c
Le Renard
4c
Haute Savoie

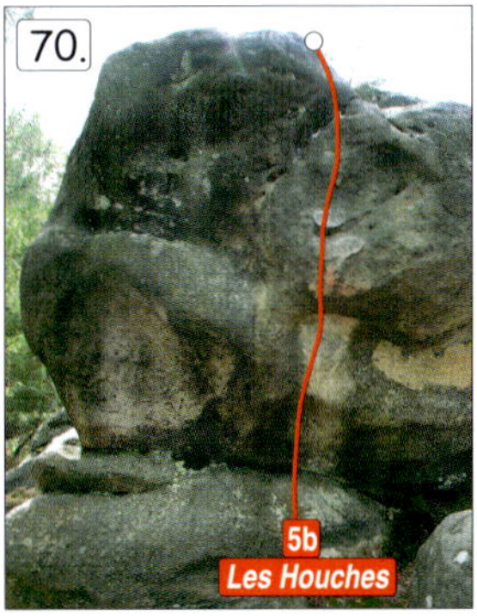
70.
5b
Les Houches

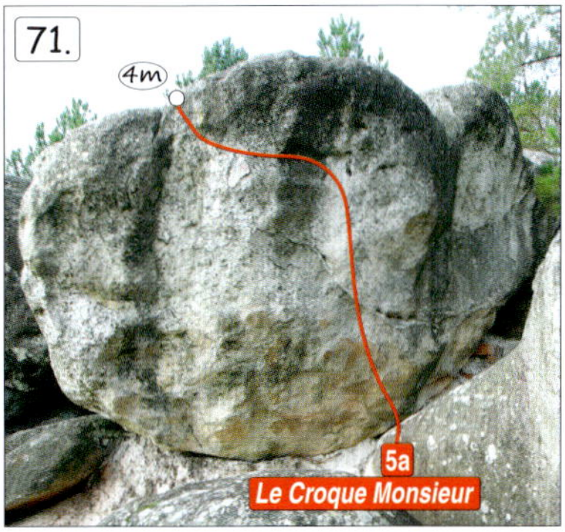
71.
4m
5a
Le Croque Monsieur

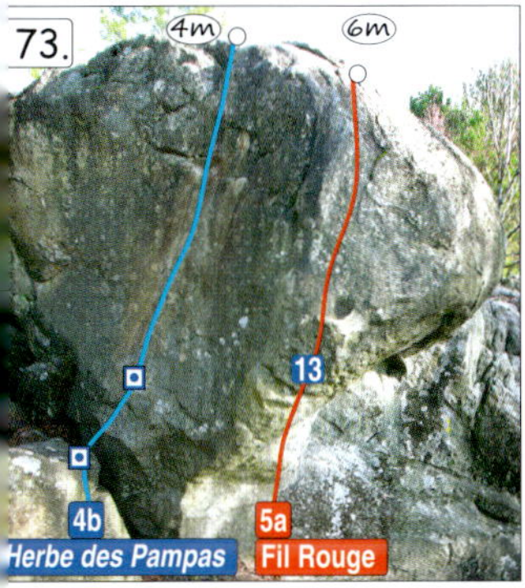
73.
4m
6m
13
4b
Herbe des Pampas
5a
Fil Rouge

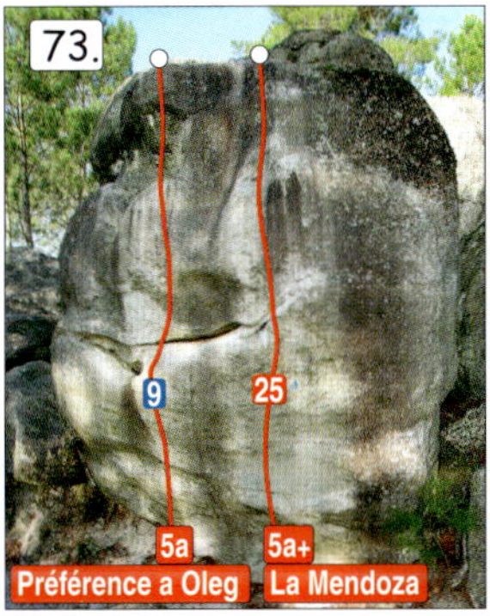
73.
9
25
5a
Préférence a Oleg
5a+
La Mendoza

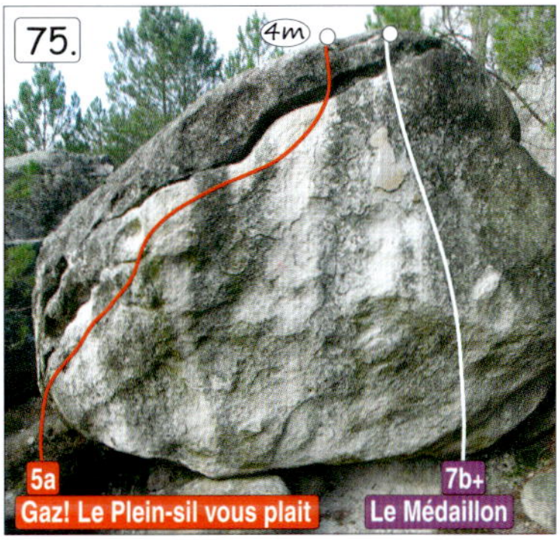
75.
4m
5a
Gaz! Le Plein-sil vous plait
7b+
Le Médaillon

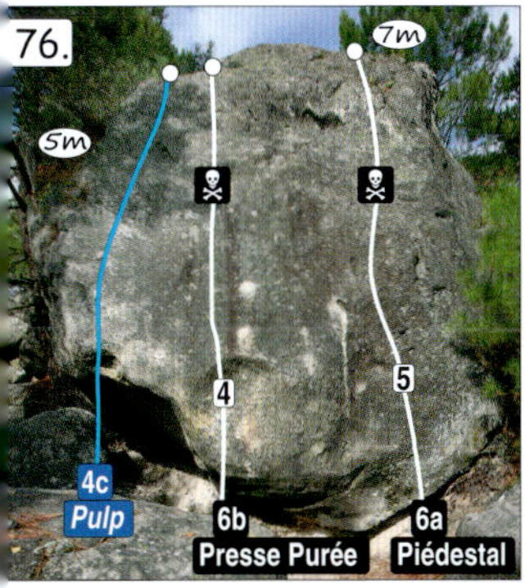
76.
7m
5m
4
5
4c
Pulp
6b
Presse Purée
6a
Piédestal

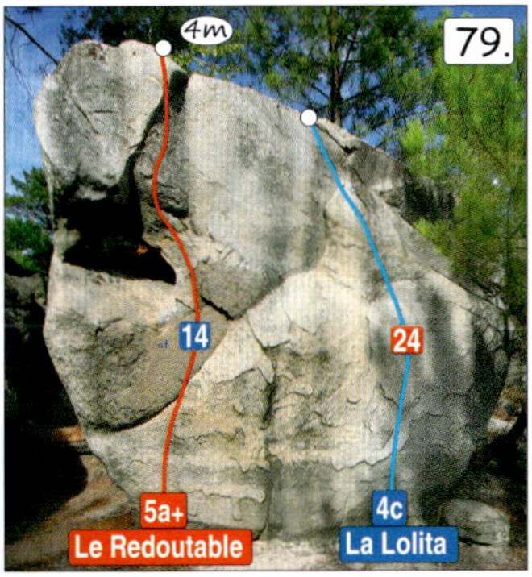
4m
79.
14
24
5a+
Le Redoutable
4c
La Lolita

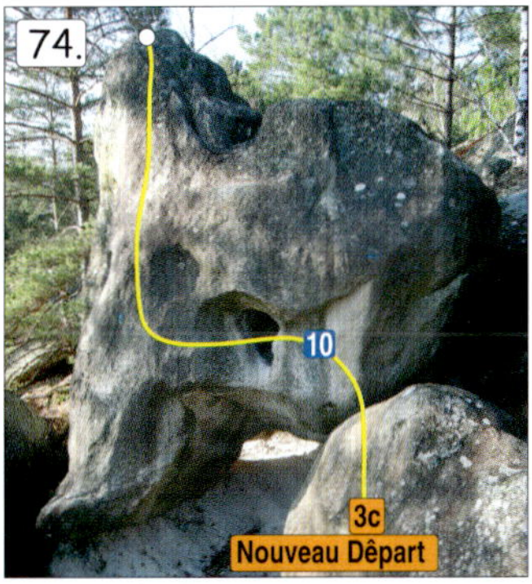
74.
10
3c
Nouveau Départ

76.
5m
6
5b
Dark Side of the Moon
6a
Time

82.
5a
Rodez

83.
4m
3a
Fay

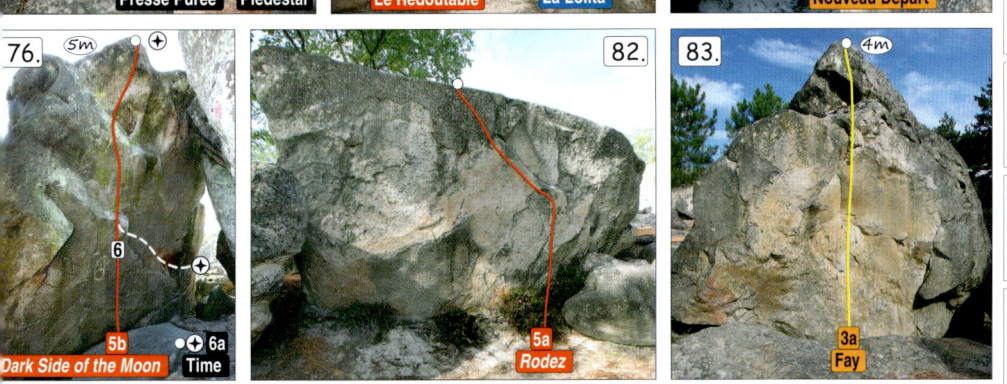

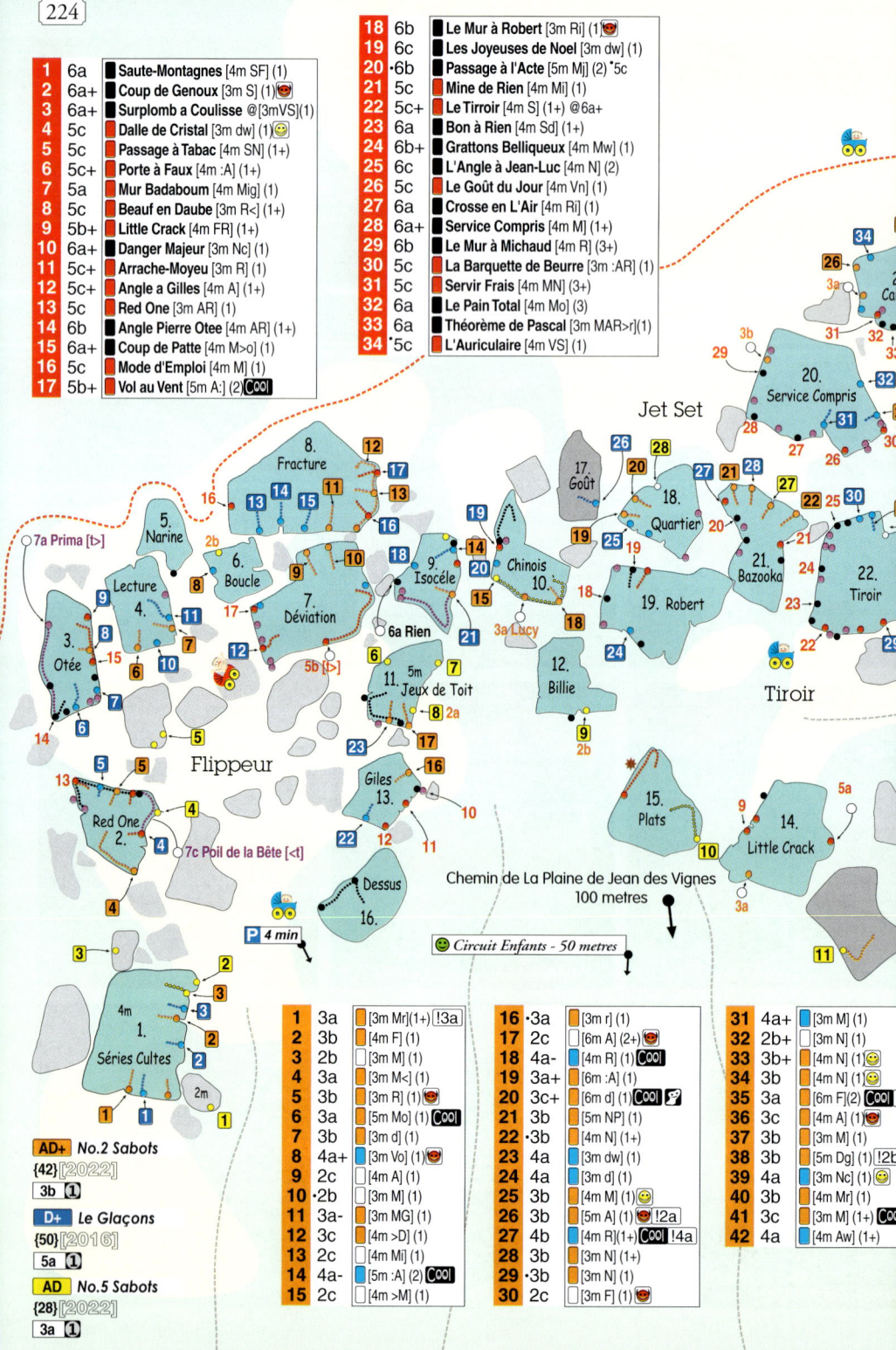

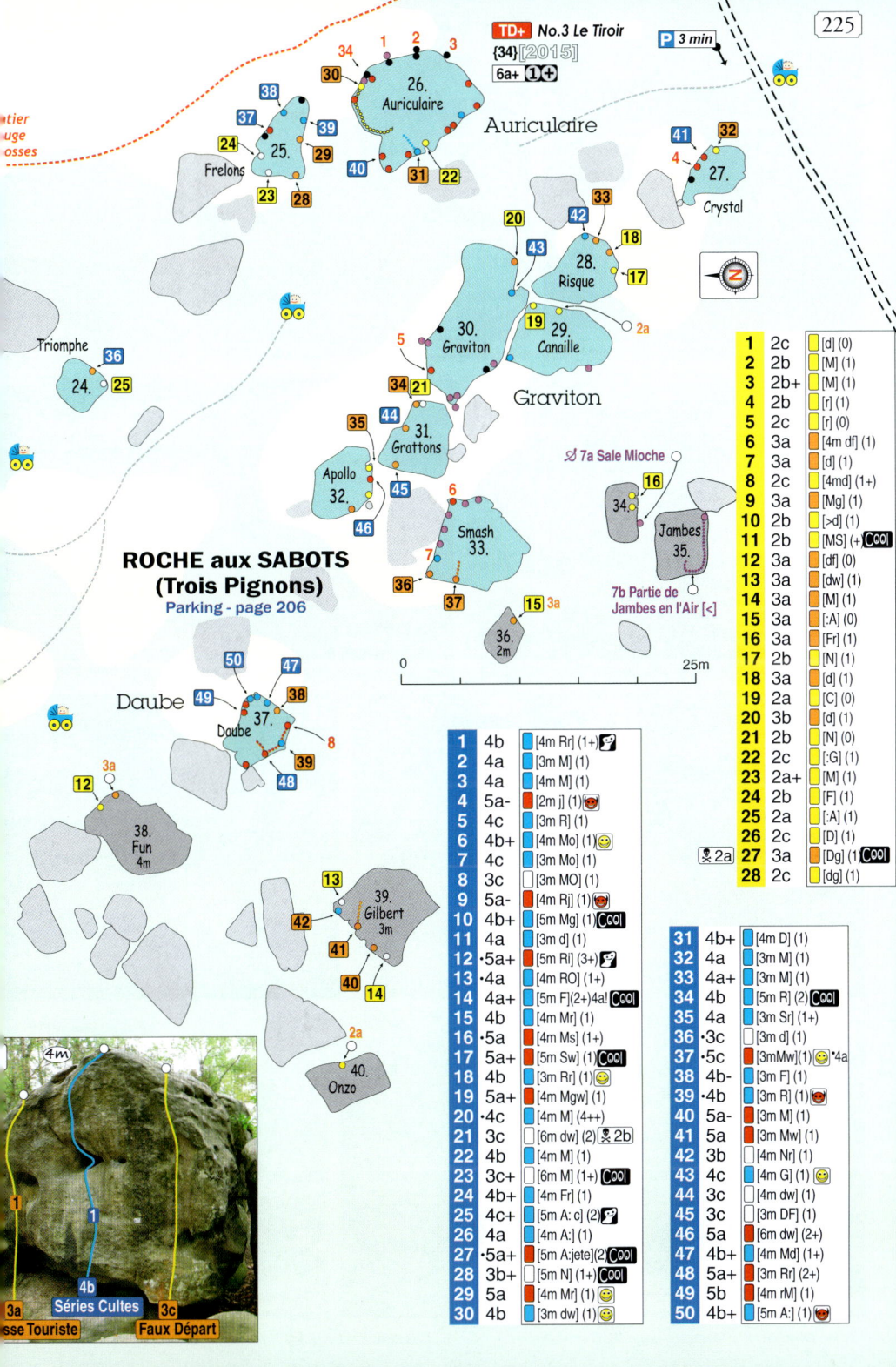

ROCHE aux SABOTS

Aerial plan - page 22

Roche aux Sabots Parking - page 206

6a CROSSE EN L'AIR 27, Yannick Stadler [Bloc 20 - Service Compris]

ROCHE aux SABOTS

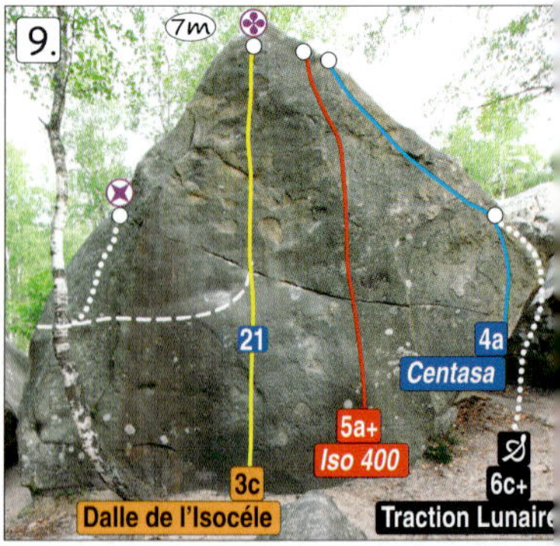

ROCHE aux SABOTS

ROCHE aux SABOTS

Aerial plan - page 22

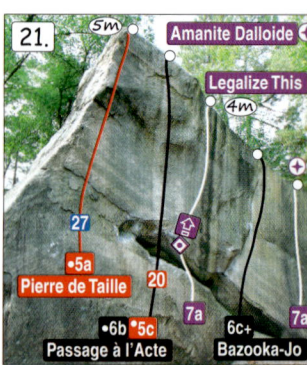

Rocher aux Sabots Parking - page 206

4c LA CHAUSSEE DES GEANTS 20, Camila Alarcon [Bloc 10 - Chinois]

ROCHE aux SABOTS

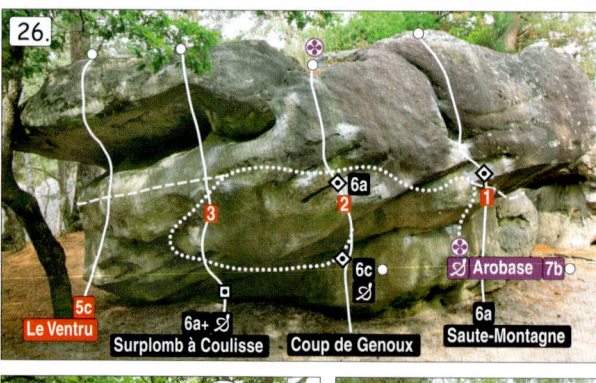

ROCHE aux SABOTS

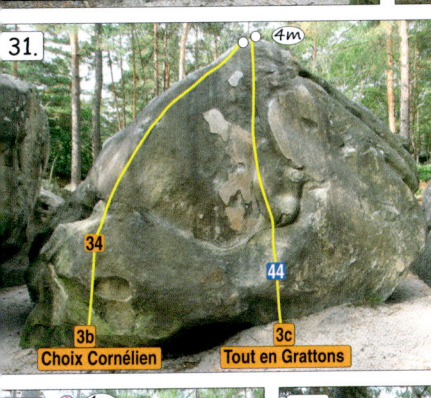

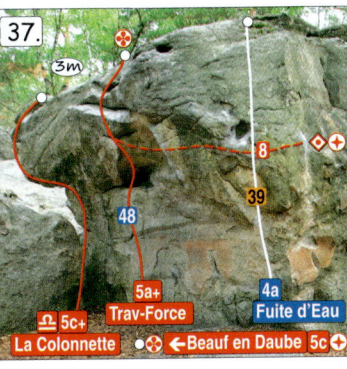

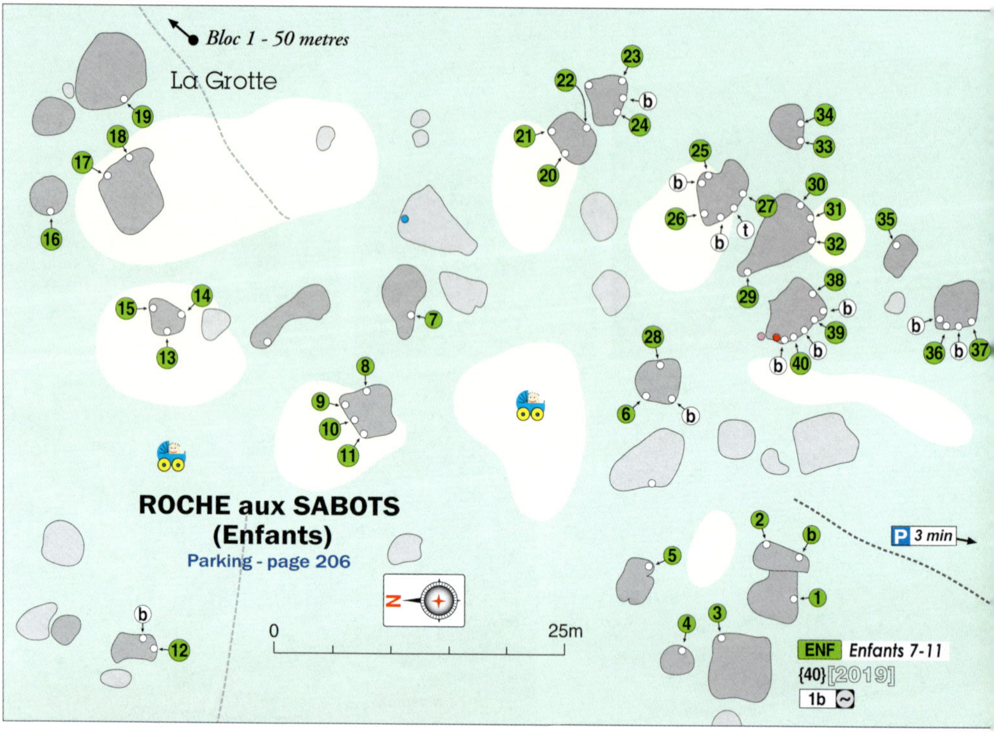
Bloc 1 - 50 metres
La Grotte
ROCHE aux SABOTS
(Enfants)
Parking - page 206
0
25m
P 3 min
ENF Enfants 7-11
{40}[2019]
1b
1
2
3
4
5
6
7
8
9
10
11
12
13
14
15
16
17
18
19
20
21
22
23
24
25
26
27
28
29
30
31
32
33
34
35
36
37
38
39
40
b
t

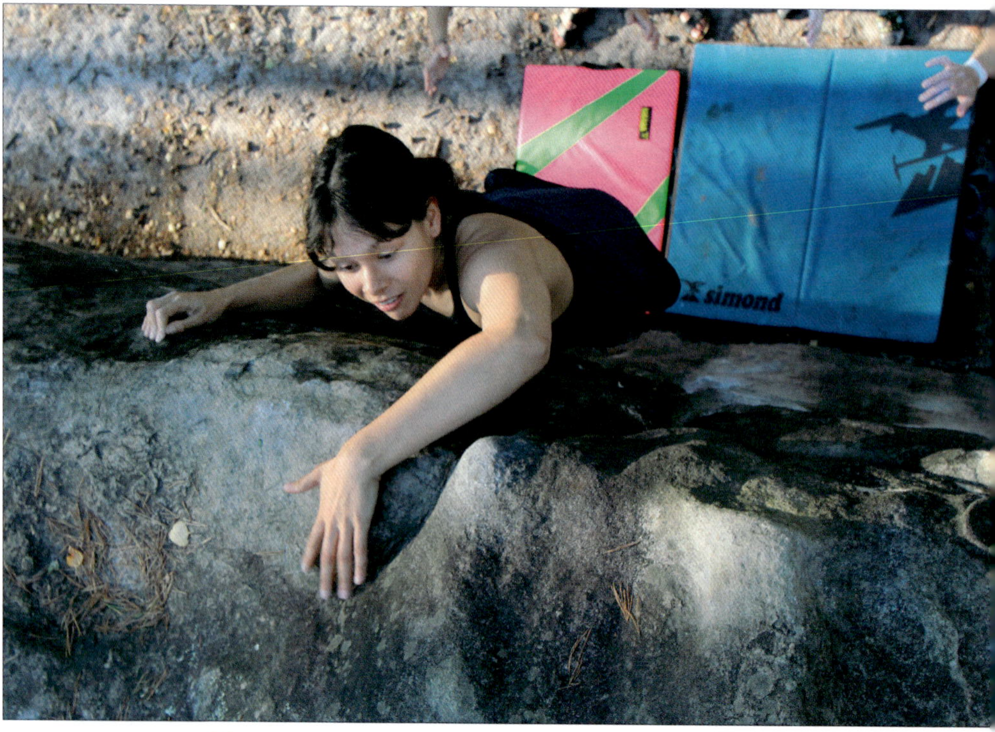
simond

⩓ 3c PLEINE PUISSANCE **41** , *Kelly van Haastere [ROCHE AUX SABOTS - Bloc 39 - Gilbert]*

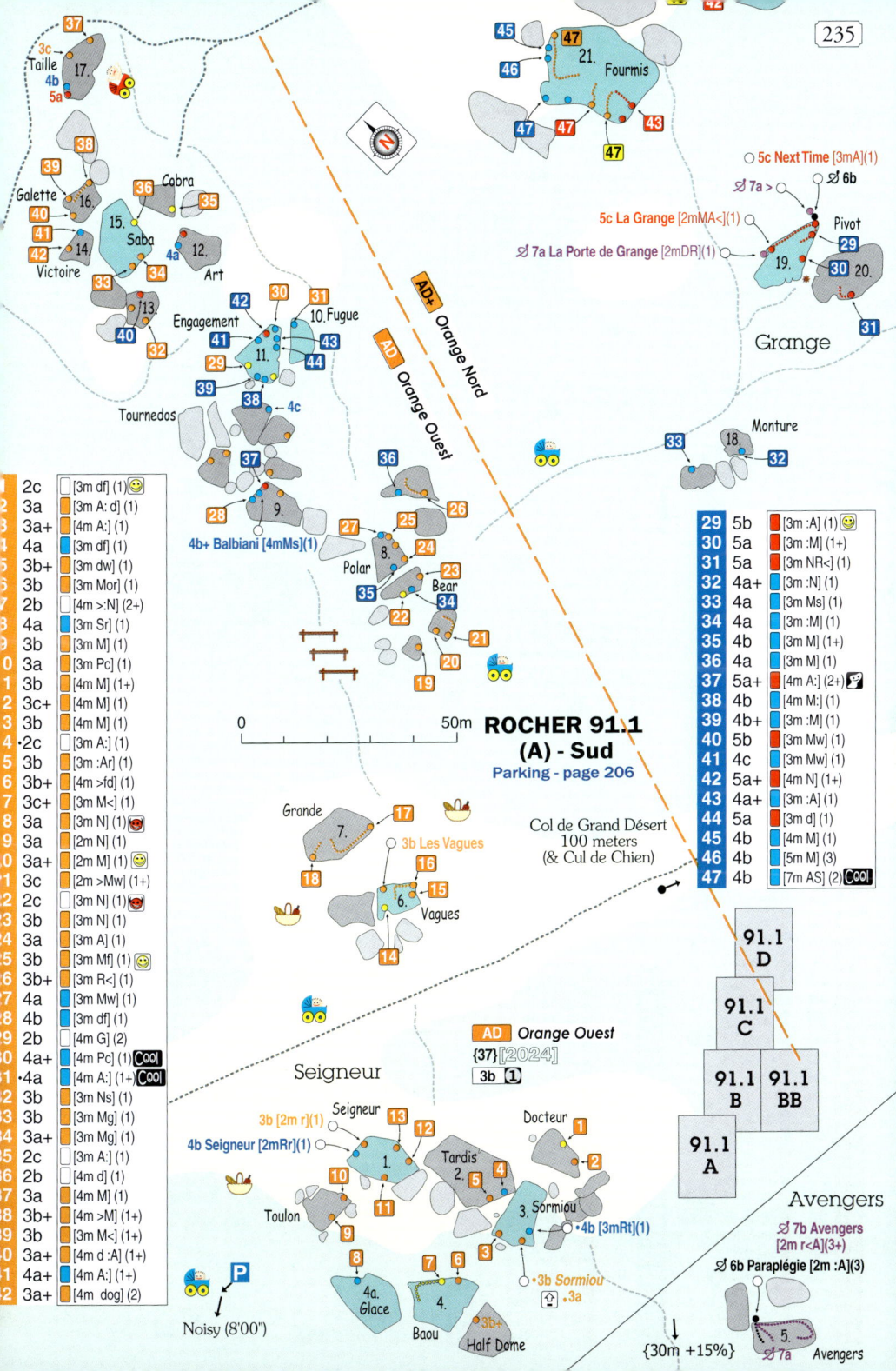

moon

Madonna 60.

59. Arts — Descente

4b L'Arête des Arts [4m :A](1)

57. 58.

56.

55.

Flipper
52. 53. Plomb
51. Gratitude — 5a [dr](1)
51a.
54. — 3b Genevive

Flip Flop

5a Péché Mignon [4mdw](1)

22. Balançoire
23. Bisou
24. Monnaie
25a.
24a.
21. Fourmis

P 10 min

#	Grade	Description
15	4c	[2m Rs] (1+)
16	6a	[4m Mw] (1)
17	5b	[4m P:] (1)
18	5c	[4m dg] (1)
19	6a	[3m M] (1)
20	5a	[3m :A] (2-5)
21	6a+	[5m :A] (3+) Cool
22	6a	[5m Dgr](3+) Cool
23	5c	[5m MF](3+) Cool
24	6a	[4m RG] (1+)
25	5b	[6m dM] (4+)
26	5b	[5m M] (4)
27	4c	[6m Dd] (3+)
28	5a	[4m Rr] (2+)
29	5a	[3m M] (1)
30	4c	[3m N] (1)
31	4b	[2m N] (1)
32	4c	[5m d] (2+) Cool
33	5b	[4m M] (2)
34	4c	[3m N] (1+)
35	5a	[4m Md] (2)
36	4c	[3m R] (1)
37	4c	[2m @M] (1)
38	5a	[2m SD] (1)
39	4c	[4m R] (4)
40	5b	[6m dM] (6) Cool
41	5a	[6m Dr N](2) Cool
42	5b	[2m NR] (1+)
43	5b	[3m MN] (1)
44	5a	[5m M] (5)
45	5a	[3m A:] (8)
46	5b	[5m PS] (2+)
47	3c	[5m dS] (2+)

#	Grade	Description
13	5c+	[3m Mw] (3)
14	5b	[4m df] (1)
15	5a	[5m df] (1)
16	5a+	[3m Mw] (1)
17	4a+	[3m :A] (2)
18	4b	[4m df] (1)
19	5b+	[4m Ns] (2+)
20	5c	[4m MA] (1+)
21	4c	[6m df] (3++)
22	5a	[3m RN] (1)
23	4b	[4m M] (1)
24	5c	[2m N] (1)
25	4a	[4m MD] (2+)
26	5a	[3m :A] (1+)
27	4b	[4m :A] (1+)
28	4b	[4m M] (1)
29	5b	[3m :A] (1)
30	4c	[3m :M] (1+)
31	5a	[3m NR<] (1)

#	Grade	Description
45	4b	[4m M] (1)
46	4b	[5m M] (3)
47	4c	[7m AS] (2) Cool

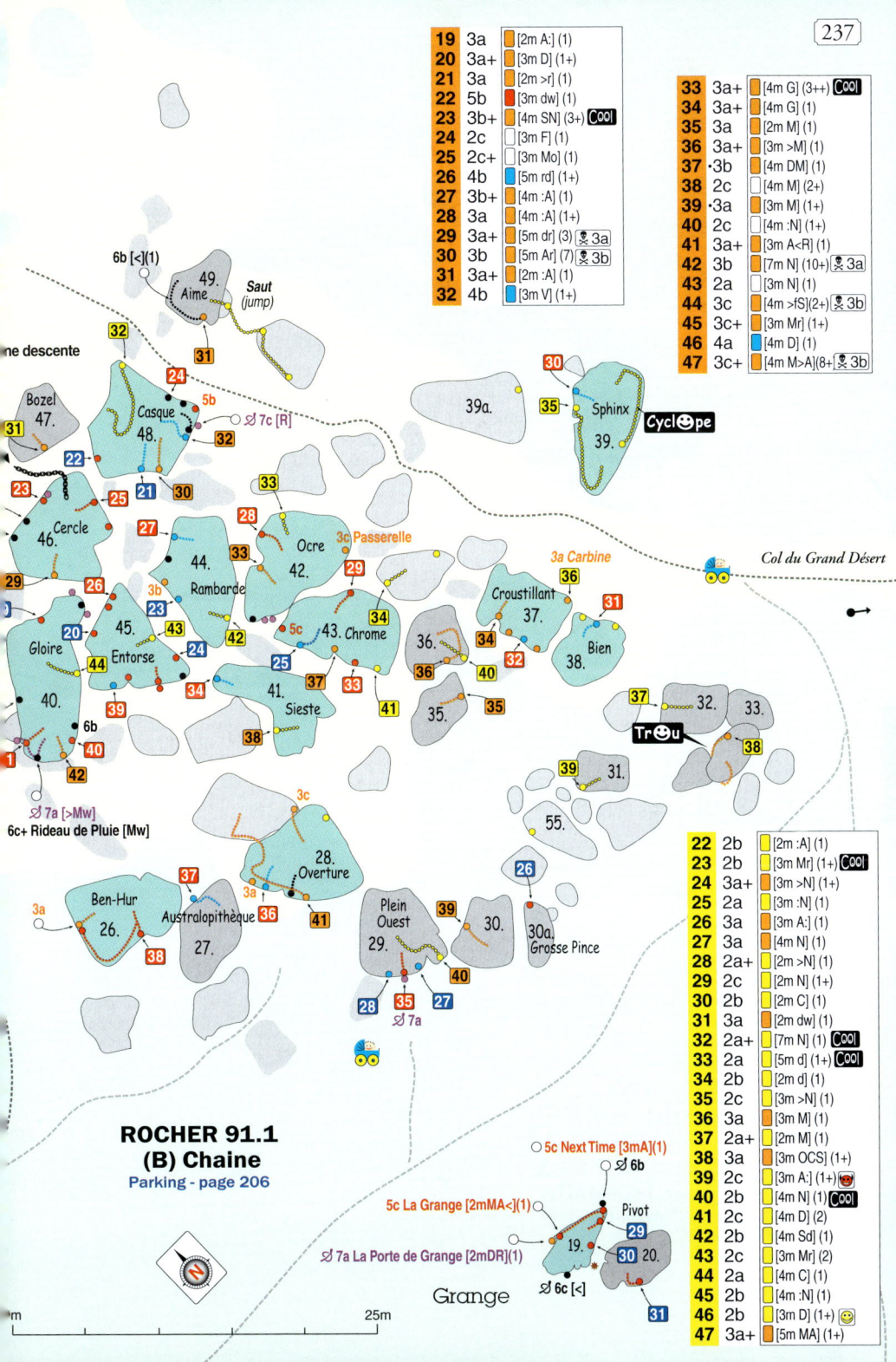

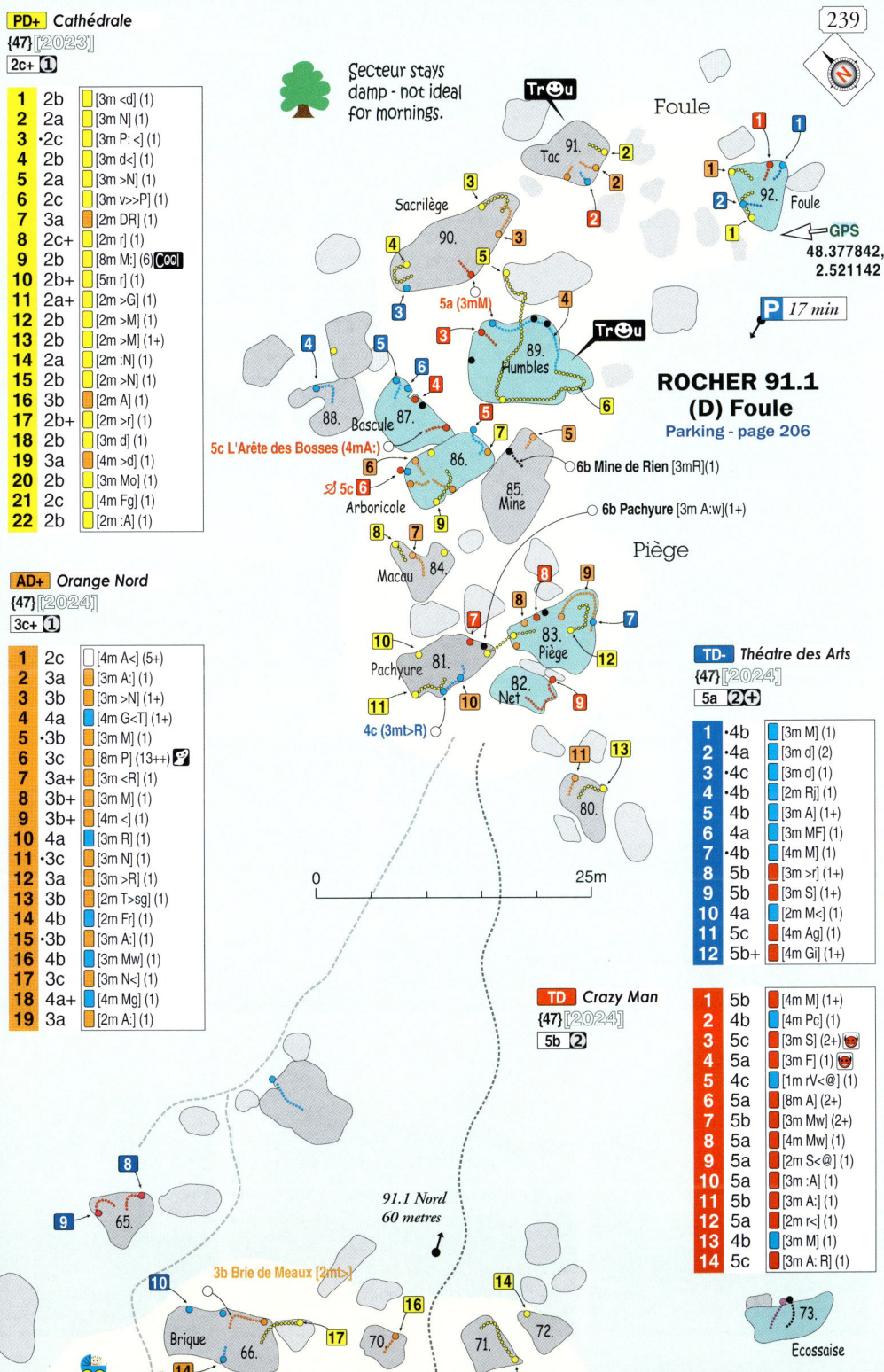

ROCHER 91.1 - A (Sud)

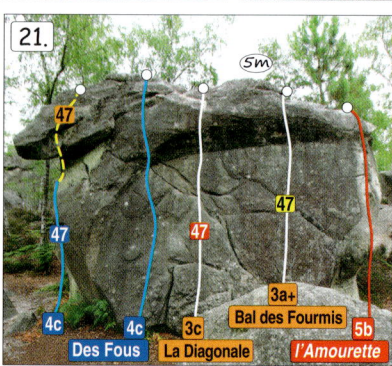

ROCHER 91.1 - B (Chaine)

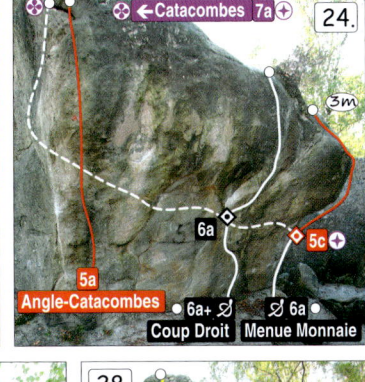

ROCHER 91.1 - B (Chaine)

Aerial plan - page 236

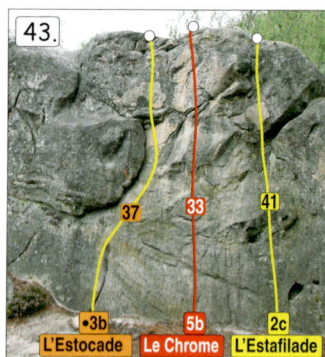

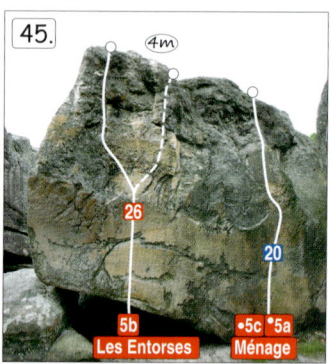

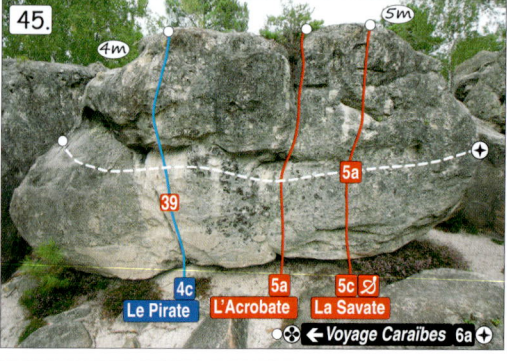

4a+ LA MONTURE 32, Carsten Joiko [Bloc 18 - Monture] ▷

ROCHER 91.1 - B (Chaine)

Aerial plan - page 236

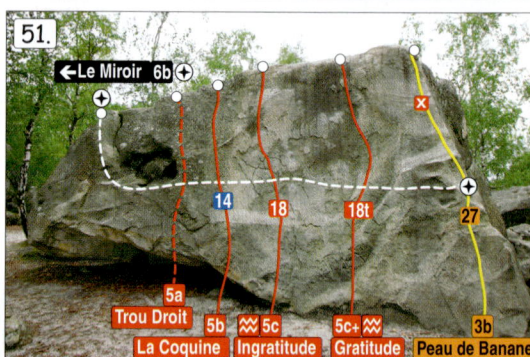

91.1 Parking - page 206

ROCHER 91.1 - C&D (Foule)

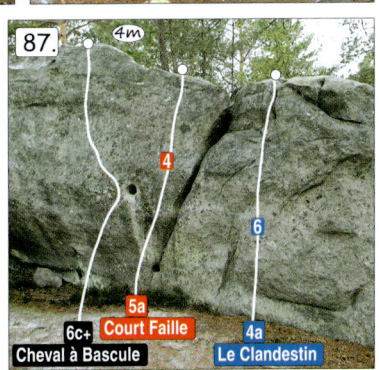
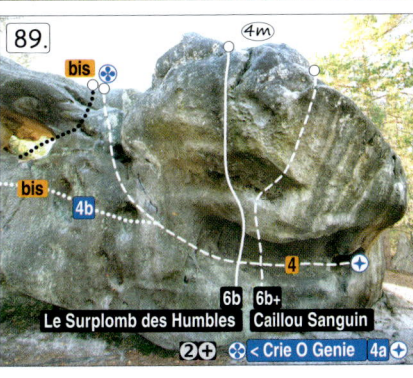

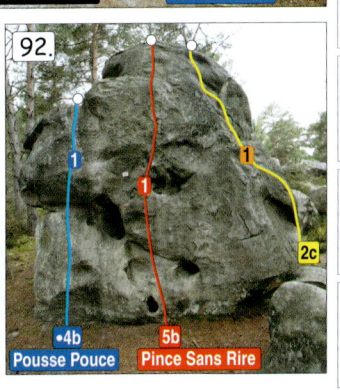

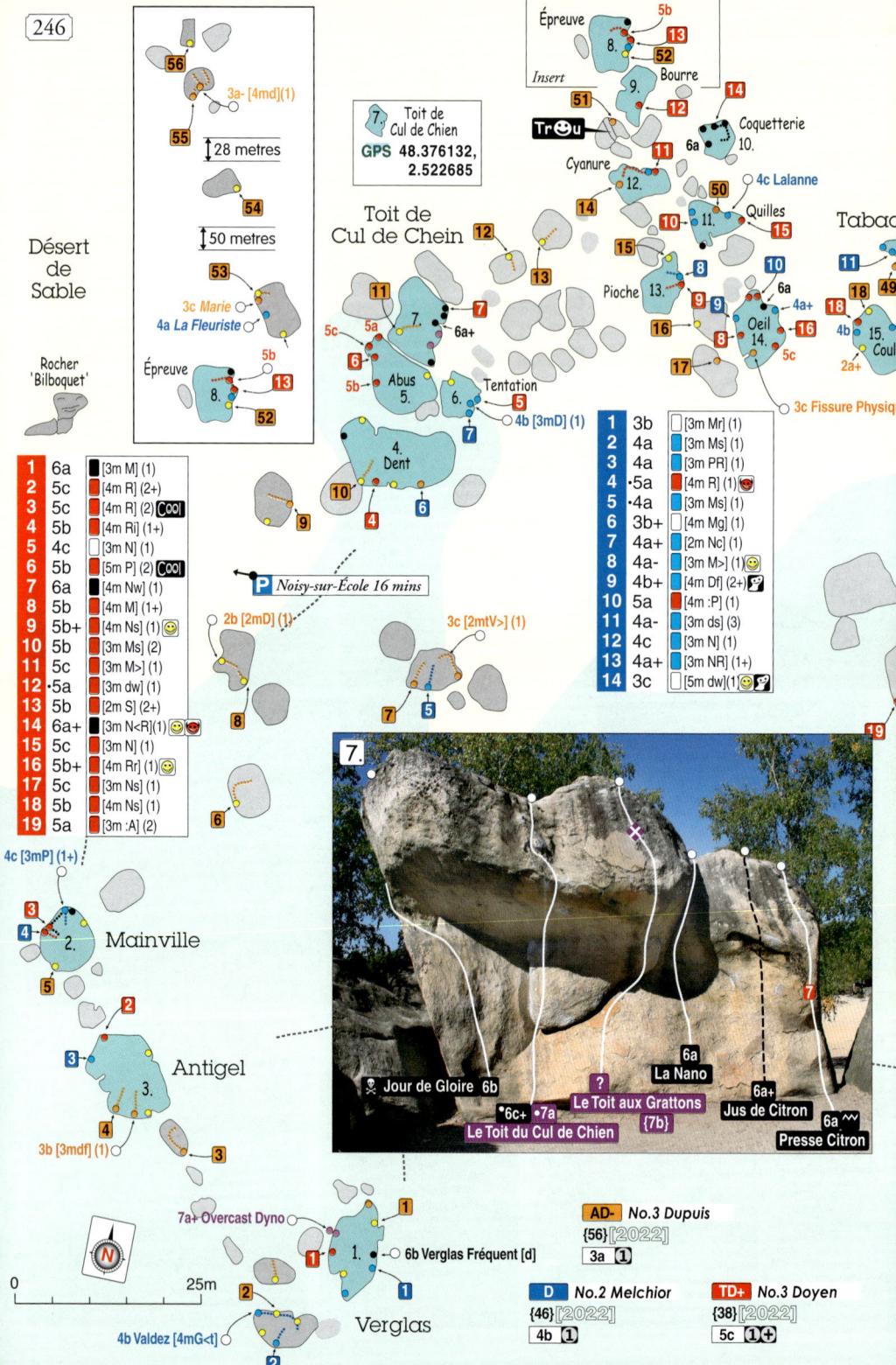

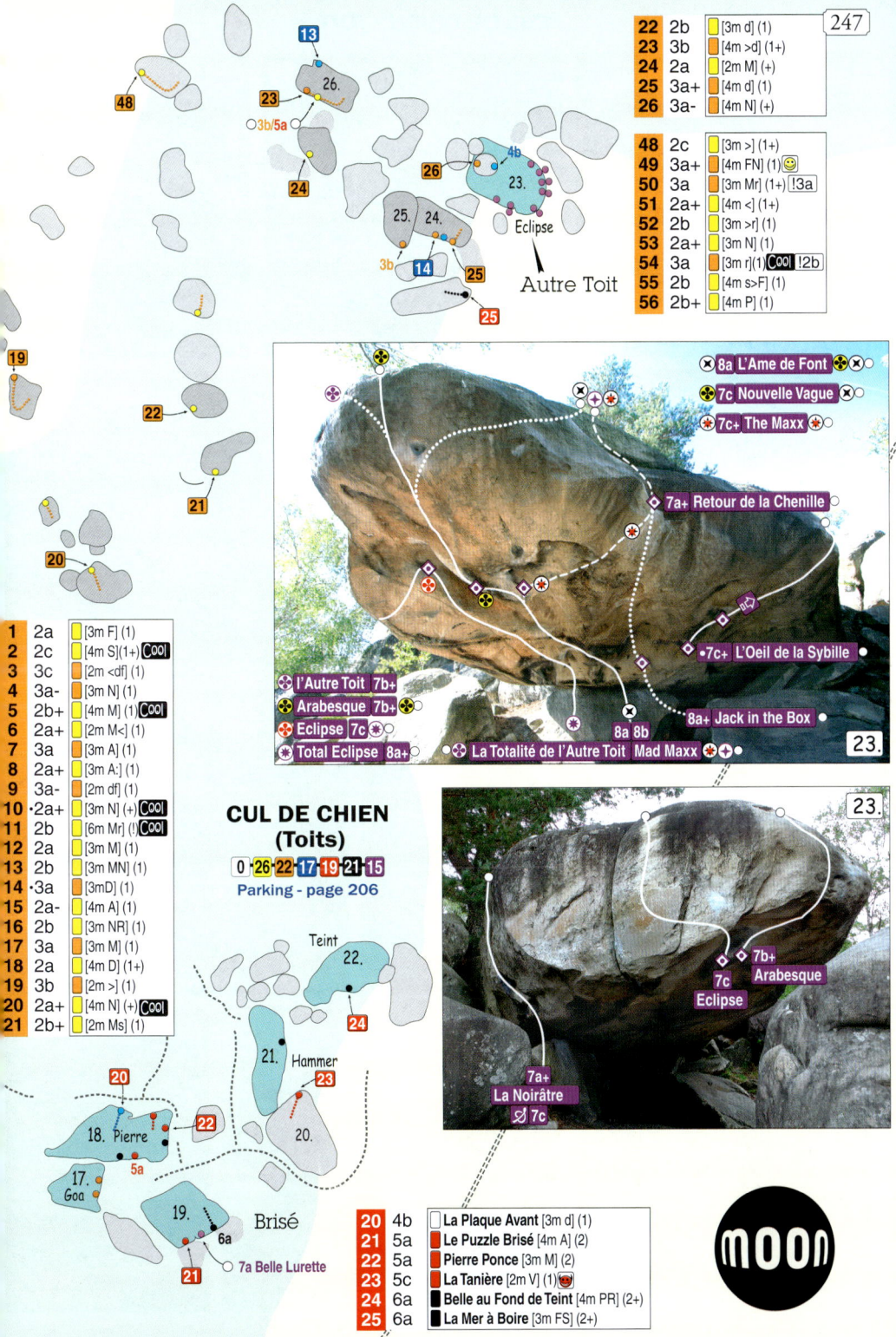

CUL DE CHIEN - TOIT

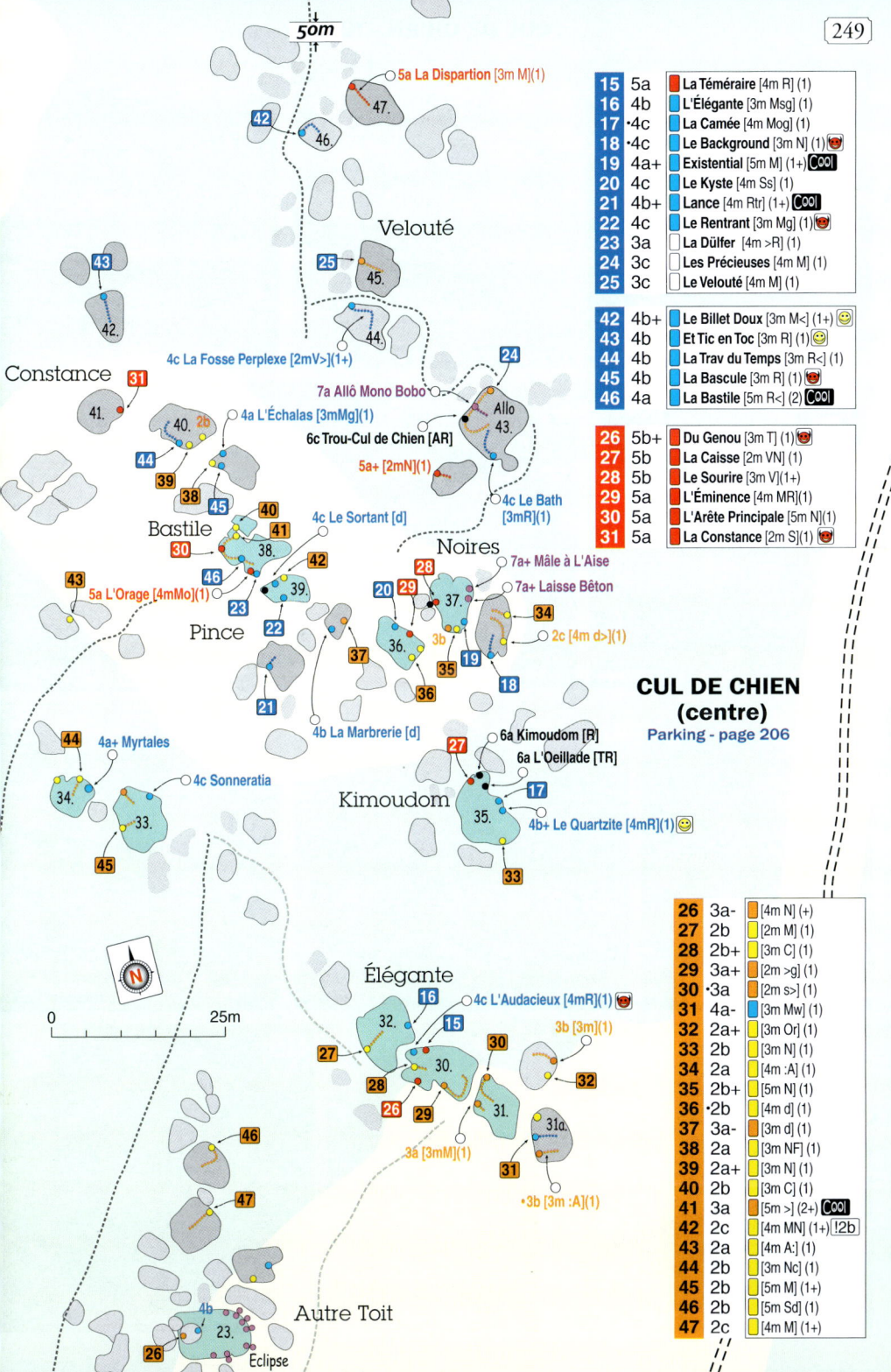

CUL DE CHIEN - TOIT

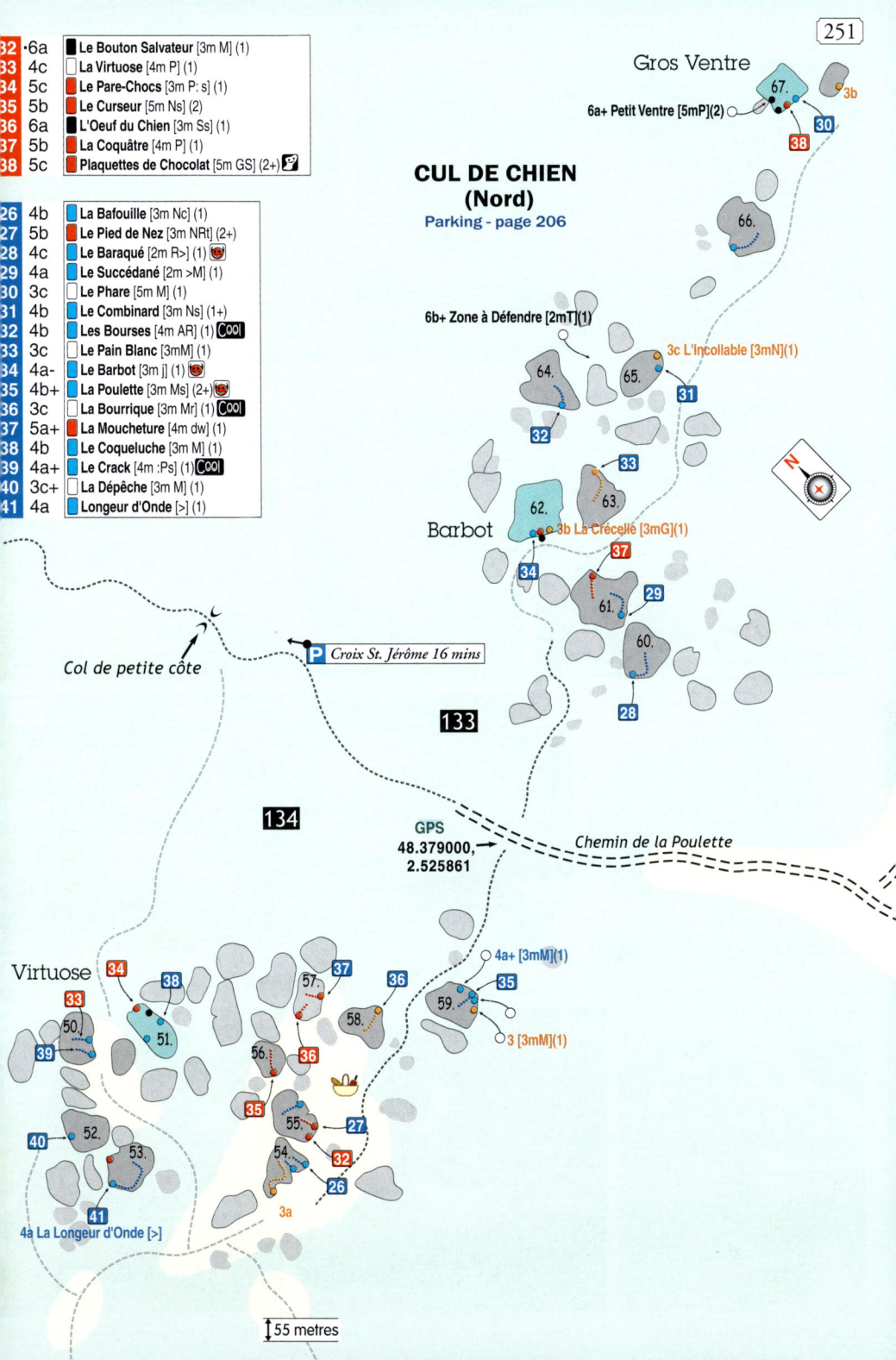

CUL DE CHIEN

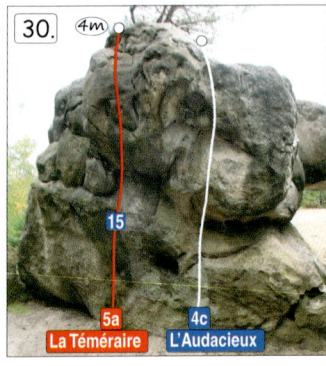

Cul de Chien Parking - page 206   7a LE TOIT DU CUL DE CHIEN, *Victor Interthal [Bloc 7 - Le Toit]* ≫

CUL DE CHIEN

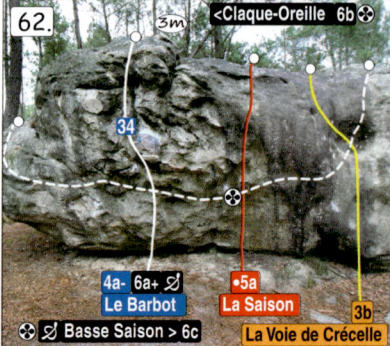
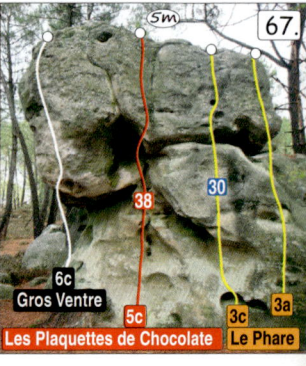

6a PINCE-OREILLE, Luca Lemarchand [Bloc 39 - Pince]

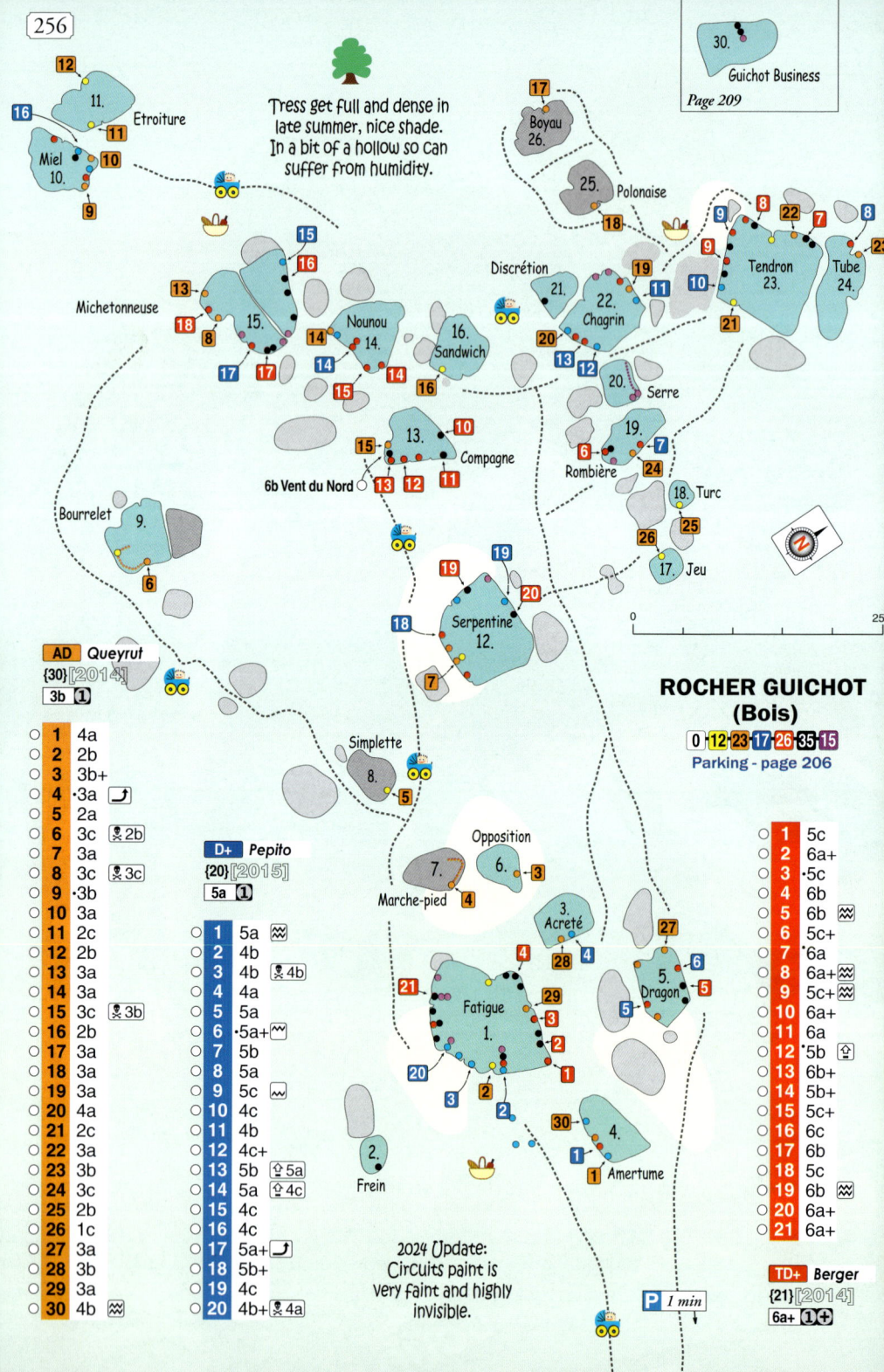

ROCHER GUICHOT

Rocher Guichot Parking - page 206

ROCHER GUICHOT

Aerial plan - page 25

Rocher Guichot Parking - page 206

5c+ **LA NOUNOU** 15, Owen Hancock [Bloc 14 - Nounou]

ROCHER GUICHOT

Rocher Guichot Parking - page 206

ROCHER GUICHOT

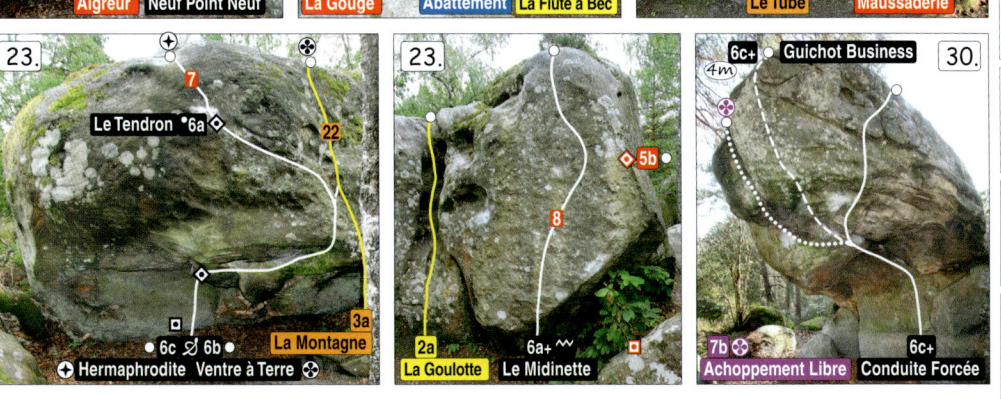

Rocher Guichot Parking - page 206

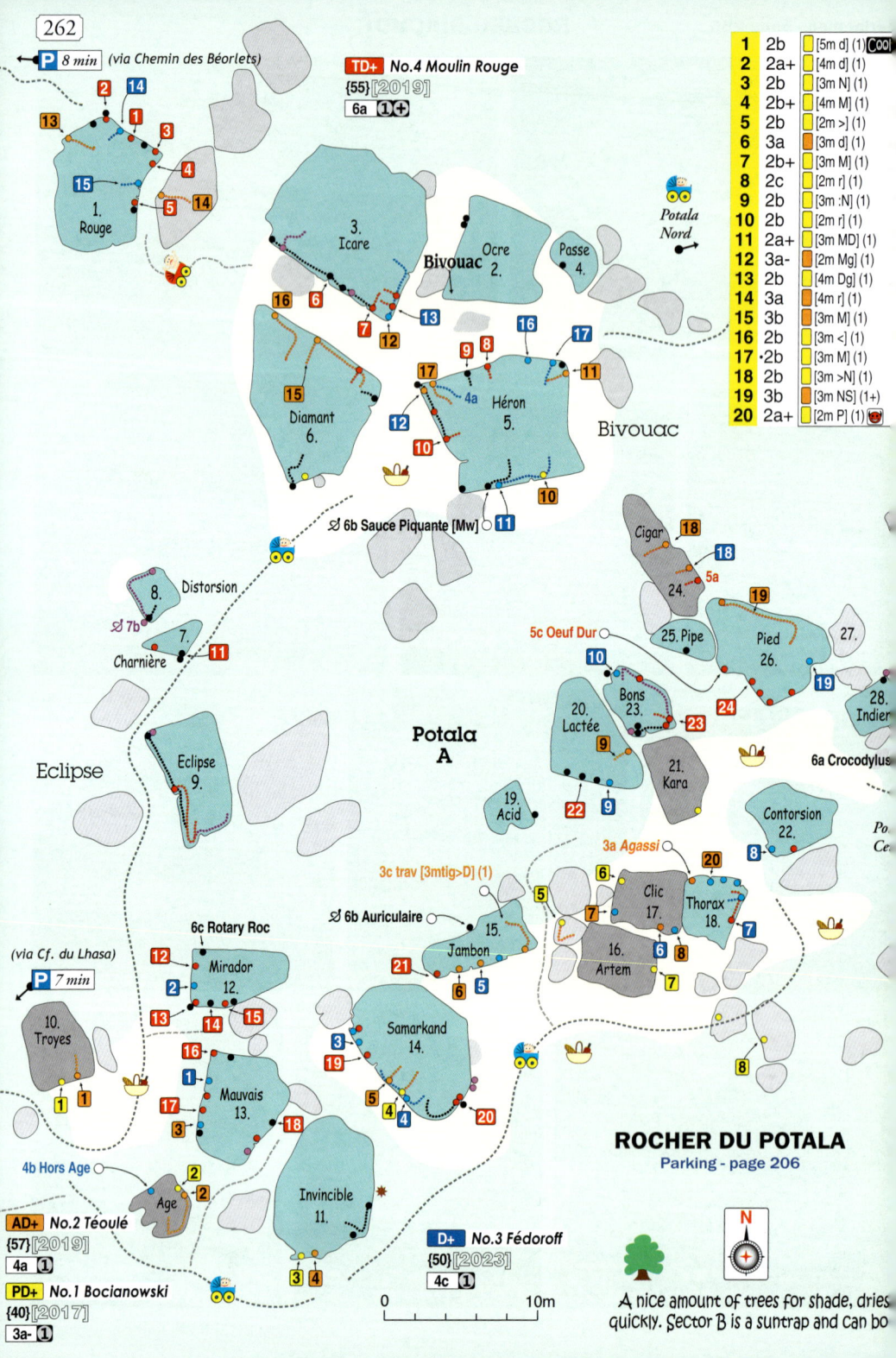

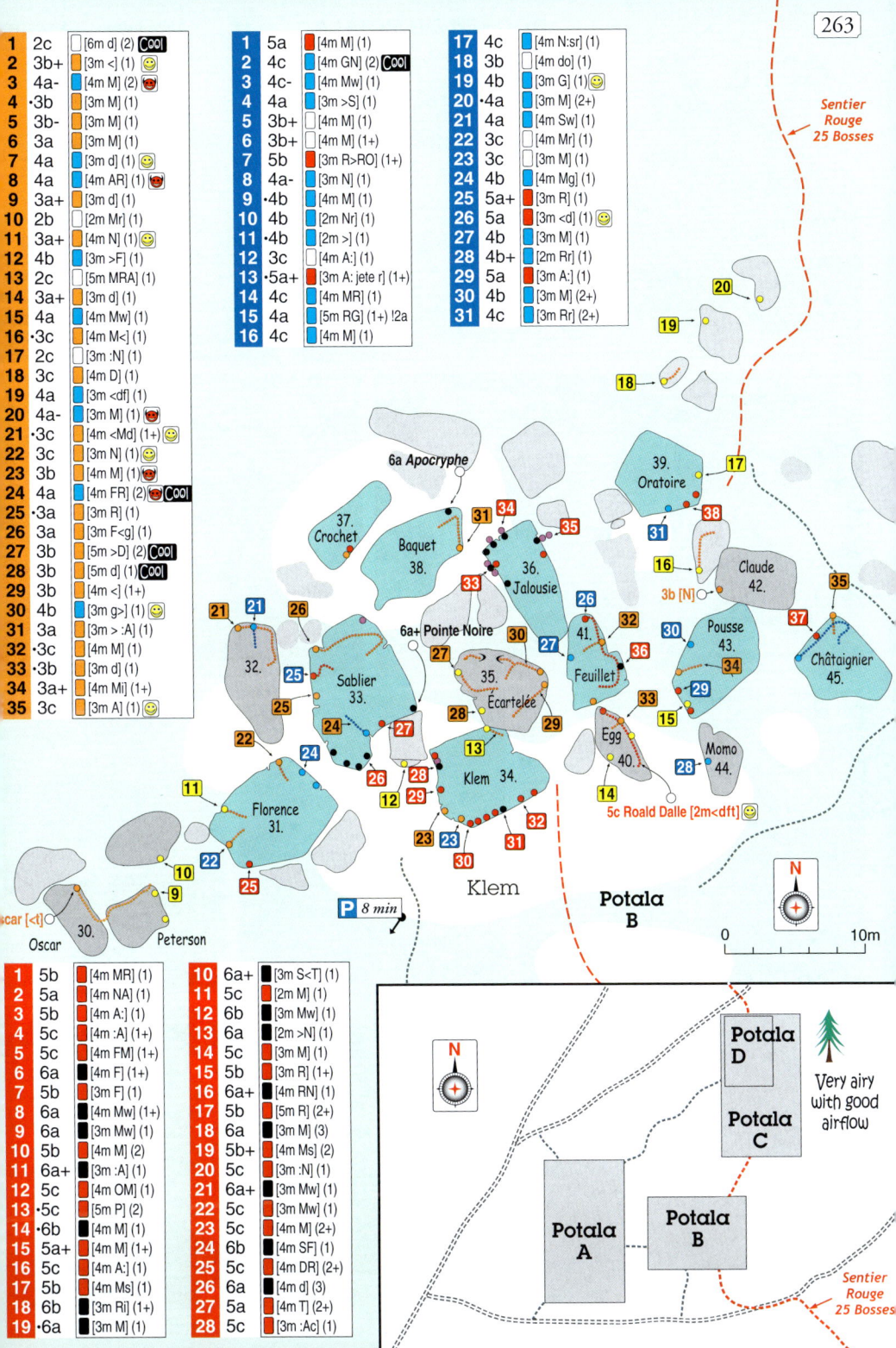

ROCHER DU POTALA

Aerial plan - page 262

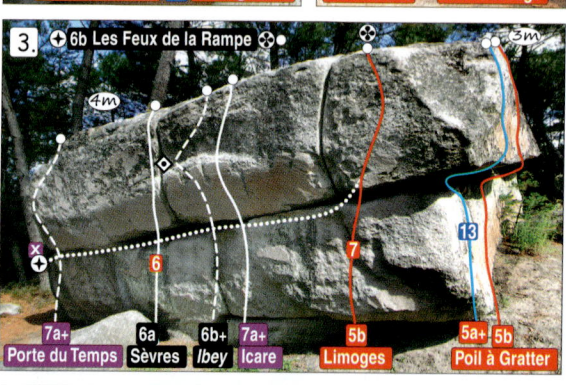

6a ACID, Mina [Bloc 19 - Acid]

ROCHER DU POTALA

Aerial plan - page 262

7b THE COMPLETE TRIP, *Leon Ben Achour* △ & *Martin Languste* ▷ [Bloc 72 - Croix]

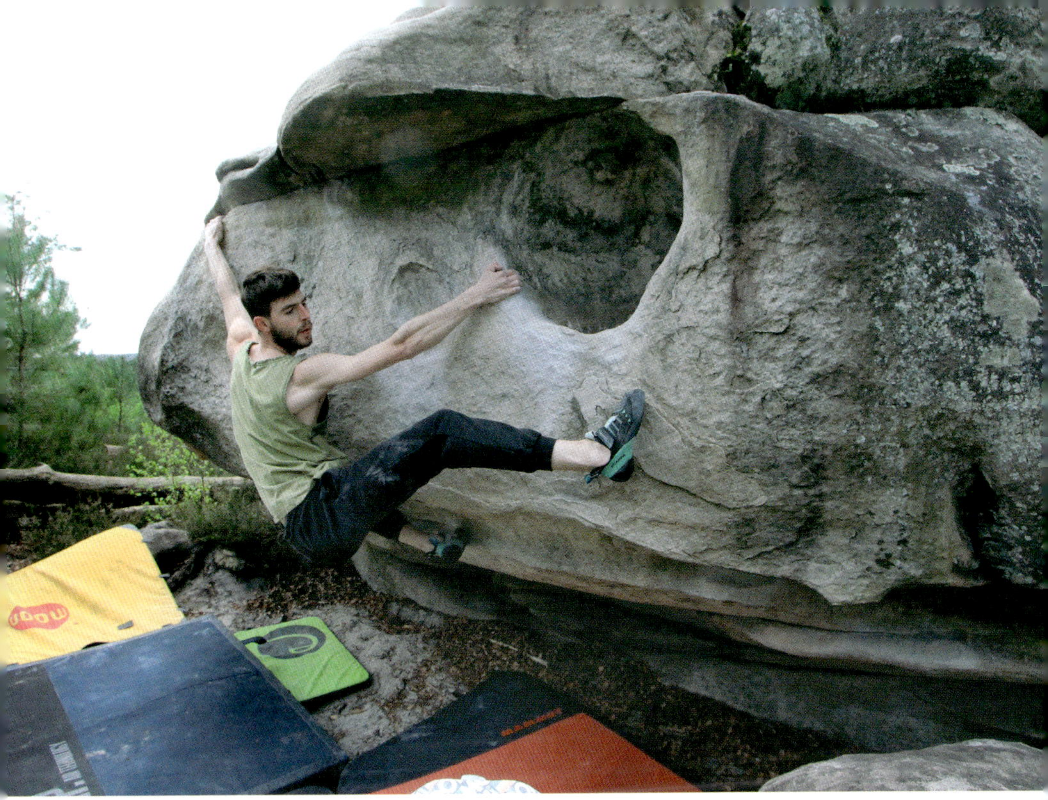

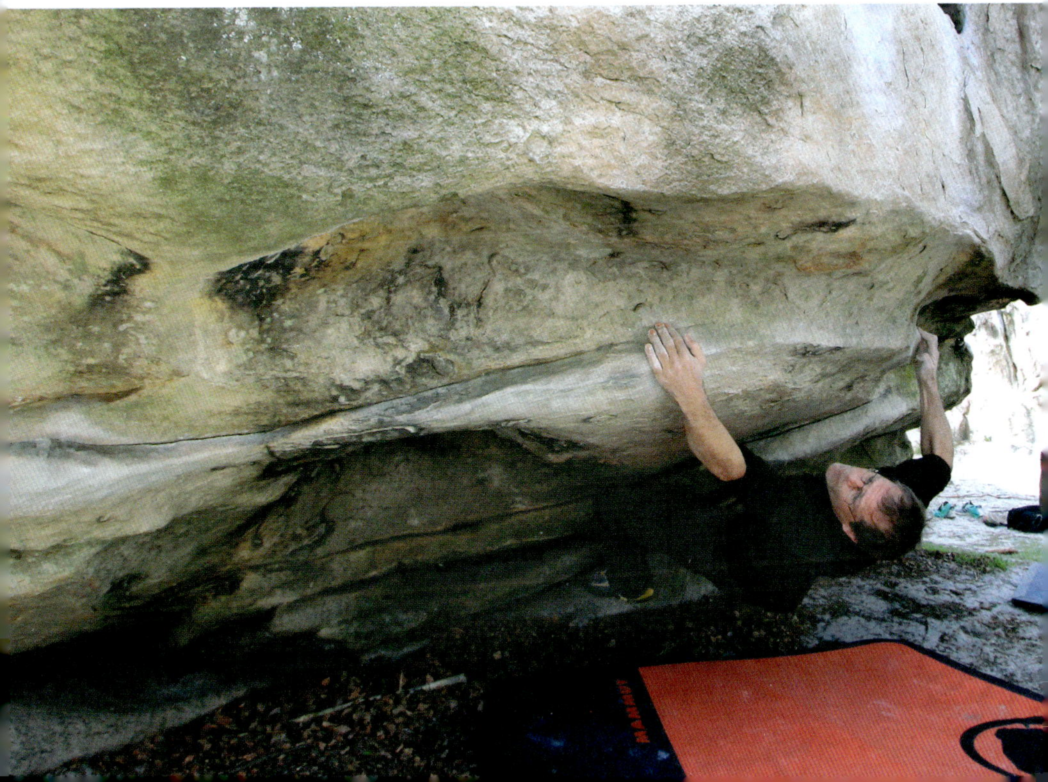

ROCHER DU POTALA

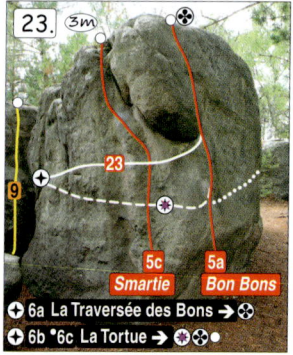

ROCHER DU POTALA

ROCHER DU POTALA

271

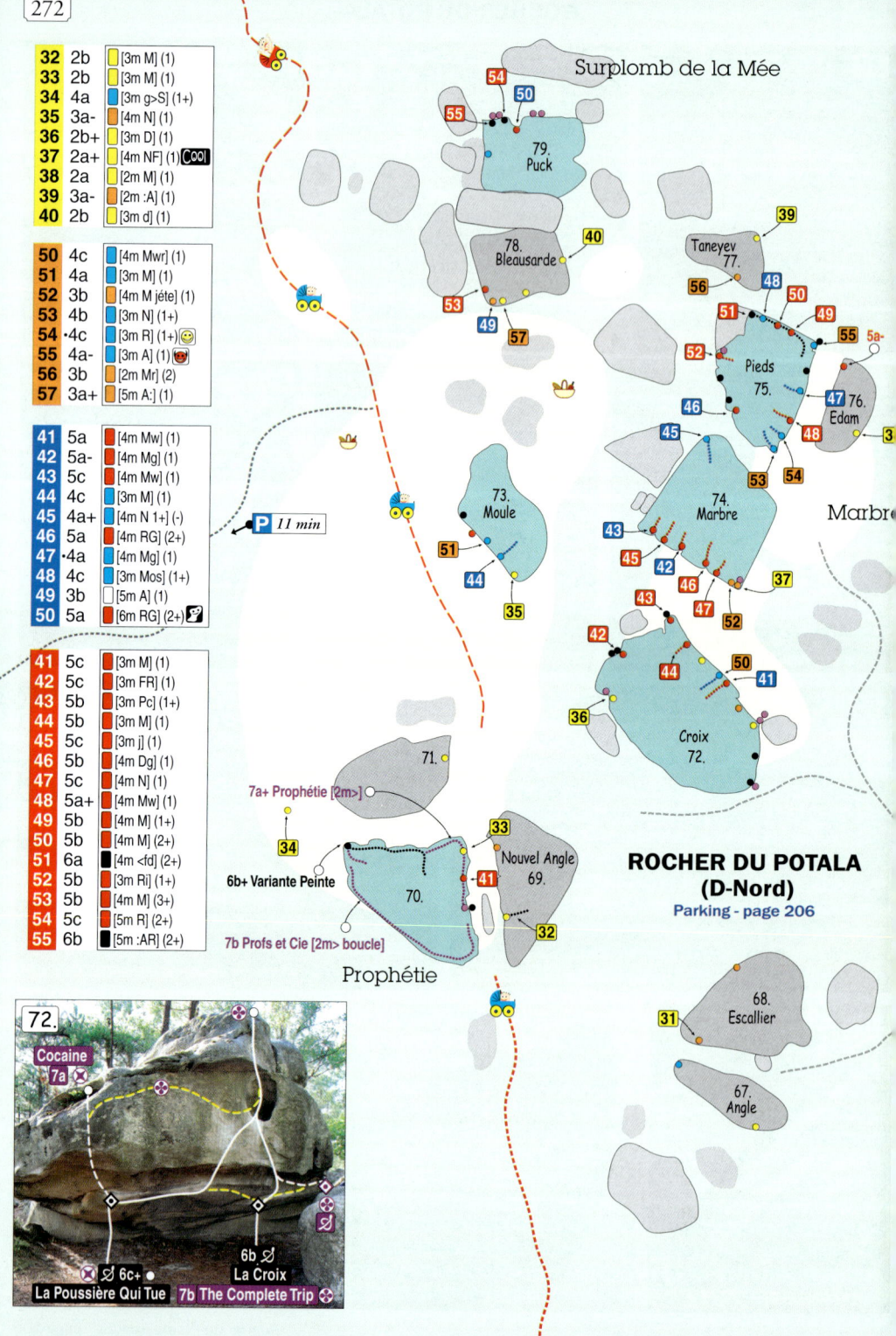

ROCHER DU POTALA - (C-Nord)

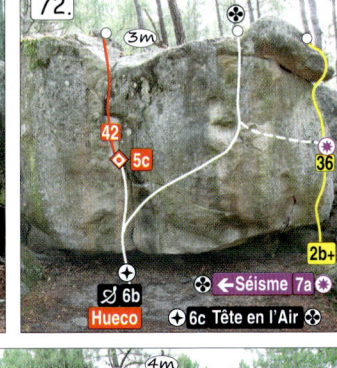

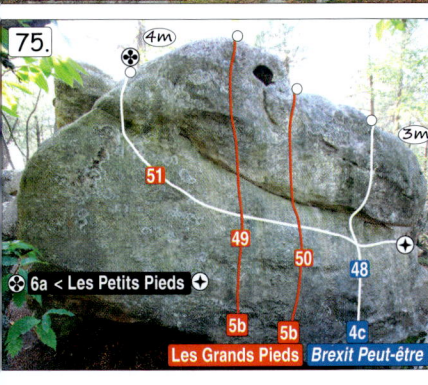
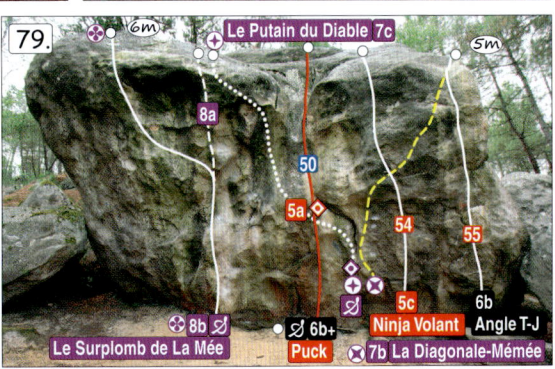

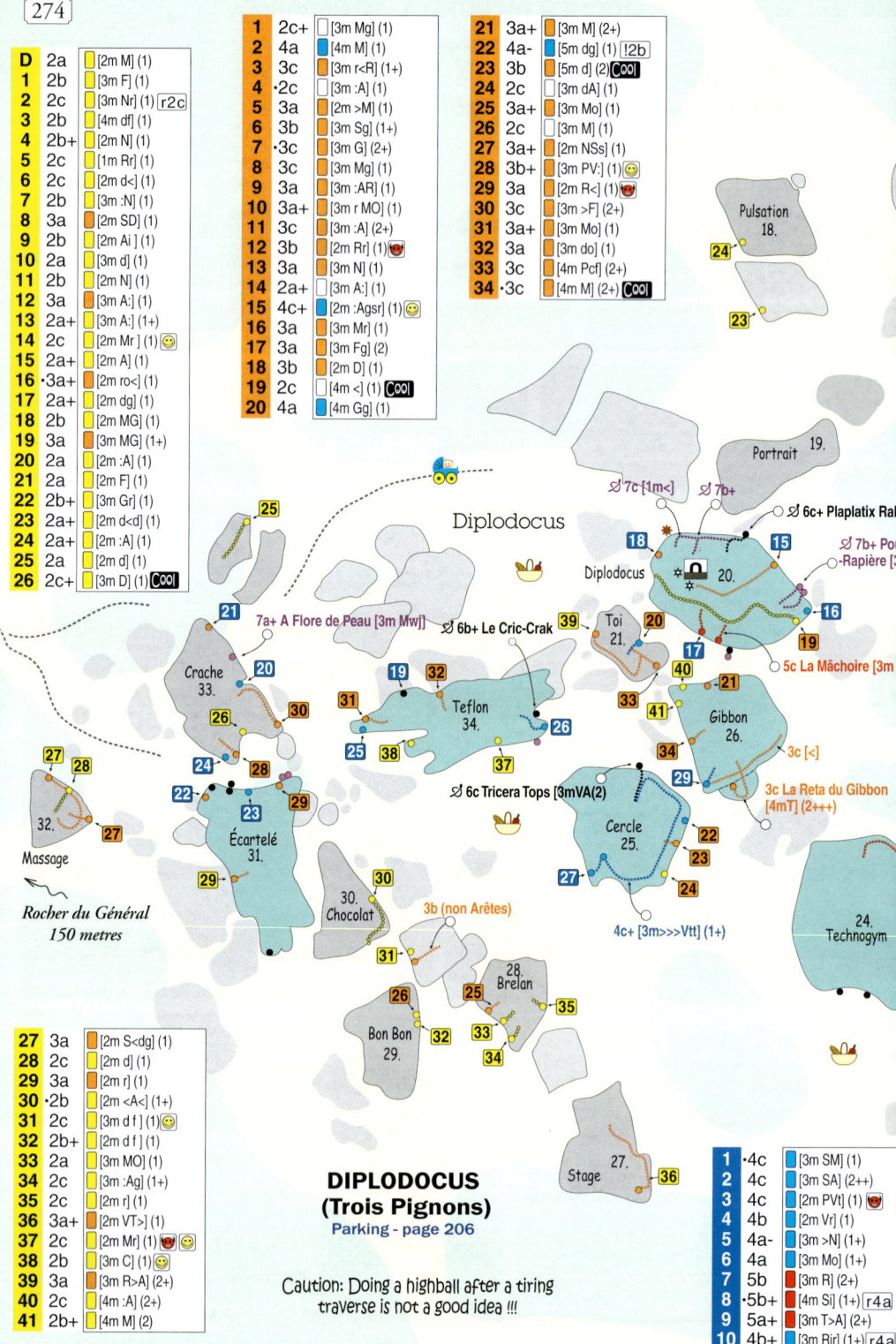

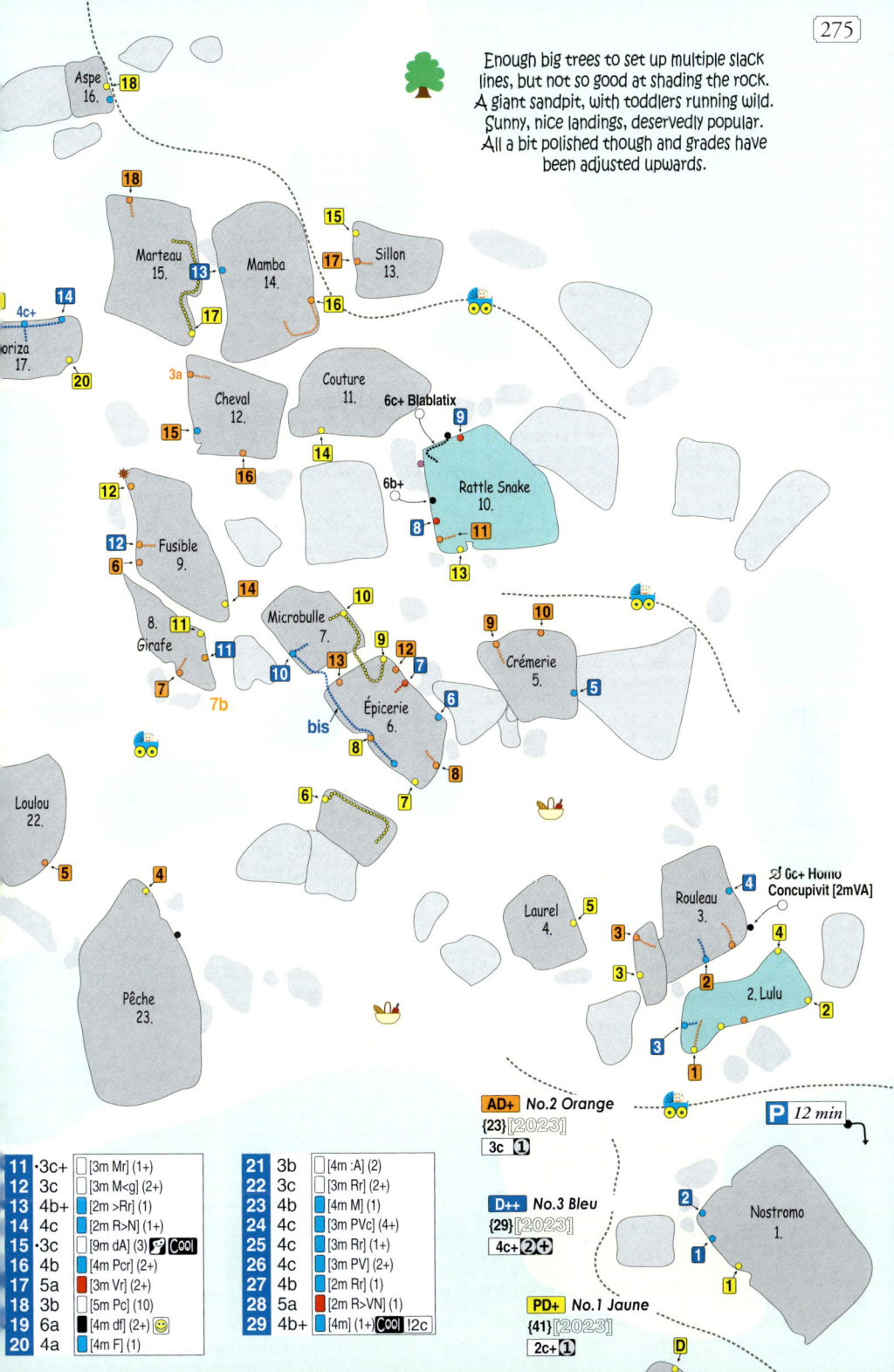

DIPLODOCUS

Aerial plan - page 274

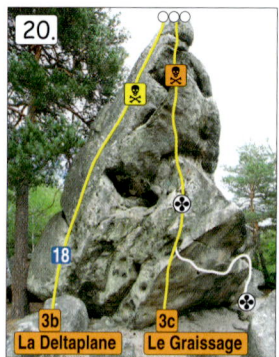

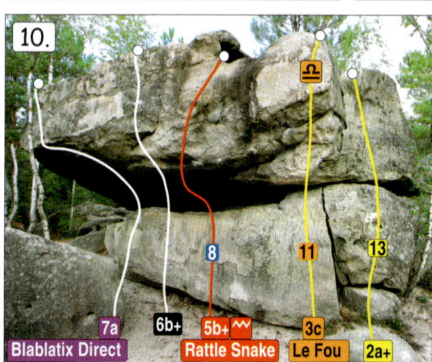

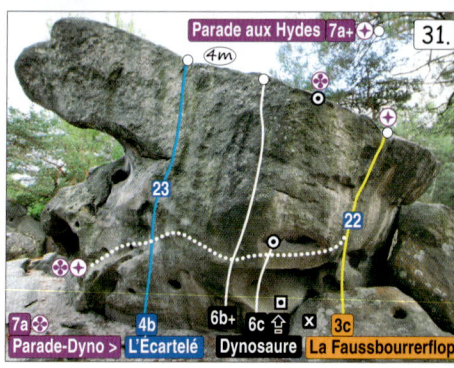

Diplodocus Parking - page 206

4c LA MURENE 3, Coline Souchon [Bloc 2 - Lulu]

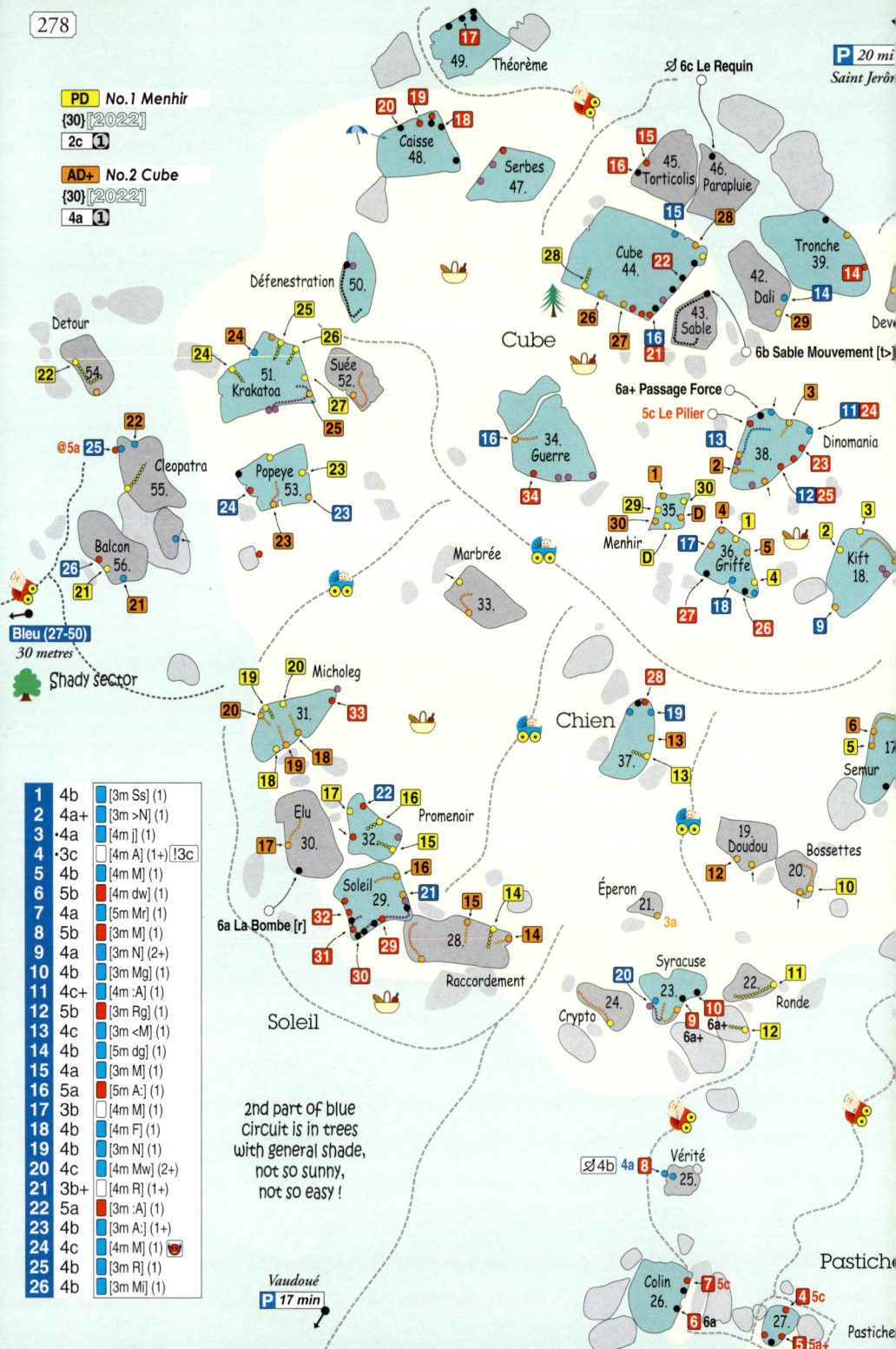

ROCHER FIN

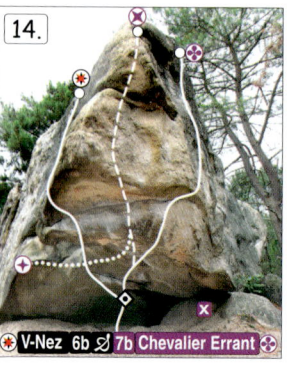
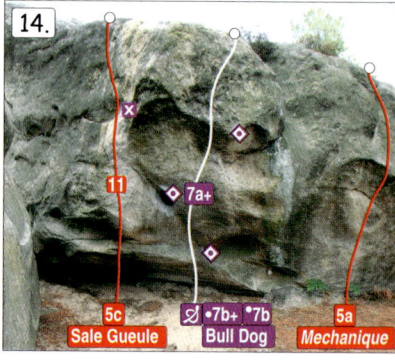

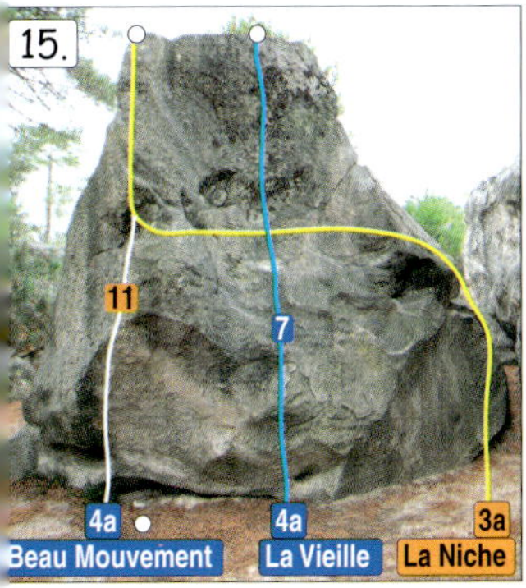

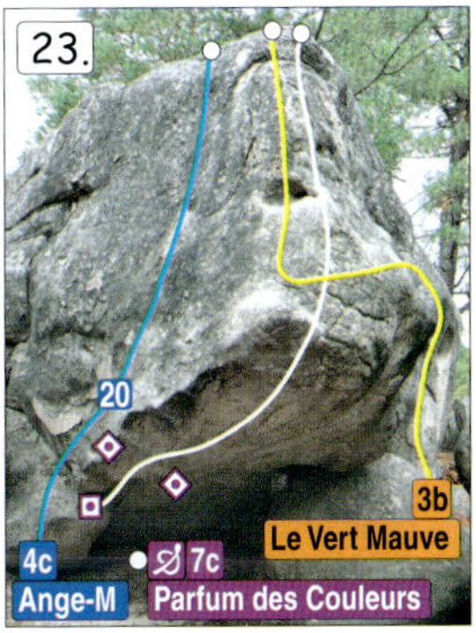

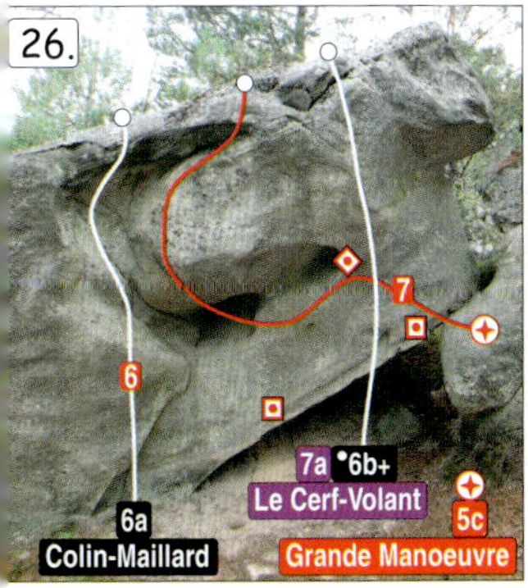

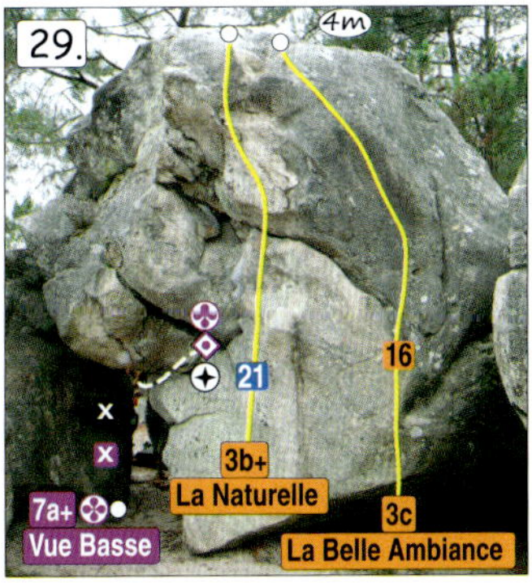

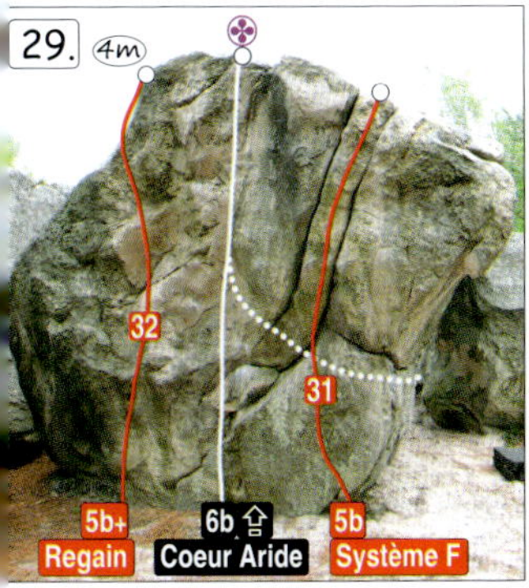

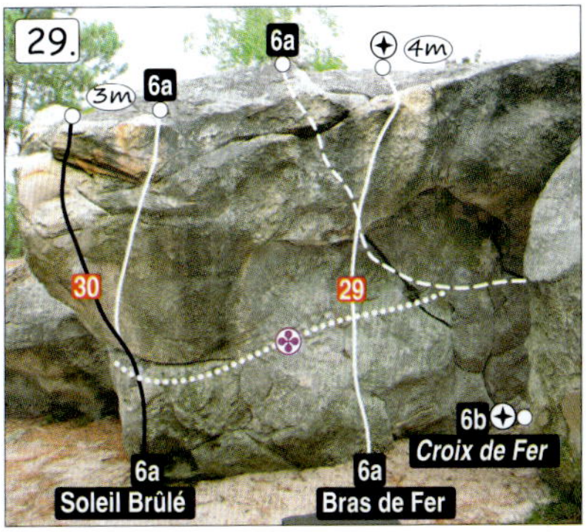

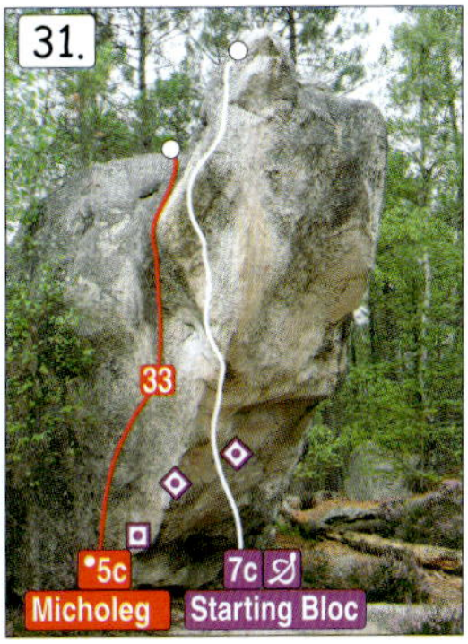

ROCHER FIN

15.
- 11 — 4a — Beau Mouvement
- 7 — 4a — La Vieille
- 3a — La Niche

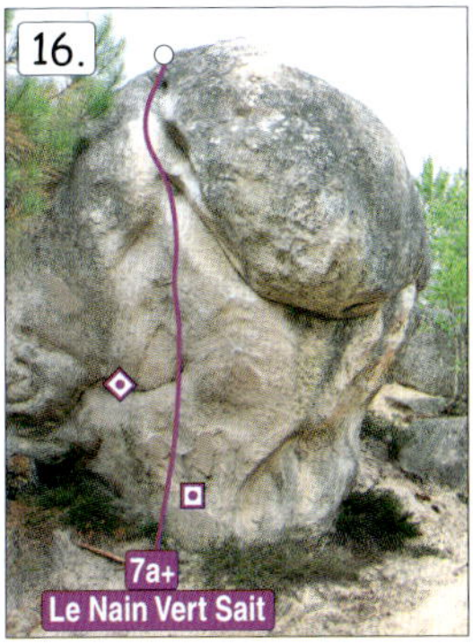

16.
- 7a+ — Le Nain Vert Sait

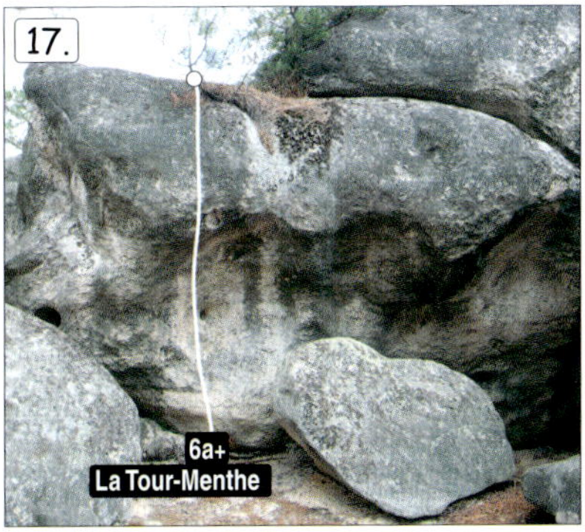

17.
- 6a+ — La Tour-Menthe

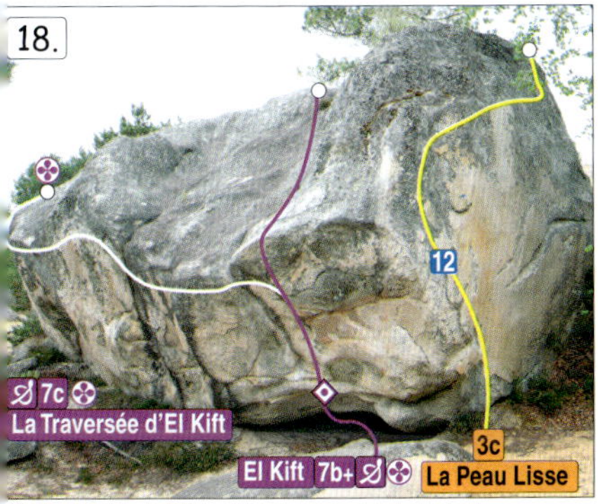

18.
- 7c — La Traversée d'El Kift
- El Kift 7b+
- 12 — 3c — La Peau Lisse

23.
- 20 — 4c — Ange-M
- 7c — Parfum des Couleurs
- 3b — Le Vert Mauve

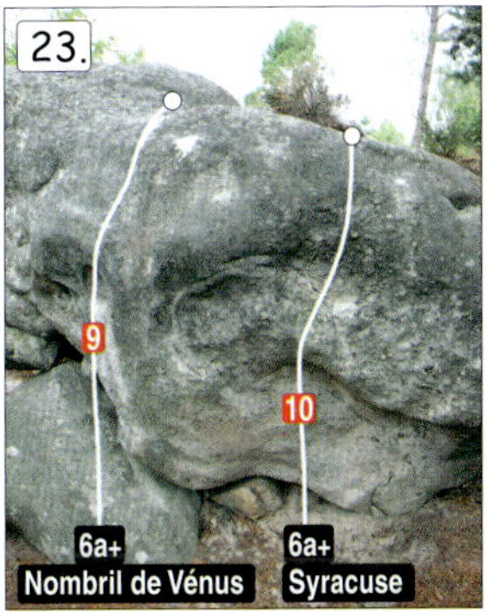

23.
- 9 — 6a+ — Nombril de Vénus
- 10 — 6a+ — Syracuse

26.
- 6 — 6a — Colin-Maillard
- 7 — 7a *6b+ — Le Cerf-Volant
- 5c — Grande Manoeuvre

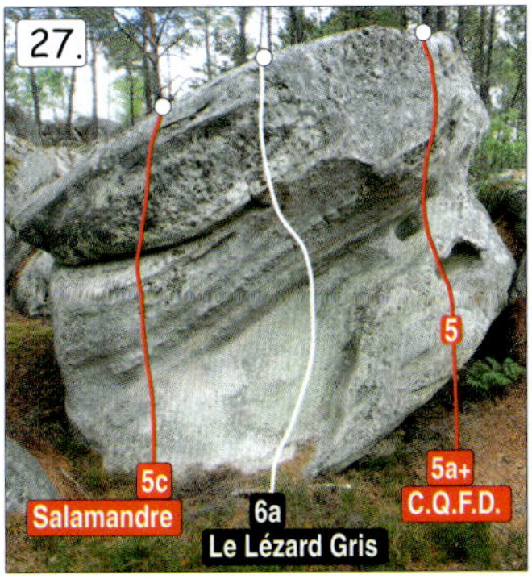

27.
- 5c — Salamandre
- 6a — Le Lézard Gris
- 5 — 5a+ — C.Q.F.D.

29.
- 7a+ — Vue Basse
- 21 — 3b+ — La Naturelle
- 16 — 3c — La Belle Ambiance
- 4m

29. (4m)
- 32 — 5b+ — Regain
- 6b — Coeur Aride
- 31 — 5b — Système F

29.
- 3m — 6a
- 30 — 6a — Soleil Brûlé
- 29 — 6a — Bras de Fer
- 6a (4m)
- 6b — Croix de Fer

31.
- 33 — *5c — Micholeg
- 7c — Starting Bloc

Rocher Fin Parking - page 206

ROCHER FIN

ROCHER FIN

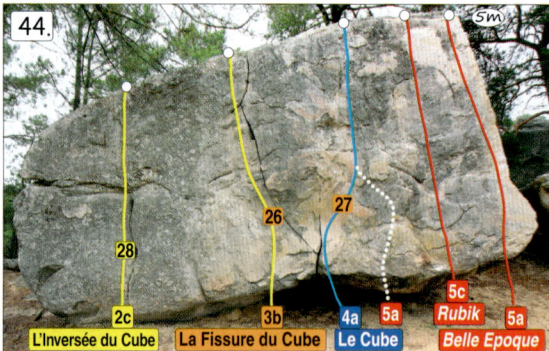

Rocher Fin Parking - page 206

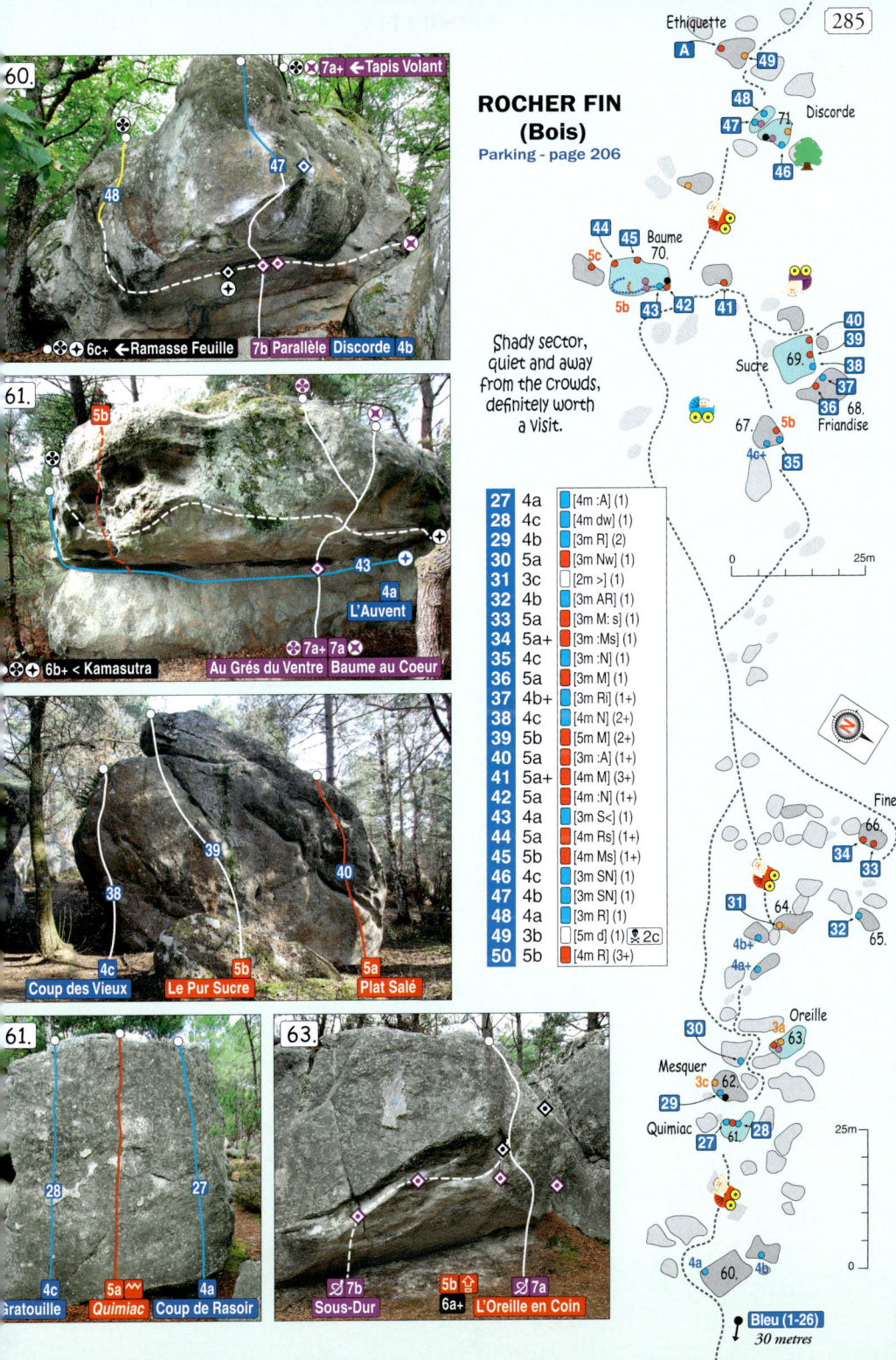

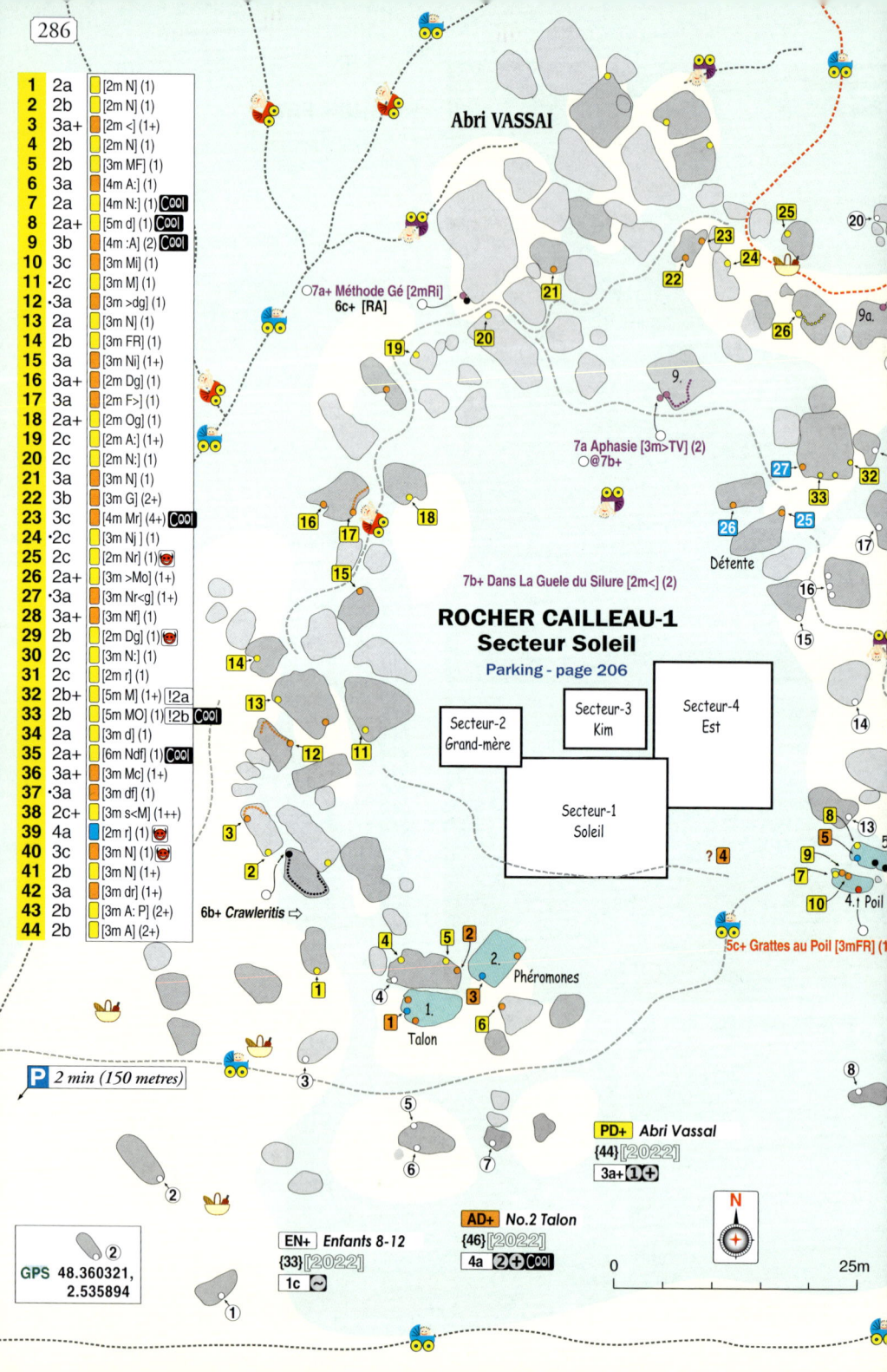

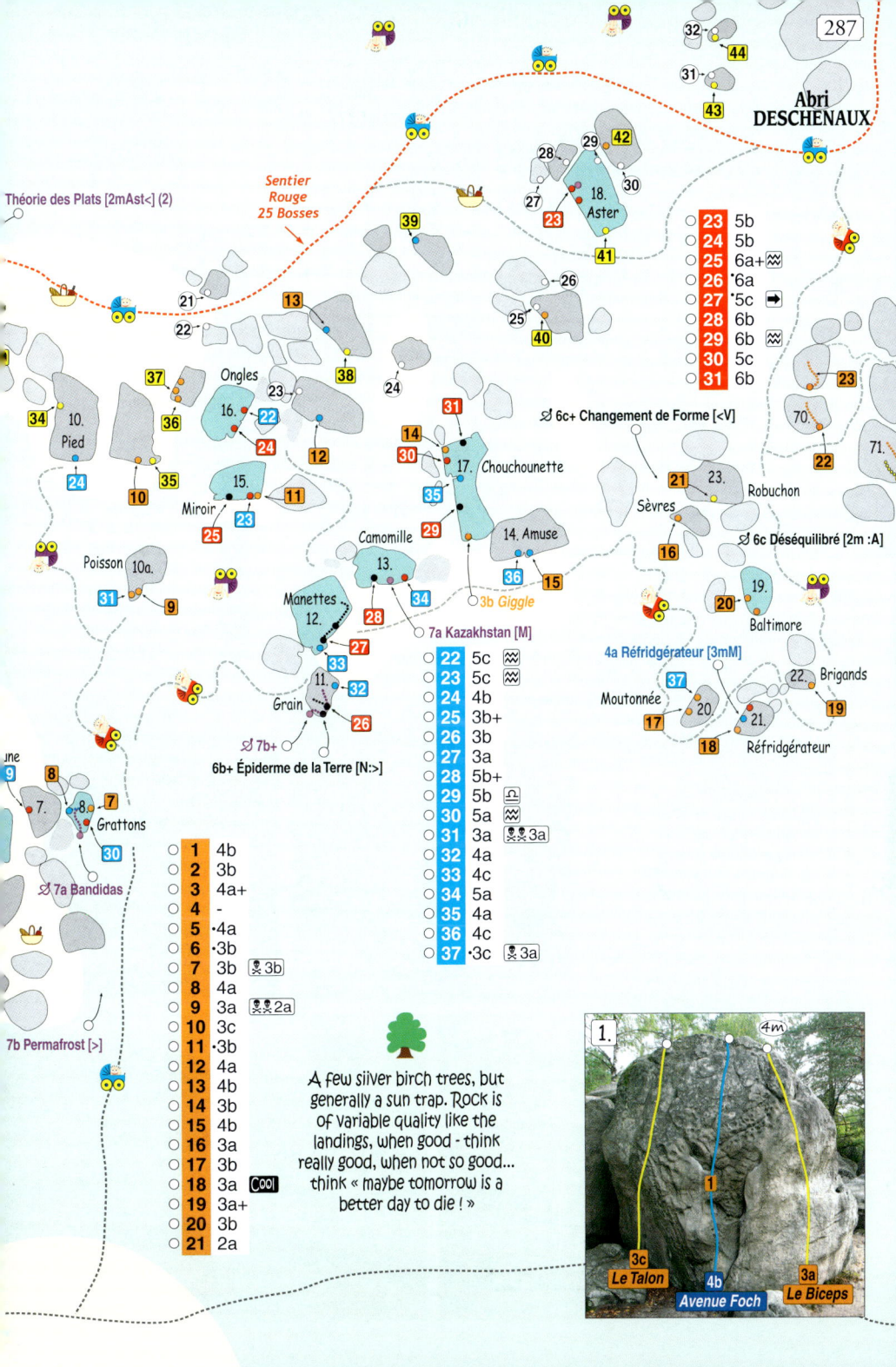

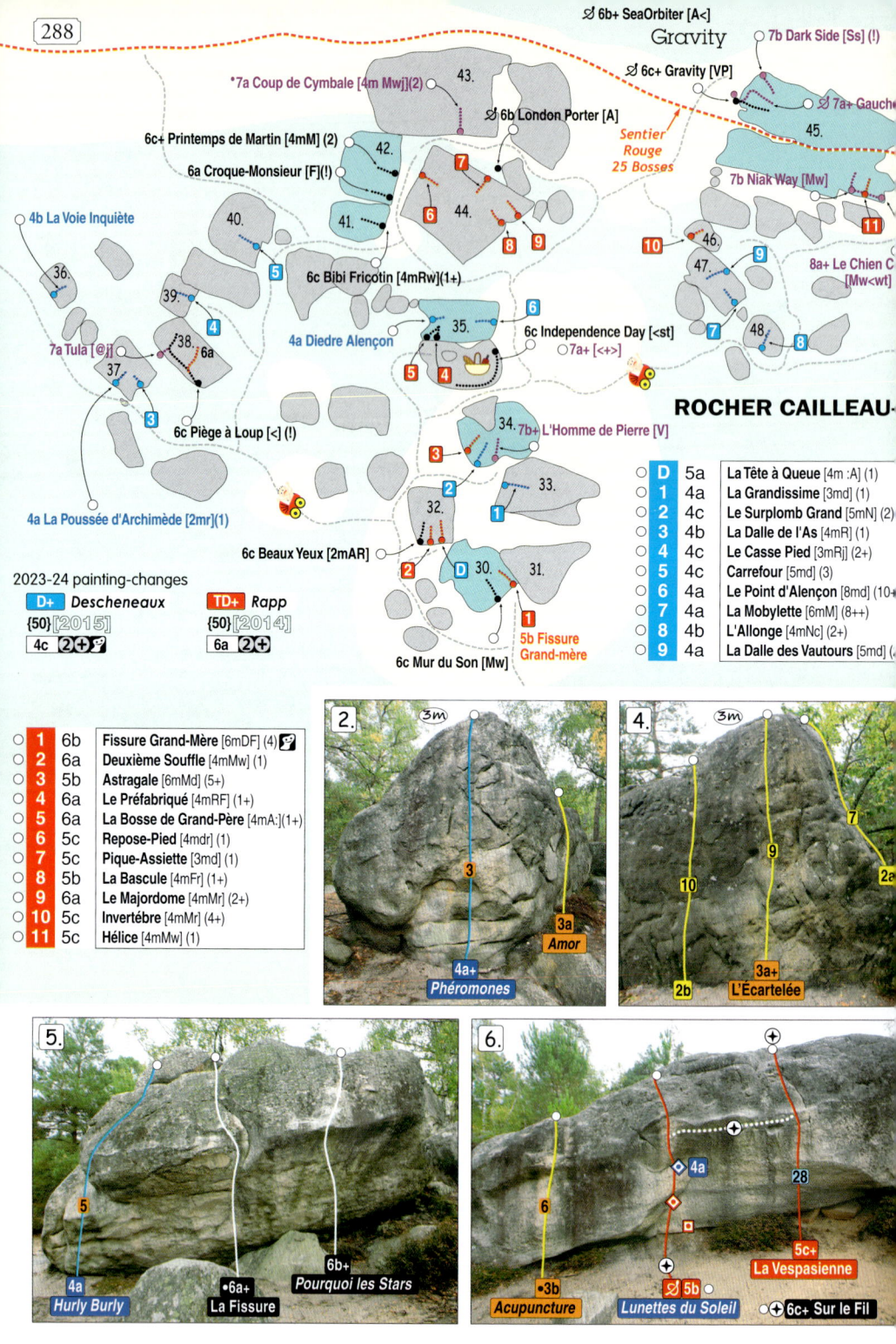

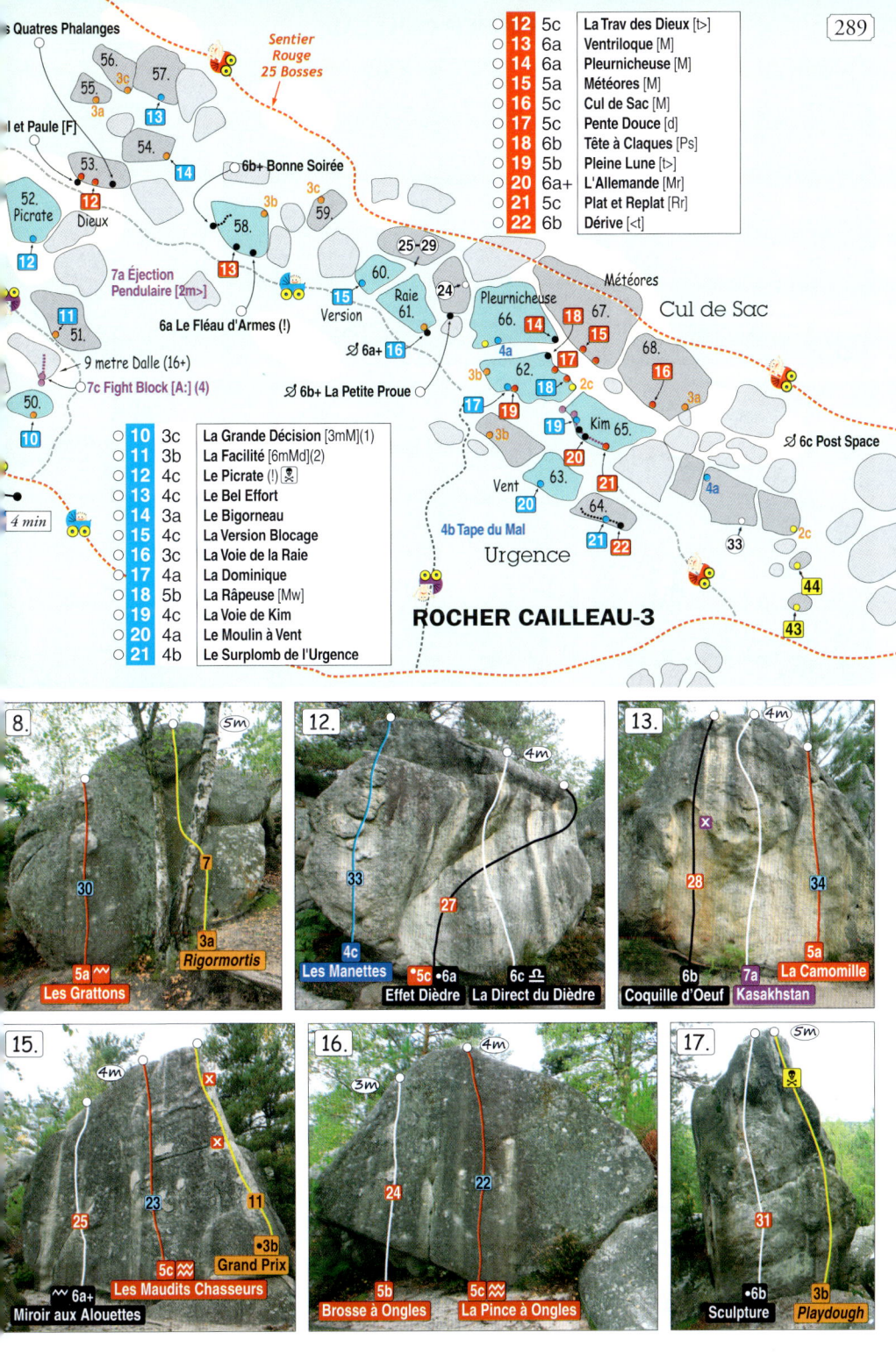

ROCHER CAILLEAU

6c BIBI FRICOTIN, Llinos Cassidy [Bloc 41 - Bibi]

ROCHER CAILLEAU

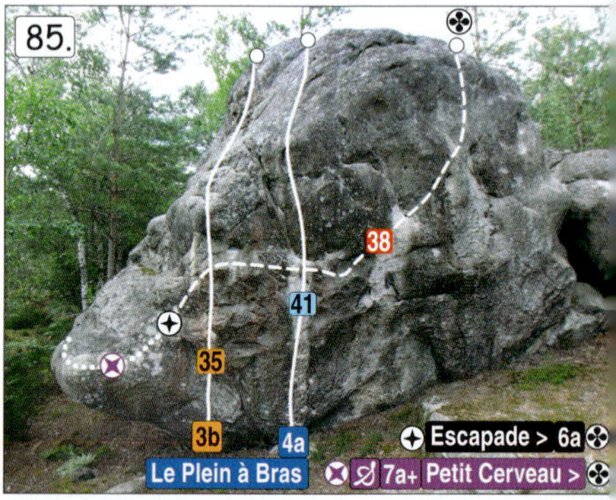

292

61. 16 / 3c / 6a+ — La Voie de la Raie

62. 17 / 4a La Dominique — 19 / 5b Pleine Lune →

63. 20 / 4a — Le Moulin à Vent

65. 7a Kim Assis / 19 / 4c La Voie de Kim / 20 / 6b+ Sur Prise de Taille / 6a+ Allemande

65. 8a L'Inutile Beauté → / 21 / 5a Plat et Replat

66. 21 / 5c — La Pleurnicheuse

67. 15 / 5a — Météores

62. 18 / 5b La Râpeuse / 17 / 5b Pent Douce

85. 38 / 41 / 35 / 3b / 4a Le Plein à Bras / 7a+ Petit Cerveau > / Escapade > 6a

Depart - Circuit No.8 Blanc - Enfants-Kids △   Rocher Cailleau Parking - page 206

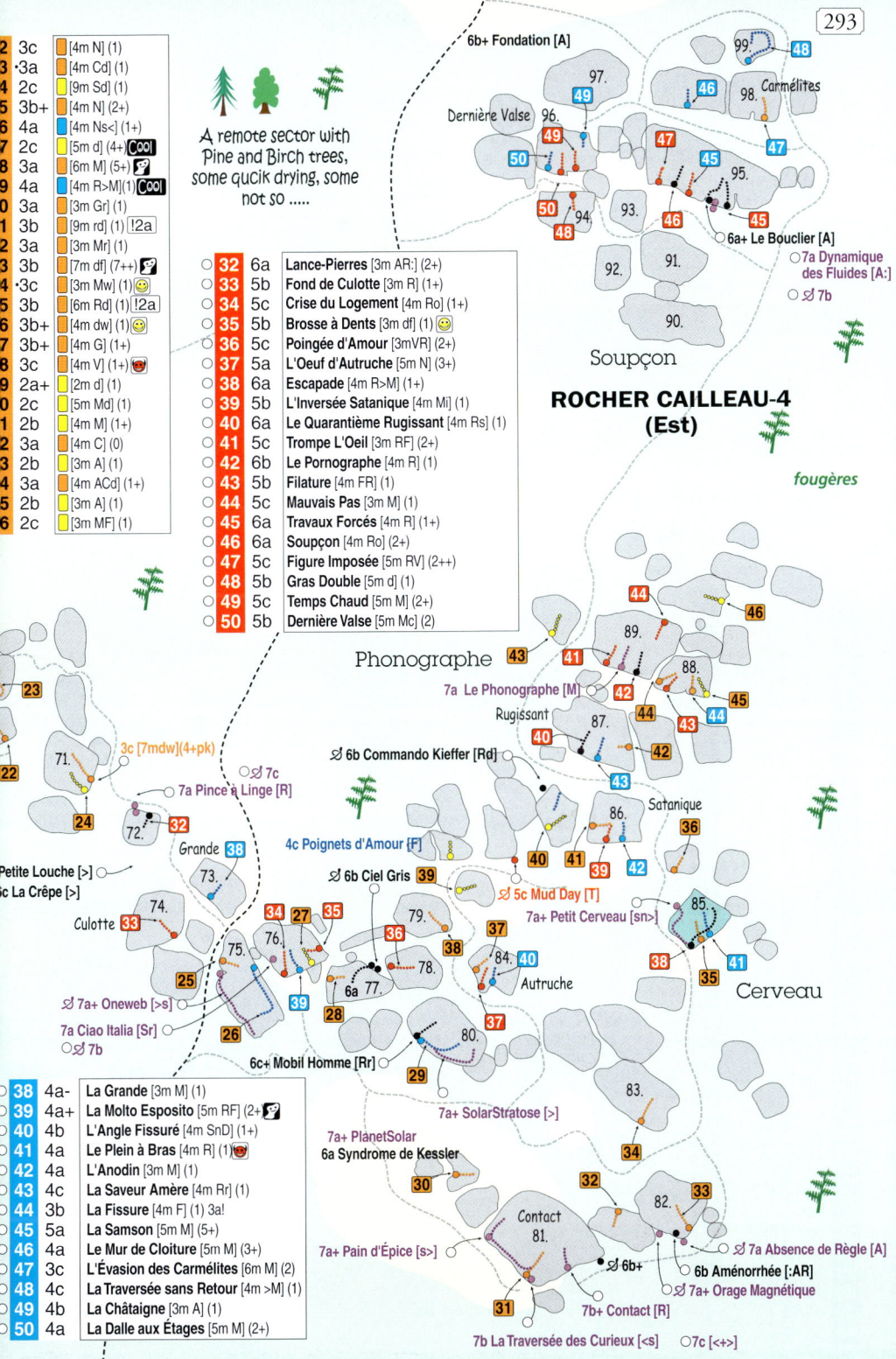

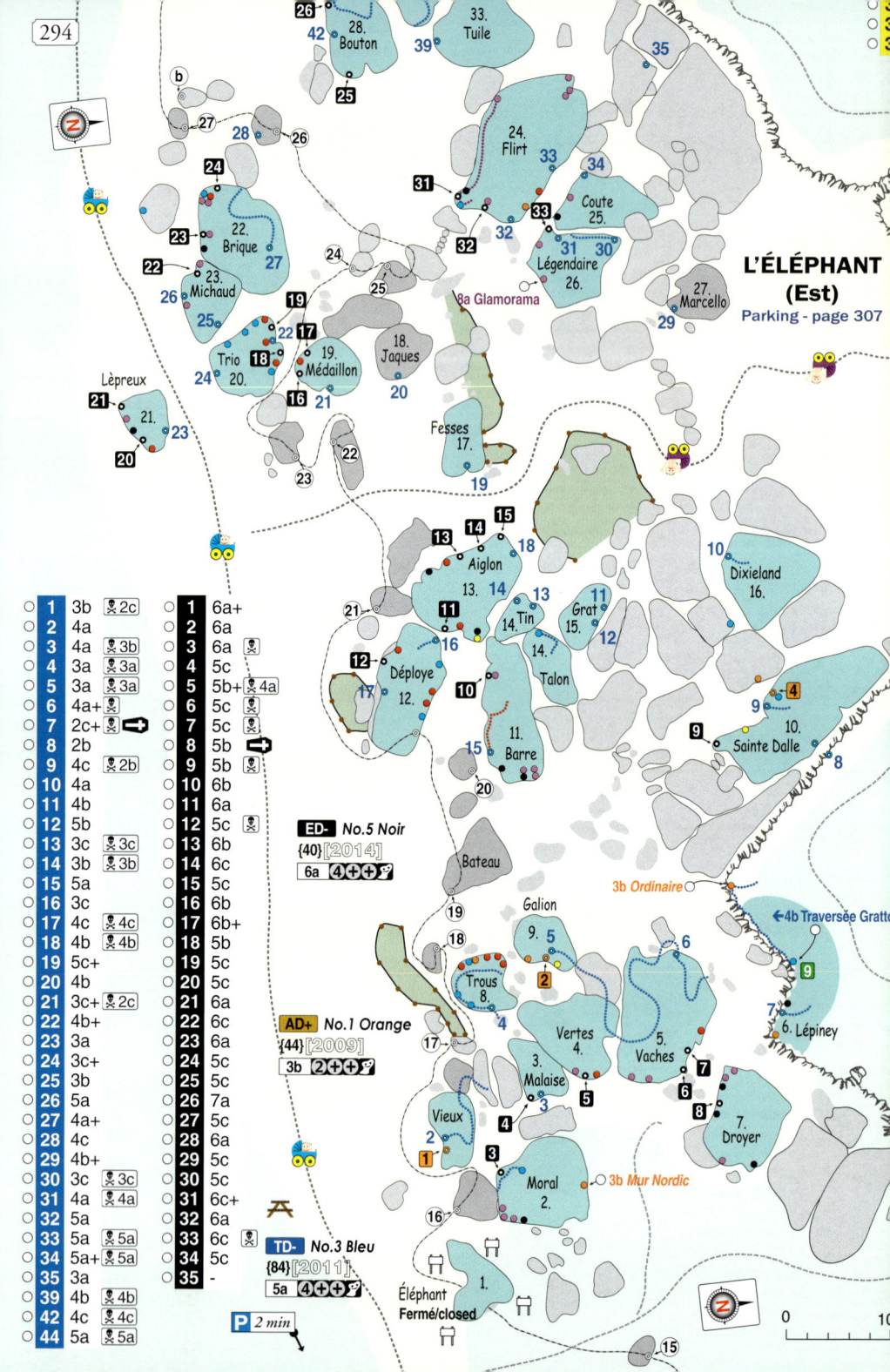

L'ÉLÉPHANT - Est

1. Elephant Bloc Fermé / no climbing - Erosion protection

1. Elephant Bloc Fermé / no climbing - Erosion protection

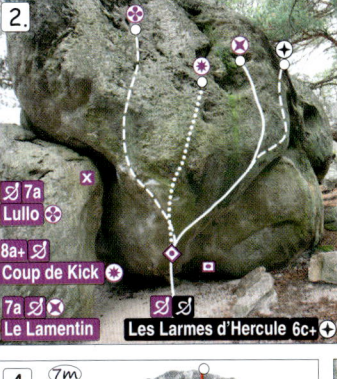
2.
- 7a Lullo
- 8a+ Coup de Kick
- 7a Le Lamentin
- Les Larmes d'Hercule 6c+

2. Descent 4a — La Chute du Moral 6a

3. Malaise 4a · L'Angle du Malaise 5c

4. (7m) Coup de Lune 7c · Fissures Vertes 5b+ · Le Trois Trou 5b

5. Vache Folles 7b+ · Égarement 7c+

5. (5m) Le Dalle Nord du Mimi 5c · Les Inversées 5b

6. (8m) Le Mur Lépiney 2c+ · Arête Sud du Pilier Lépiney 3b

7. Ouverture en Quatuor (8m) · Figure de Proue 7a · 6c Directe · Le Mur de la Mort 5b

7. (6m) Dans Les Bois Éternels 7b · Le Pilier Droyer 6c · 7a

L'ÉLÉPHANT - Est

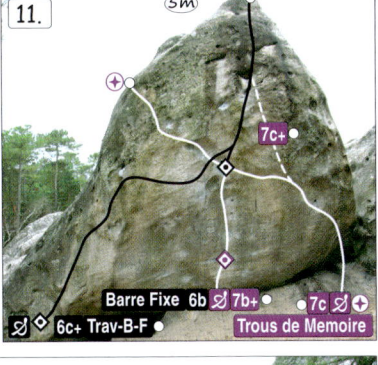

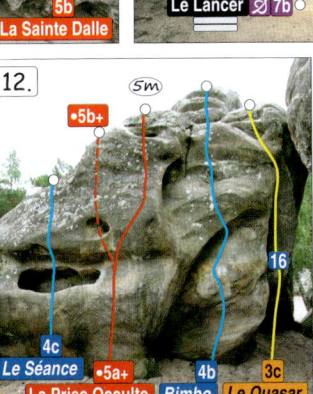
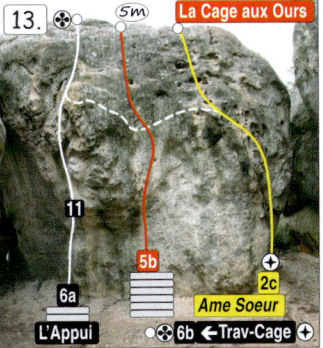

◁ 7a **FIGURE DE PROUE**, Benedikt Stadlbauer [Bloc 7 - Droyer]   Éléphant Parking - page 307

L'ÉLÉPHANT - Est

Aerial plan - page 294

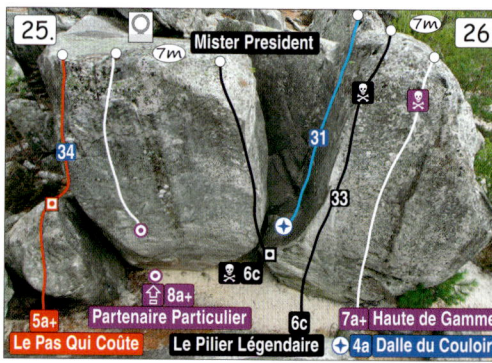

Éléphant Parking - page 307 — 6c LA VOIE MICHAUD, Adrien Echiffre [Bloc 23 - Michaud] ▷

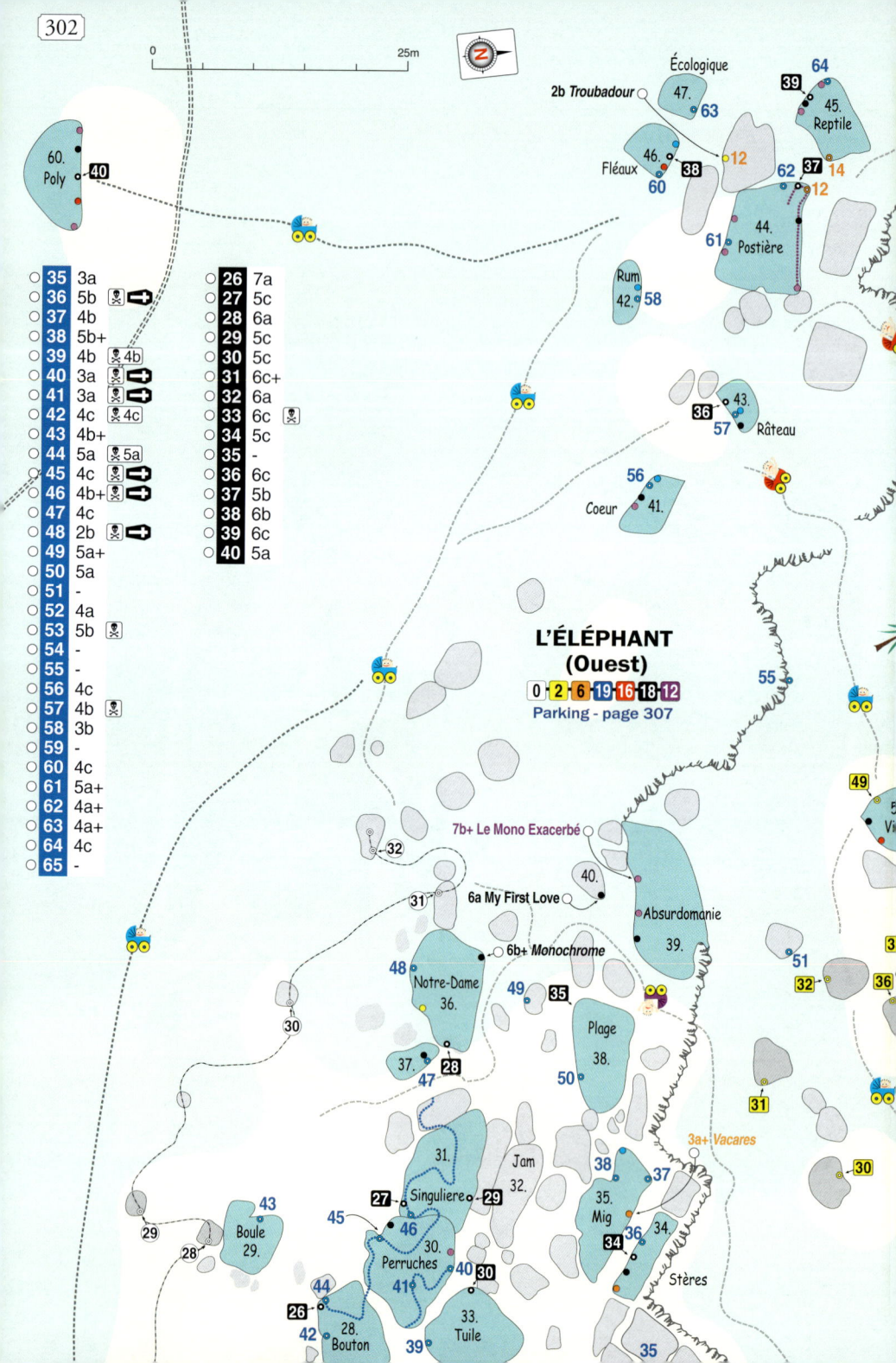

L'ÉLÉPHANT - Est

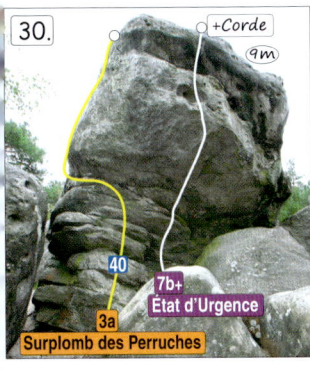

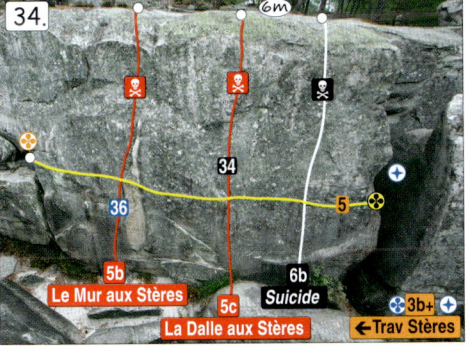

Éléphant Parking - page 307

L'ÉLÉPHANT

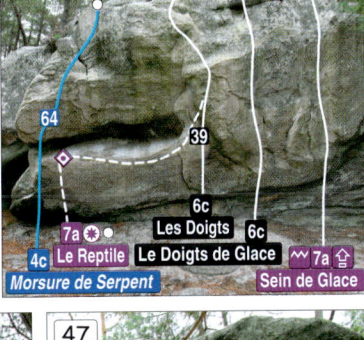

◁ 7a ENVIE d'ANGE, Geoffrey Van Kriekinge [Bloc 44 - Postière]

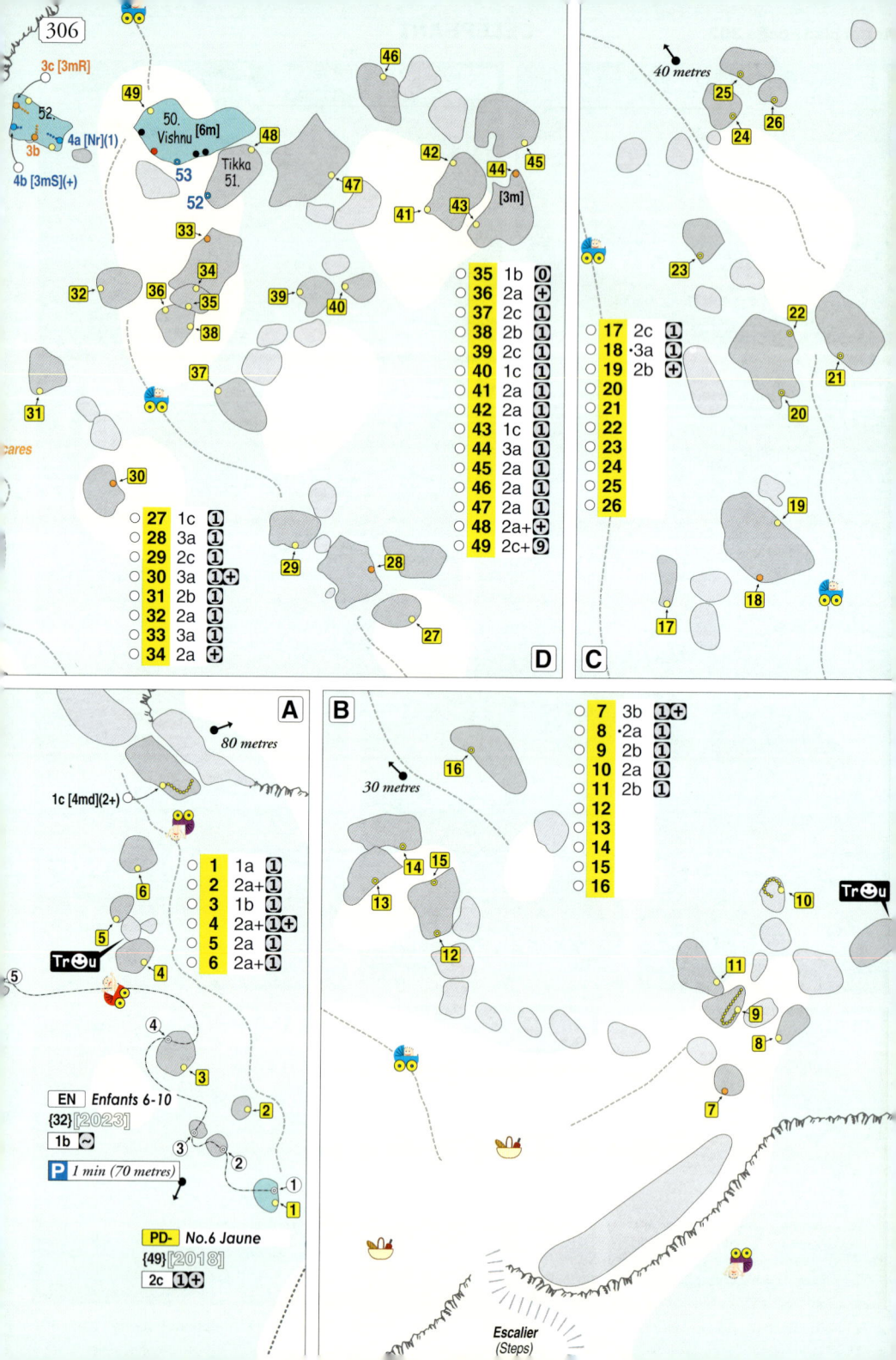

L'ÉLÉPHANT

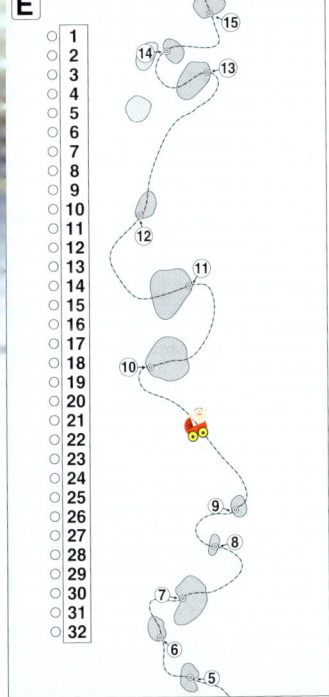

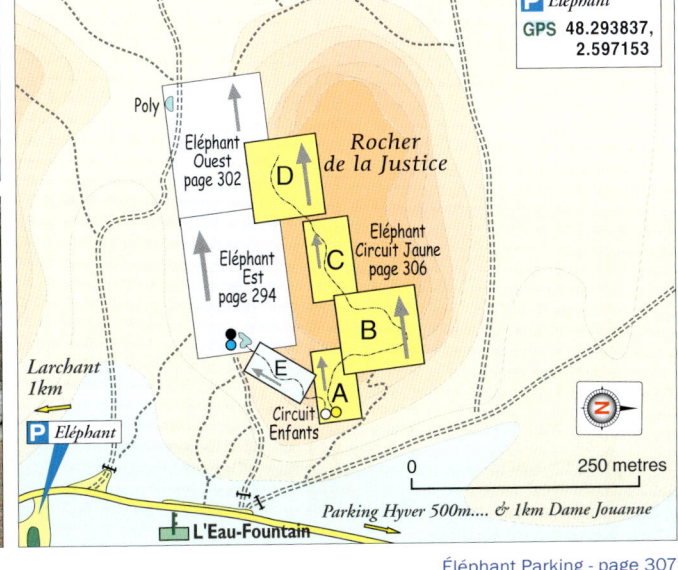

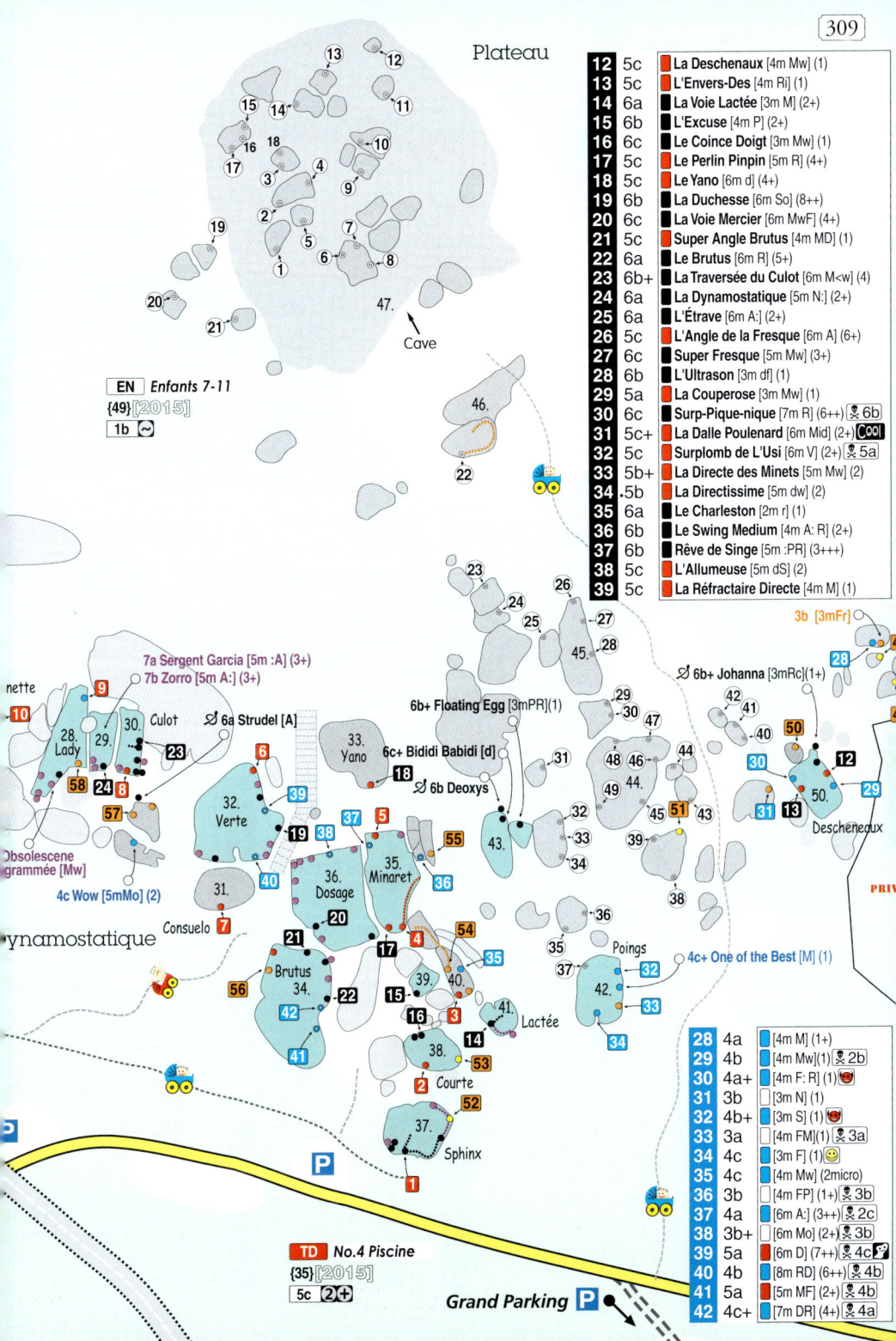

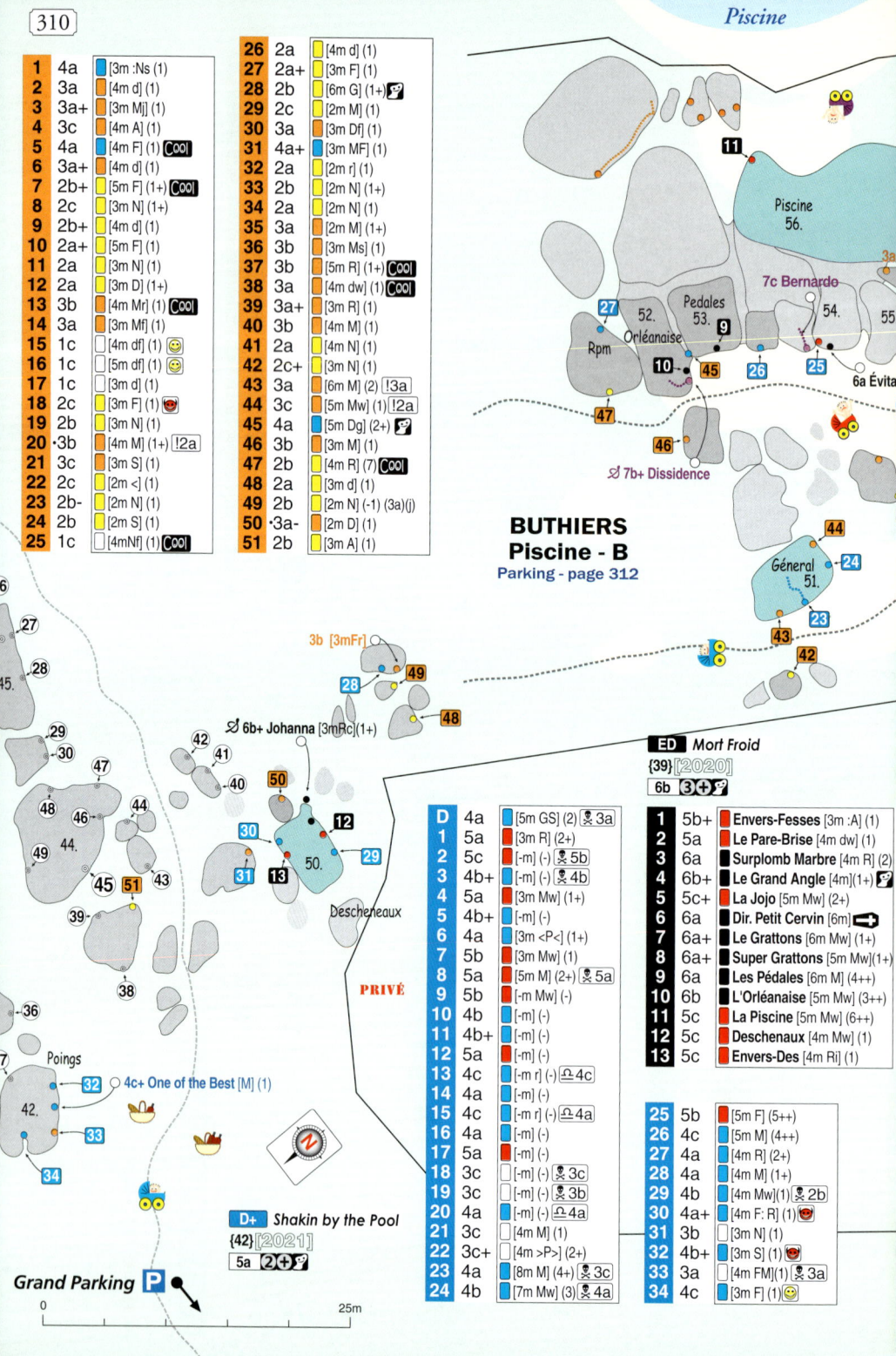

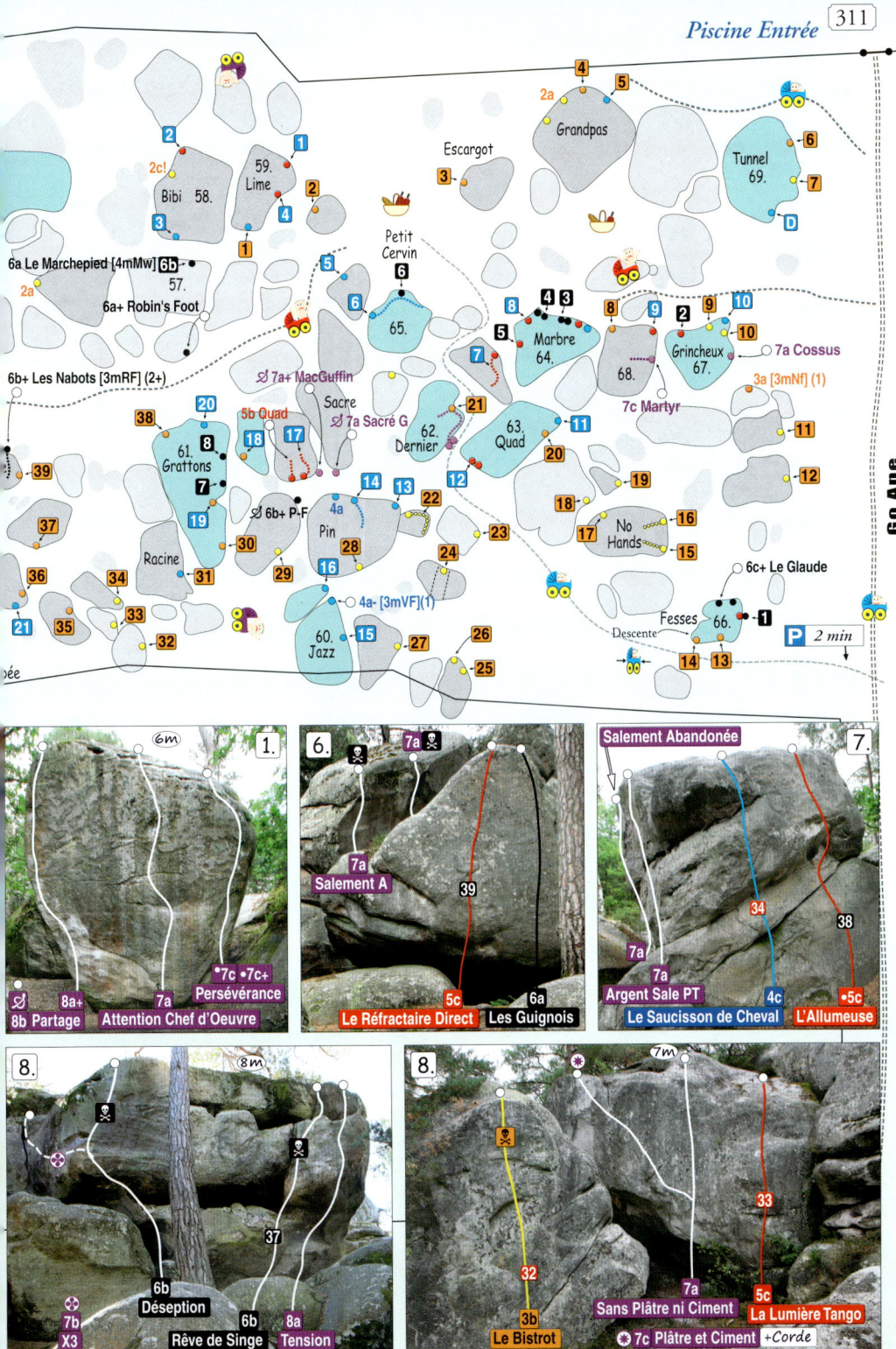

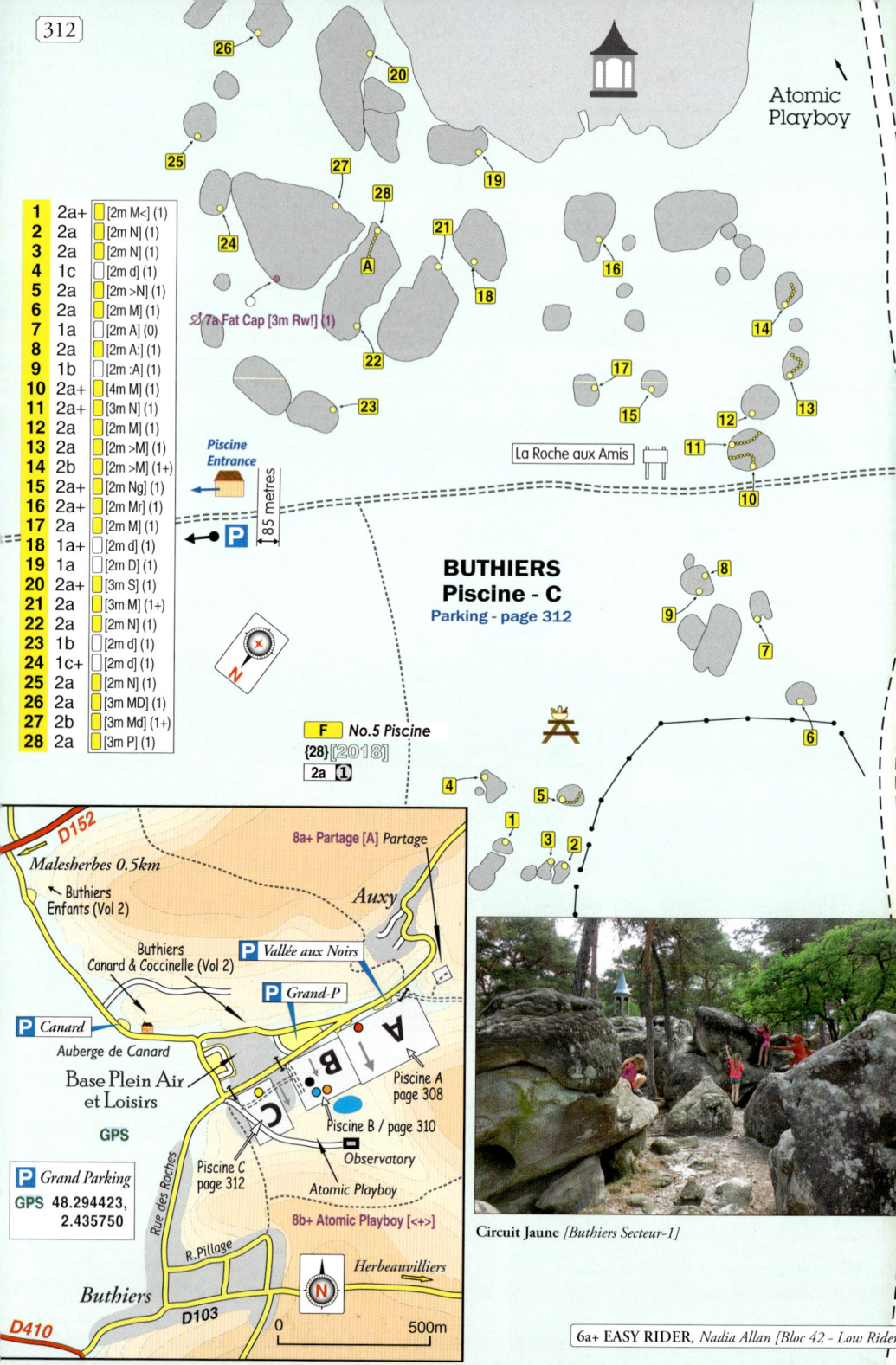

BUTHIERS - Piscine A

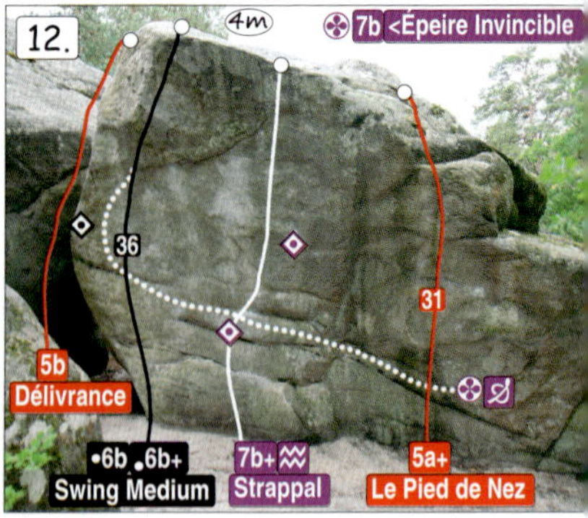

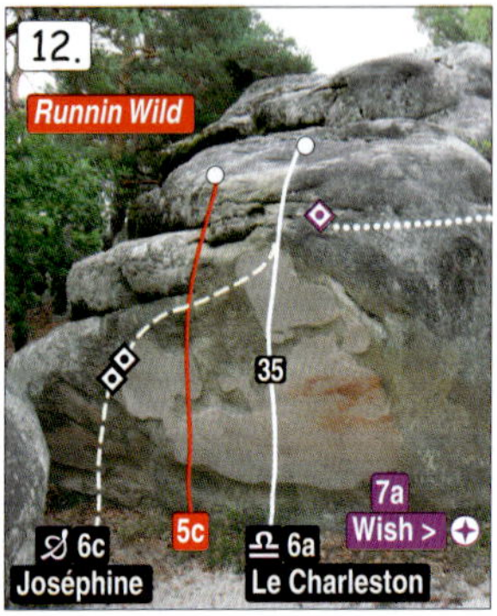

BUTHIERS - Piscine A

Aerial plan - page 308

Buthiers Parking - page 312

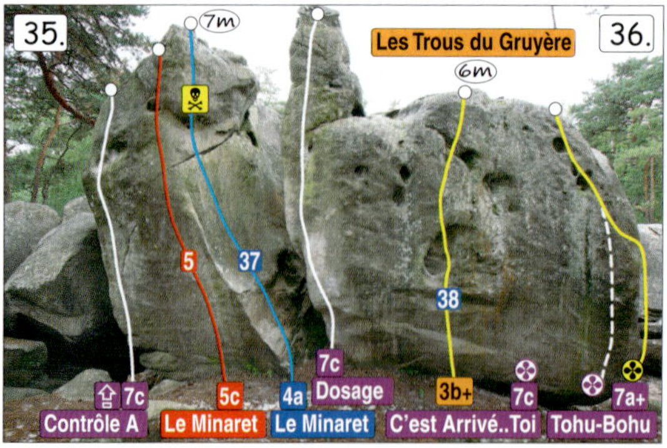

BUTHIERS - Piscine A

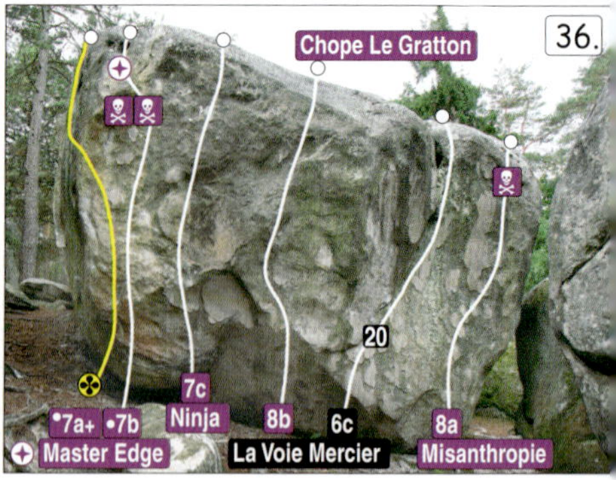

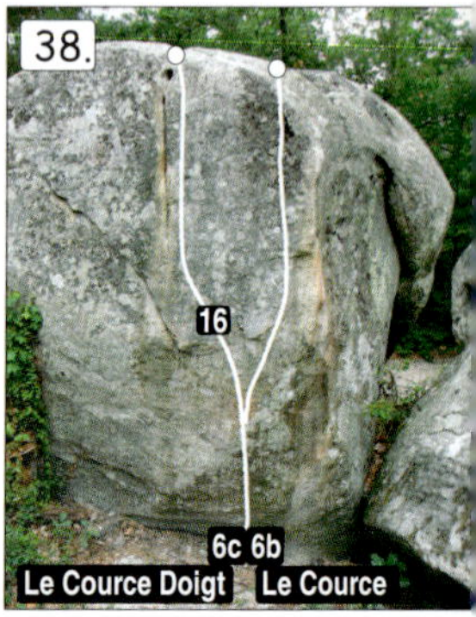

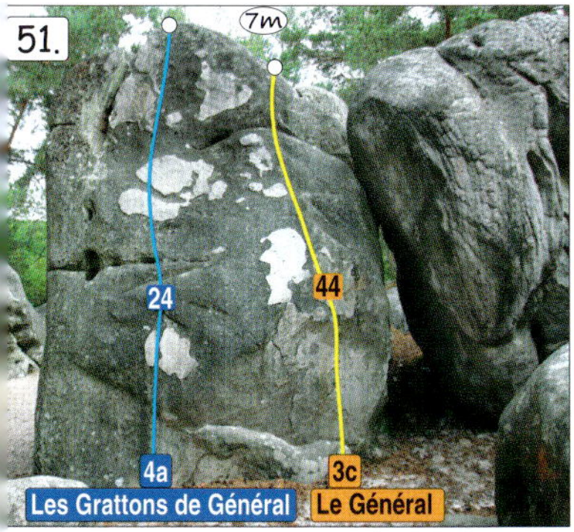

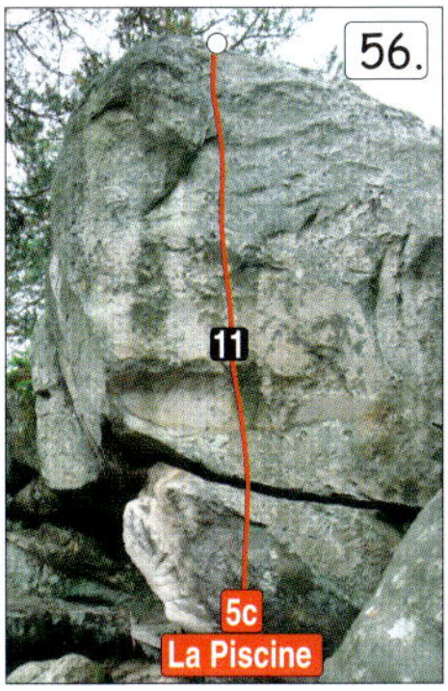

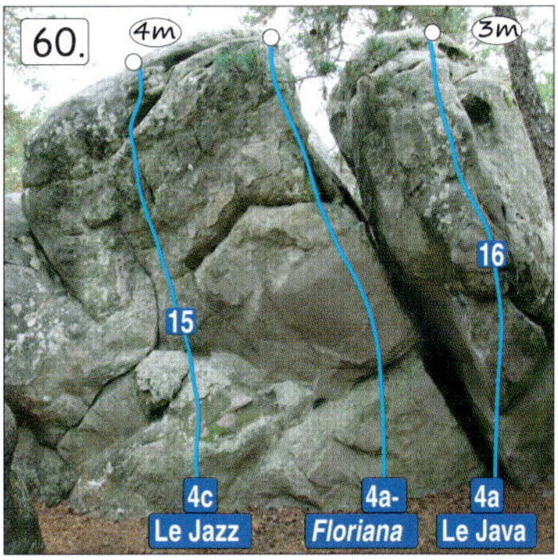

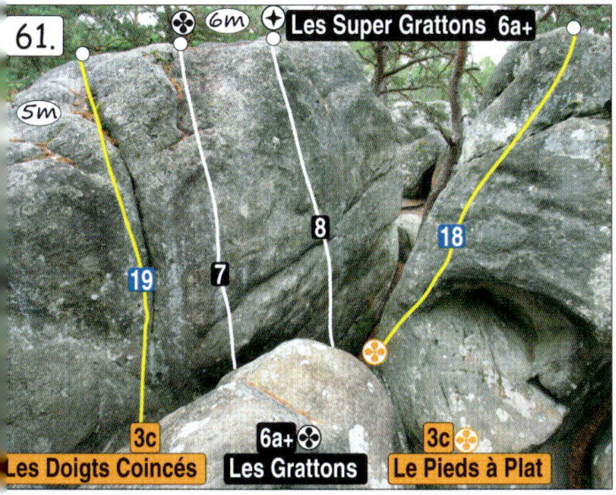

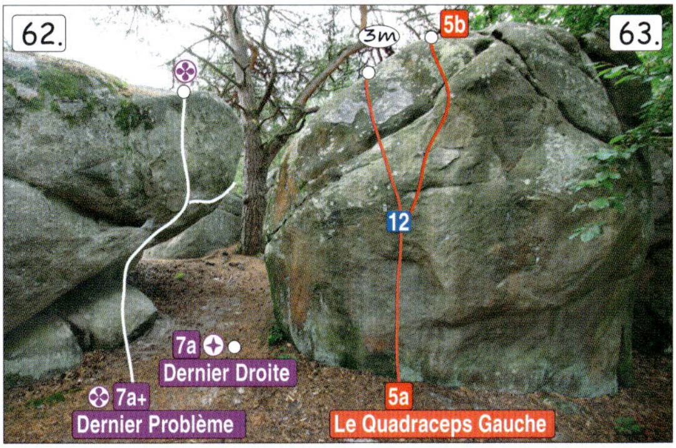

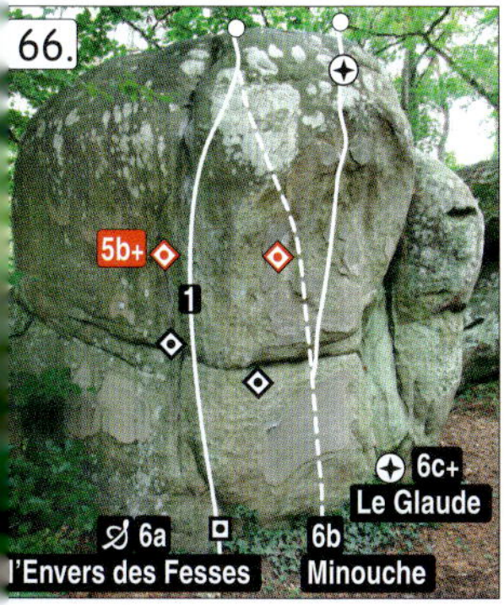

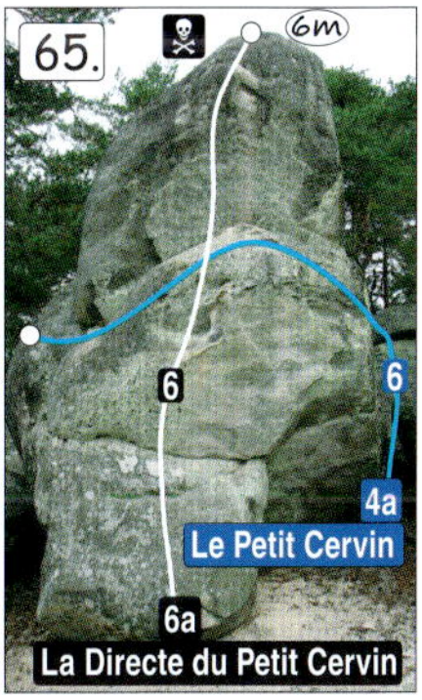

BUTHIERS - Piscine B

INDEX

Abattoir 75
Abbé-Résina 74
Abdolobotomy 140
Absent Friends 305
Absurdomanie 305
Absynthe 213
Acariâtre 260
Achille Talon 233
Acrimonie 258
Adrénaline 108
Aérienne 241
Aérodynamite 68
Aéro Beuark 197
Agliato 155
Aigle Déployé 297
Alta 131
Amanite Dalloide 230
Americain 241
Amertume 257
Amoche Doigt 122
Amoco 17
Anar'Chic 202
Angélique 162
Ange Naïf 222
Angle-Giles-Sabots 228
Angle à Jean-Luc 230
Angle Ben's 134
Angle-Pierre Otée 226
Angle de Marbre 284
Angle Incarné 73
Angle Obtus 86, 177
A-Tortues Jumelles 273
Anglomaniaque 228
Anglophile 83
Anthracite (7a) 27
Anti-gel 141
Appartenance 315
Appui Acide 188
Appui et le Battant 195
Arabesque-Bizons 102
Arabesque (C-Chien) 247
Araignée 51
Arbiste 245
Arbuste Sacré 200
Arc de Cercle 242
Arrache-Moyeu 228
Arrache Coeur 136
Artificier 32
Art de Vivre 280
Ascendance 279
Aster 290
Asterix 268
Astragale 50
Astrolabe 116
Atome Crochu 174
Attrape-Mouche 58
Audacieux 271
Authenac 85
Autoroute du Sud 170
Babaobab 54
Bâbord 196
Baccalaureate 213
Back in the Game 314
Bagdad Café 21
Balafre 17
Balafre Rouge(91.1) 242
Balance 74
Balançoire 240
Baleine-Canche 179
Baleine-Canon 63
Baquet-Cuvier 84
Barre Fixe 297
Bascule 104
Basses Fréquences 96
Basse Tension 164
Bastogne 51

Bateau Ivre 51
Bateau Pilote 48
Batman-Canche 174
Baume au Coeur 285
Bazar 219
Bazooka-Jo 230
Beatle Juice 142
Beauf en Daube 233
Beau Pavé 176
Beginenette 204
Belle Lurette 252
Ben-Hur 241
Bengale 46
Beurre Marga 127
Be Bop Euh Lula 301
Bibi Fricotin 290
Biceps Mou 73
Bicoiffe 203
Bidule 86
Bijou 39
Bisou le Rongeur 241
Bissouflante 138
Bizarre-Cuvier 77
Bizarre Bizarre 155
Bizon Futé 105
Bizuth 86
Black Out (7a) 23
Blatte Runner 25
Bleurb 152
Blocage Mental-Cuis 150
Bloc à Bertrand 222
Boeuf Carrottes 27
Boîte à Lettres 160
Bonzai 29
Boomerang 149
Bornioll 78
Bouboules 211
Bouddha 141
Bouddha Peste 188
Boule de Glace 173
Boule de Nerfs 132
Bourgeoise 260
Bowling 241
Bras de Fer 281
Bras Plat à Bras 142
Bretelles 85
Brevitate Vitae 141
Brosse à Ongles 289
Brutus 315
Butor 93
Buthiers 312
Cadavre Exquis 48
Calcul Mental 116
Câlins de Kim 51
Cappuccino 17
Cappuccino-Cuis 158
Caravane 204
Caresse 128
Carie Dentaire 226
Carlota 299
Carnage 74
Carré d'As 96
Carton Blanc 162
Casa Nova-B-Rond 190
Casse-croûte 123
Casse Dalle-Isatis 134
Catacombes 241
Cave Nicolas 104
Cendrier 160
Cerf-Volant 203, 281
Cervin-Canon 59
Chaînon Manquant 15
Chaires Mobiles 29
Chair de Poule 154
Chalumeuse 83
Chapeau Chinois 228

Charcuterie 73
Charleston 314
Charleston-Canon 63
Charleuse (Elep) 301
Charlie Brown 209
Charmer-Serpent 197
Chasseur de Prises 63
Chatterley 84
Chevalier Errant 280
Cheval à Bascule 245
Cheval d'Arçon 48
Cheval de Troie 222
Chicorée 85
Chien-Apremont 117
Chien Fou-R Fln 282
Chimpanzée 84
Chocolate 87
Chope le Gratton 316
Chop Suey 305
Chouchounette 290
Chouchou Chéri 179
Choucroute Garnie 123
Chute du Moral 295
Cinzano 85
Citation du Jour 213
Clair de Lune 111
Claquettes 217
Clavicule 80
Clé-Cuvier 80
Clin d'Oeil 110
Clotilde 315
Cocaine (95.2) 222
Coeur 305
Coeur Aride 281
Coeur Croisé 307
Colin-Maillard 281
Colombine 258
Comète 150
Compagne 260
Compos-Forces 124
Compressman 61
Conque-Canche 176
Consolation-Chats 203
Cons-Amoureux 197
Contorsion-Potala 268
Contortion 105
Contrôle Technique 16
Copains d'Abord 57
Coquetterie 250
Coquille d'Oeuf 289
Coq Gauche 70
Cordier, Mur-Cuis 158
Corps a Corps 194
Cortomaltèse 77
Coule Douce 250
Coupelle 88
Coup de Feel 84
Coup de Fou 248
Coup de Genoux 232
Coup de Kick 295
Coup de Lune 295
Coup de Rouge 130
Courage (95.2) 216
Courage Fuyons 78
Courtisane 257
Crabe Volant 203
Crackle 213
Crampes 84
Crawl 19
Crème Fraiche 203,
Crevette 66
Crime Passionnel 159
Crimp Like Fuck 268
Crise de la Dette 266
Croates 284
Crochet-Potala 271

Crocodile (bloc 9a) 120
Croisé Magique 172
Croix de Fer-R Fln 281
Croque-mort 90
Croque Monsieur 105
Culot 315
Cure-Dents 242
Cyclope-Chats 203
Cyclope-St.G 37
Dallain 202
Dalle à Poly 307
Dalle de Cristal 232
Dalle Teflon 276
Dangler-Cuis 145
Danse Macabre (7a) 17
Dark Side 290
Débonnaire 170
Dérape Sec 170
Déchirure 136
Défenestration 284
Déferlante 162
Défi Suppliment.. 245
Défroquée 77
Déli-Carte 150
Délit de Fuite 156
Délivrance-Canon 58
Deltoïde 273
Dénoyautée 58
Dépravation 159
Dérapage 176
Dernière Probleme 317
Dernière Tentation 267
Destin d'une Pulsion 307
Dévergondée 128
Deverminage 215
Déviation 226
Dévissante 90
Dexoys 316
Diéséliste 19
Dinomania 282
Discréte 128
Divine 149
Divine Déchéance 124
Doigts - Cuvier 66
Doigts de l'Homme 174
Doigt dans L'Oeil 282
Dominat-Intellectuelle 111
Dosage-Buthiers 316
Douche Froid 124
Douche Froide 188
Drôlesse 257
Dromadaire-Canon 57
Dru Direct 137
Duchesse 315
Duègne 257
Dulcinée 257
Dune-Isatis 136
Durandal 117
Duroxmanie 96
Dynamostatique 315
Dynosaure 276
Easy Rider 314
Ébène 17
Échec et Mat 51
Échine-Cuis 165
Éclipse-Cuis 156
Éclipse-Potala 267
Éclipse (C-Chien) 247
Ectoplasme-Cuvier 80
Ectoplasme (95.2) 212
Edam 219
Effet Dièdre 289
Égarement 295
Egoiste 114
Égomoije 179
ÉLÉPHANT 294

Éloge (7a) 21
Élucubration 233
Emprise 111
Enchaîné 242
Enclume 266
Enfants d'Abord 188
Enfer des Nains 178
Engagement 240
Ensorcelée 241
Entorse 152
Entorse (91.1) 242
Envie des Betes 126
Envie d'Ange 305
Envol du Martinet 282
Epée de Sable 23
Équilibriste-Canche 180
Été Indien 268
Étrave-Buthiers 315
Étrave Étrange 269
Eugster Jovial 155
Explos- Bonheur 136
Excalibur-Cuis 142
Fanfou 202
Fantôme 80
Fauchée 79
Faucon 219
Fausse Danse 220
Faux Baquet 132
Fay (95.2) 223
Femme Infidèle 152
Ferrite 267
Festin de Pierre 94
Figure de Proue 295
Filles-Trav 19
Fil à Tordre 117, 156
Final (Elep) 299
Fissures Vertes 295
Fissure du Marbre 273
Fissure USA 164
Fizzy Fingers 204
Fléaux 305
Fleur de Rhum 117
Flexible Friend 219
Flicxion 273
Flipper (91.1) 244
Flippeur-Sabots 226
Flip Flop 244
Floating Egg 316
Fokker 222
Folie des Rondeurs 197
Folle 83
Footrix-Cuis 165
Footrix Le Retour 137
Forge 83
Fosse aux Ours 220
Fosse Septique 59
Fossoyeur 16
Fourchette 116
Fou du Roi 155
Frein de Parking 257
Frelons-Sabots 232
French Cancan-Canon 58
Fresque-Buthiers 315
Frites 71
Fritz Angle 188
Froggy Dick 140
Full Metal Jacket 61
Furyax 107
Fuséologie 273
Garétatov 260
Gâteau Royale 241
Gazomètre 70
Genouillère 70
Ghost Train 159
Gigabyte 267
Gigi 202

Ginseng 217
Glasnost 192
Glop-Cuis 149
Glycolyse-Canche 174
Gnossienne 124
Golgotha 57
Golgotogratte 203
Gouge-Guichot 261
Goulette (91.1) 242
Goulotte à Dom 170
Goulotte sans 66
Grand Chauve 192
Grand Dièdre 242
Grange 240
Gras Double 282
Gratiche-Cuisse 201
Gratinée 132
Gratitude 244
Gratonnade 130
Gratton-Chronique 130
Grattons Invisible 219
Graviton 233
Gravity 290
Greta Garbo 219
Grève des Nains 204
Gros Bras 301
Gros Cerveau 126
Gros Ventre 254
Gruyère 307
Guêpe Ride 134
Guerre et Paix 282
Gueulard 208
Gugusse 71
Guichot Business 261
Guingos 19
Guirlande-Revolver 164
Gumbolt the Villan 240
Gymnopédie-Isatis 124
Gym Tonic 205
G Force 248
Hale Acab 192
Haltérophilie 220
Hammer's Break 252
Happy Boulder 111
Hareng Saur 149
Harry Potter 215
Hatari 174
Haut-Cal-B-Rond 194
Haute de Gamme 301
Haute Pression 124
Haute Tension 162
Hebegibies 158
Heister's Dive 179
Hélicoptère 74
Hercule 117
Héros-Bois Rond 194
Hésitation-Canche 177
Hipposarse 164
Hirondelle 222
Holey Moley 73
Homo Cavernicus 39
Houches 223
Hueco 116
Hueco-Potala 273
Humbles 245
Hyde 202
Hymne à Mort 45
Hyperplomb 116
Hypothèse 73
Icarus 128
Iceberg 140
Idées Noires 254
Impasse du Hasard 152
Impulsion 152
Indestructible 217
Indigestion 74

INDEX

fusion du Soir 170
gratitude 244
nominata 50
nominata-Cuvier 86
acadi-Canche 178
alousie 269
érémiades 110
été d'Or 242
été Michaud (95.2) 222
et Set 229
eu de Quilles 250
eux de Toit 228
eu de Dalle 219
u Jitsu 110
)'Special 162
oker 86
ouiss- Massetar 150
our de Gloire 246
) Dalton 190
our de Rêve 258
us d'Orange 233
us-Citron (C-Chien) 246
amikaze 279
angaroo City 134
ansas City 219
arma-Cuis 155
arma-Little-Isatis 126
ilo de Beurre 80
ilo de Beurre (95.2) 222
im Assis 292
rakatoa 284
rill 244
acrima 32
ady Big Claque 315
amentations-Isatis 124
angouste Royale 66
angoustine 195
armes d'Hercule 295
eininger 85
épiney 295
épreux 301
évitation 7
ézard - Chats 200
hassa 271
ibre Service 250
ili 66
ime à Ongles 226
ittle Miss Cheeky 204
ong Fleuve Tranquille 188
une 117
une de Fiel (7a) 50
Macadam 54
Mâchoire 132, 276
Mach 3 152
Madiene 301
Magic Bûche 315
Magifix 48
Magneton 200
Magnifique 165
Mambo Italiano 217
Manyata 257
Marbre-Buthiers 317
Marbrée-Isatis 128
Marbre Brisée-Isatis 140
Marchand de Venise 220
Marche à Pied 230
Marco 85
Mardi Gras 179
Mare Droite 58
Marginal 111
Marie Rose 86
Marquis de Sade 59
Marteau Fou 290
Maschine 45
Master Edge 316
Mastodompté 192

Mathilde 25
Mathusalem 158
Matière et Mémoire 280
Matière Grisée 151
Maudite Arête 202
Maudits Chasseurs 289
Maudit Manège 165
Mauvaise Pioche 250
Mauvais Temps 267
Maxx (C-Chien) 247
Médaille en Chocolat 116
Médaillon (95.2) 223
Megawatt 130
Meglomanique 177
Mémel 138
Mémoire-Tombe 280
Mémorium 170
Ménage à Trois 78
Mendoza 223
Menhir 282
Merci les Gags 156
Mer de la Tranquillité 188
Metatarsal 220
Mexican Hat 202
Michel Ange 96
Michetonneuse 260
Michodière 117
Micholeg 281
Midinette 261
Minos 314
Minotaure 282
Mirador 267
Miroir-Potala 269
Miroir-Alouettes 289
Misanthropie 316
Miséricorde 154
Mise à Pied 124
Mise en Suif 172
Mister Dynamite 155
Mister Proper 219
Molaire-Cuis 161
Môme 261
Monde Perdu 276
Mongolito 316
Moondance 142
Moonshadow 267
Moriturí 48
Morphoillogique 173
Morphotype 50
Mots Croisés 172
Motus Vivendi 110
Mouche-Beauvais 25
Moule, La 126
Moulin à Vent 123
Moulin Rouge 266
Mouton à 5 Pattes 152
Mouton Noir 21
Multichops 201
Mummery 93
Murmure 80
Mur-Michaud-Sabots 229
Mur à Robert 229
Musique de Dance 219
Myosotis 162
Nano (C-Chien) 246
Nationale 88
Navigation 250
Navuku 316
Neige d'Automne 200
Nescafé 85
Nez-Canche 177
Nezzo-Isatis 141
Nezzundorma 132
Nicablocaglory 232
Ninja 312

Noix de Coco 269
Noix de Pécan 244
Nombril de Vénus 281
Nonameyet 282
Nostromo 114
Nouvelle Vague 247
Obli-Yettes 197
Oblique 230
Oeil de Çiva 45
Opéra Tchétchène 202
Orca 63
Orgueilleuse 267
Outlandos d'Amour 212
Ovomaltine 70
P'tite Mousse 216
P'tit Toit 217
Page en Braille 86
Paillon Directe 88
Pain Total 230
Parafine 180
Parapluie 177
Paris Texas 222
Partage 315
Partenaire Particulier 301
Passage à Tabac 250
Pensées Cachées 158
Pente Douce 266
Père Lachaise 156
Perlinpinpin 316
Pernod 213
Petits Pieds-Potala 273
Petits Plats-Canche 176
Petit Cervin 311
Petit Chauve Sourit 162
Petit Plats-Sabots 229
Piano à Queue 114
Picrate 290
Pieds Nickelés 242
Pied à Coulisse 104
Pied à Coulisse-Isatis 134
Pierre Bénite 135
Pierre Douce 252
Pierre Ponce 253, 269
Pierre Précieuse 212
Pif Paf 80
Pilier Droyer 295
Pilier Légendaire 138, 301
Pince-monseigneur 130
Pince-Oreille 227, 254
Pince-oreille 127
Pince à Ongles 289
Pince Genou 130
Piscine-Buthiers 317
Pitt Bull 155
Plastikman 141
Plâtre et Ciment 311
Plats de Saison 202
Plats Tonitrus 68
Plein Pot 284
Pleurnicheuse 292
Pofinage 96
Pogne 68
Poincenot 222
Poinçonneur- Lilas 68
Poing 32
Poire 128
Pokemon 200
Poly (Elep) 307
Ponction Lombaire 195
Popeye 284
Porte du Temps 266
Portugaises 162
Postière 305
Pot de Fer 51
Poussah 136
Poussée Occulte 196

Poussière Qui Tue 272
Poussif 136
Power-Lolotte 124
Précieuse 261
Présom-Innocence 201
Presse-Citron (Canon) 63
Presse Citron (Chien) 246
Presse Purée 223
Prestat 88
Prise de Bec 126
Prise de Becquet 195
Proue de la Passion 161
Psyssure 93
Pubis Infernal 219
Puce-Canche 178
Puck 273
Puzzle-Cuis 164
Quatre Cents Buts 299
Quille 194
Radio Crochet 177
Rage-Dent (C-Chien) 248
Ramasse Feuille 285
Rampe 314
Rampe Infinie 135
Rapido 285
Rataplat 124
Râteau 305
Rattle Snake 276
Ravensbruck 68
Razoirbaque 269
Razorback-Bois Rond 196
Reblochon 219
Récupéractive 174
Red One 226
Regain 281
Réta Authenac 71
Réta du Gibbon 276
Retour aux Sources 211
Rétrofriction 152
Réveil-matin 74
Réveille Matin-Chats 200
Rêve de Chevaux 177
Rêve de Toit-Canche 179
Rhomboïde 164
Rhume Folle 83
Ric Rac 202
Rideau de Pluie 240
Rien ne Presse 179
Rigolade 124
Ritz 212
Rodez 223
Rognure d'Ongles 122
Rombière 260
Roquefort 200
Rotule 204
Rouleau-Chats 203
Rouleau Californien 269
Roxane 94
Rubis Sur l'Ongle 203
Rudeboy 210
Rumsteak en Folie 230
Sable Émouvant-Cuis 154
Sablier-Potala 269
Sablier (95.2) 215
Sainte Dalle 297
Salade 71
Salamandre 116
Sale Gosse 233
Sale Gueule-R Fln 280
Samarkand 267
Samouraï 84
Sanglier-Chats 200
Sangria 152
Sanguine 45
Sang Lisse 77

Sarkopabo 102
Saucisson Beurre 102
Saute-Montagne 232
Saut de Puce 132
Sauteuse Trav - 102
Sa Pelle au Logis 202
Scampi Fritti 71
Scarface 96
Science Friction 117
Scream (Chien) 152
Secouer la Tête 217
Selle-Chats 204
Sensation 192
Serbes 284
Séries Cultes 225
Service Compris 229
Siamoise 79
Siesta des Biceps 242
Siliceuse 137
Silver lago 190
Sisyphe-Cuis 149
Sitstart is Best 196
Smash 233
Snoopy 209
Soleil Brûlé 281
Soleil Couchant 280
Sonnet Posthumes 46
Sortie de Secours 124
SOS Glycogène 48
Soubrette 258
Soufflet 83
Soupe au Lait 132
Soupir 117
Sous-Plomb 244
Sphincters Toniques 230
Sphinx 316
Spinatus 196
Spoutnik 71
Stalingrad 88
Starsky 124
Statique (91.1) 241
Stères 303
Stormroc 204
Strappal 314
Styrax 48
Superlative 58
Super Bouze 86
Super Joker 124
Super Vista 197
Surmenage 257
Surplomb à Coulisse 232
Surplomb de La Mée 273
Surplomb Ocre 242
Surp-Rouge-Souris 209
Surprise 122
Sur le Fil 284
Suzanne 85
Symbiose 211
Syndrome Albatros 29
Syracuse 281
Système F 281
T.G.V.-Sabots 233
Talon d'Achille 61
Tanks 116
Taupé 284
Technograte 78
Technomaniaque 108
Tékit Izi 96
Temps Modernes 50
Tendance 201
Tendron 261
Tension 311
Tentation 211
Ten Eleven 154
Tequila Sunrise 137
Terminator 301

Terre Promise 160
Théorème 284
Théorie-Nuages 196
Théorie du Chaos 63
Thorax 268
Ticketyboo 93
Tire-Bouchon 242
Tire au But 141
Tiroir 231
Toboggan 37
Toho-boho 316
Toit (C-Chien) 246
Toit des Braves 178
Toit du Loup (Elep) 301
Toit Tranquille 111
Toubib 196
Tourmalet 195
Tourniquet-B-Rond 195
Tour de Pise 78
Toutatis-Canche 172
Tranche de Lard 142
Travaux Forcés 203
Tremb-Rapido 160
Tripes 90
Triplette 213
Tristesse 261
Trois Lancers 267
Trompe-Oeil 134
Trompette 245
Tronche à Noueux 282
Trous de Memoire 297
Trou du Tondu 66
Trou Simon 65
Ultimatum 104
Ultime Secret 137
Undertow 161
Uranus 160
Urticaire 116
Vache Folles (Elep) 295
Vague Patatras 34
Valse aux Adieux 61
Vaudou Surprise 74
Vélo de Max 188
Ventriloque 290
Ventru 130
Verglas Frequent 248
Version Blocage 290
Vespasienne 288
Vibration-Apremont 117
Vieille Fille-Guichot 258
Vielle Canaille 232
Vin Rouge 127
Visa (95.2) 219
Vishnu 307
Vita Beata 140
Vodka Martini 217
Voie du Flirt 301
Voie du Pin 156
Voie Lactée-Potala 268
Voie Michaud (Elep) 301
Vol-au-Vent 226
Voltige 93
Vol au Vent 227
Vol de Mort 117
Voyageur 150
Wall 152
Washington Sniper 93
Water Polo 158
Yapludju 132
Yoga-Souris 209
Zip Zut 125
Zorro 315
Zyno 210

GAD système - Sport Escalade & Bloc

Arête/Angle	**A**	**a-retour**	aller-retour/ there and back [>+<]
Boulder style/style Bloc	**B**	**b**	bien equipée/very well protected
Chimney/Cheminée	**C**	**c**	compression movement
Corner/Dièdre	**D**	**d**	dalle/slab
Endurance style/style Endurance	**E**	**e**	avec corde/best climbed with a rope
Crack/Fissure	**F**	**f**	à piéds/good footwork needed
Smooth groove/Goulotte	**G**	**g**	glissant/slippery and polished
stays green-wet after rain/**Humide**	**H**	**h**	horrible
		i	inversée/undercut
JINGO - power	**J**	**j**	jété/dyno-grade colour coded
No equipment-Nuts cams/Coinceurs	**K**	**k**	cool-you need to stay cool and calm
First pitch/Première Longeur	**L1**		
Vertical Wall/Mur vertical	**M**	**m**	mètres/metres
Rouded Nose/Nez-Boule	**N**	**n**	talon-crochet/heel hook
Large Hole-pocket/Trou	**O**	**o**	mono-bidoigt/finger pockets
Pillar-Prow/Pilier-Proue	**P**	**p**	panique/scary
Cliff unstable/Falaise Instable	**Q**	**q**	rocher mauvaise/dodgy rock
slightly leaning-overhanging/Raide	**R**	**r**	réta/mantleshelf
Overhang-bulge/Surplomb	**S**	**s**	plats/slopers
Roof-Ceiling/Toit	**T**	**t**	talon/ heel hook (replacing t=traverse)
Best on top rope/Escalade moulinette	**U**	**uh**	malaisé en moulinette/bad on a top rope
Constantly steep-overhanging/Dévers	**V**	**v**	descend/climb down
WOBBLY - technique	**W**	**w**	réglettes-grattons/sharp crimps
Danger of Death/Grand danger	**X**	**x**	danger-hôpital/you may survive-just
Abseil down/Rappel	**Y**	**y**	scellements en résine/resin bolt
Jump across boulders/saut	**Z**	**z**	plaquettes/expansion bolt with hangars
Départ assis		**@**	Sit start
traversée à droite		**>**	traverse to the right
traversée à gauche avec talon		**<**	traverse to the left
traversée à droite dans un mur,		**M>**	traverse across a wall, going to the right
traversée à droite et finir dans le mur		**>M**	traverse to the right, finish up the wall
grimper l'angle par la droite		**A:**	Climb right side of angle
cotation 4a eh haut du bloc		**!4a**	High move of 4a

- prise pour la main/handhold
- prise pour le pied/foothold
- prise interdite/not allowed
- repère de voie/route marker
- (2) crash pads [maximum 24]
- parade recommandée/spotter please

- ✵ broche en résine/resin bolt
- ✶ arbre/tree
- **B** Lettrine de sentier/footpath letters

Example:
7b Bleau's Art [3m PVc] (2)
[3 metres, Pilier Dévers compression] (2 crash pads)

D+ No.2
{36} [2015]
4c **①+**

{nombre de voies} [année de peintre]
{number of problems} [year of paintin
Bonne cotation - grade to do 80%

P GPS (google)
Decimal WGS 84